Marching Dykes, Liberated Sluts, and Concerned Mothers

Marching Dykes, Liberated Sluts, and Concerned Mothers

Women Transforming Public Space

ELIZABETH CURRANS

UNIVERSITY OF ILLINOIS PRESS
Urbana, Chicago, and Springfield

1 2 3 4 5 C P 5 4 3 2 1
♾ This book is printed on acid-free paper.

Library of Congress Cataloging-in-Publication Data
Names: Currans, Elizabeth, 1973– author.
Title: Marching dykes, liberated sluts, and concerned mothers: women transforming public space / Elizabeth Currans.
Description: Urbana, Chicago, and Springfield: University of Illinois Press, 2017. | Includes bibliographical references and index. |
Identifiers: LCCN 2017011914 (print) | LCCN 2017025041 (ebook) | ISBN 9780252099854 (ebook) | ISBN 9780252041259 (hardback) | ISBN 9780252082801 (paper)
Subjects: LCSH: Feminism—United States. | Protest movements—United States. | BISAC: SOCIAL SCIENCE / Gender Studies. | SOCIAL SCIENCE / Women's Studies. | HISTORY / United States / 21st Century.
Classification: LCC HQ1236.5.U6 (ebook) | LCC HQ1236.5.U6 C87 2017 (print) | DDC 305.420973—dc23
LC record available at https://lccn.loc.gov/2017011914

Contents

Preface

Sitting next to my computer as I write is a memo to "members of proposed settlement in class action lawsuit involving the 2004 Republican National Convention." Within this document, I'm supposed to find myself in "Mass Arrest Subclass Six: August 31, 2004, on 16th Street between Union Square East and Irving Place, between 7:00 p.m. and 10:00 p.m." I was with seven others. Most of us were part of a direct action–oriented group created in response to the 2003 bombing of Iraq called ARISE, which I've written about elsewhere.[1] We'd discussed the possibility of arrest, left contact information with a local ally, and buddied up based on different comfort levels with risks of bodily harm and arrest. As part of the more risk-averse half of our group, I was paired with another graduate student, Frank.

Our buddy system became particularly important once we arrived at Union Square, where we planned to take part in a street party. This party, one of many simultaneous protests around the city, sought to demonstrate collective playfulness in the face of stern warnings from the New York City Police Department. We wanted to enact another way of being in the city and in the world, an impetus similar to the now iconic protests against the World Trade Organization (WTO) in Seattle and anarchist events worldwide.[2] The party was short-lived; we hadn't even moved a block out of the park before we were met by police in riot gear. As they closed in on us from both sides, Frank and I were among a group of people pushed up against a wall on the south side of 16th Street. As the police advanced, they told us to disperse, yet there was no place to go. This tactic, I now know, is called "kettling."[3] In front and on both sides of us were police holding orange netting; behind us was a concrete wall. I held Frank's hand as we were pressed tighter and tighter against the wall. My feet left the ground as I was mashed between other bodies, and I lost hold of Frank's hand. I don't recall how we peeled ourselves apart and found ourselves sitting on the sidewalk in small groups with arresting officers assigned to us. I do remember Frank being led away with some other men. I remained on the sidewalk with two other women from our group.

As we were searched, we watched people being led away with their hands bound behind them. Soon we too were cuffed, herded onto waiting buses, and driven to a holding facility at Pier 57. There I was separated from the rest of the women in my group and spent ten hours inside a large cage made out of chain-link fencing on the grease-covered floor of a former airplane storage facility. We women watched from our cages as the men were led, group by group, out of the facility. We later learned from a guard that the city had more official facilities for holding men, which is why they could be booked and moved through more quickly than women. After fifty-two hours I was released to find my seven friends and one friend's mother waiting outside. We took the subway uptown, giddy with exhaustion. Frank and the other two men in the group serenaded us with pirate-inspired songs as we walked from the subway station two blocks west and five floors up to my friend's apartment.

I begin with this story to set up a few important features of the time period during which most of the events discussed in this book occurred. First, the nation was at war, and military aggressions abroad were at the forefront of public discussions. (As I write in 2016, we're still at war, a fact that seems so normal as to be unremarkable.) Then, many people were actively engaged in defending or contesting U.S. military presence in Iraq and Afghanistan, as chapters 4 and 5, focused on Women in Black and CODEPINK, explore in more depth. Second, protesting was a contested activity fraught with risk of arrest and abuse by bystanders. This affected how people approached their public presence and the tactics they employed. Protesting was also not new. As Don Mitchell and Judith Butler each reminds us, public space is not given; it is always the result of struggle.[4] The state is also closely involved in regulating who can say what and when and where they can say it.[5] Third, and most important for this text, gender matters even in mixed-gender events focused on seemingly ungendered issues. Our gendered socialization affects how we interact with others. Additionally, criminality is primarily associated with men, especially men of color and working-class white men. Our judicial and prison systems, like most social institutions, also rely on a rigid gender binary that not only treats men and women differently but also fails to recognize genders that depart from narrow understandings of masculine men and feminine women. All these factors affect why and how women engage in protest activities and how people respond to women's public presence.

In the United States and globally, 2004 was a particularly fraught moment. Wars in Iraq and Afghanistan were at the forefront of many people's minds; there was still widespread debate about how the United States should respond internationally and domestically to the attacks of September 11, 2001; and it was a presidential election year complete with large conventions for both major political parties. Not only did the U.S. media have a lot to say about such issues, but commentators around the globe did too. Like people in the United States, people in numerous other countries took to the streets and published commentary in newspapers and magazines addressing U.S. militarism and their hopes and fears for the U.S. election. Accordingly, the demonstrations described in this book provided an opportunity to think about how women-dominated groups addressed a variety of issues at a time when civil liberties were being renegotiated.

Feminism in the Twenty-First Century

Activists in 2004 struggled with long-held anxieties about feminism and activism, as well as the issues particular to the post-9/11 era. The comment below from Heather, a forty-four-year-old white heterosexual officer in the Twin Cities (Minnesota) chapter of the Million Moms March, highlights some of the perceptions of activism in U.S. culture at the time, views that have changed little in the past decade.

> I hate to say that us being active as moms is a way of us keeping our role, but it is less threatening for a lot of women to be out there marching as a mom than marching as an activist. It's my guess that a lot of Million Moms don't consider themselves activists. And for me, I think I got to be more comfortable using [the term "activist"] being involved in the peace movement, where to be an activist is really something you work towards, where with the Million Moms it's more like we're volunteers. There is a real difference there. Obviously, in the peace movement you're volunteers too. But really you're a peace protester. You're a peace activist. You're an antiwar activist. And we're Million Moms. We're volunteers. We're ordinary people. . . . It's a less threatening way to be seen in the general public, it's a more open and inviting way to bring more people in.

As her comments indicate, "activist" is not a label all people are willing to accept even if the work they do is seen by others as activist. Additionally, people who might be seen by outsiders as activists have distinct relationships to the term and to cultures of respectability. Antiwar protesters see themselves as contesting the status quo and therefore are more likely to embrace a label such as "protester" or "activist." The Million Moms, who enter the political sphere in the name of children, are invested in maintaining ties to people who see activists as outside of acceptable norms. This respectability might have felt more important in 2004 than in early 2001. Media scholar Marita Sturken explains: "September 11 has become a marker of change, the day when the society we live in was divided into a before and an after. . . . Before September 11, the images of gender roles that circulated within the media were of casually dressed dot-commers and young professional men and women. After September 11, the images of gender shifted to an emphasis on traditional working-class masculinity and wives holding down the home front."[6] While then president George W. Bush and his party emphasized traditional gender roles before the attacks, and feminism has never been part of the mainstream, traditional gender norms were reified by the new media focus. Patriotism required clearly defined gender roles in which both hypermasculine men and domesticated women supported war efforts.

The distinction Heather makes between activist and volunteer is important for understanding people's resistance to being "activists." An activist attempts to change social structures that cause individual problems, while a volunteer seeks to help people without necessarily questioning the structures that create need.[7] For example, a volunteer might feed the homeless without attempting to change economic or other conditions that cause homelessness. The stigma of activism even reaches into feminist communities. In the prologue to *Grassroots: A Field Guide for Feminist Activists*, Jennifer Baumgardner and Amy Richards discuss their initial ambivalence about using the term "activism." They considered using a term like "volunteerism" or "charity" instead: "The word 'activism' sounds so dramatic, as if this book was for people who chain themselves to trees or ruin dinner by lecturing to their family and friends about factory farming."[8] Even these well-known feminists are uneasy with the label "activist," which seems somewhat ironic, given how many women resist the label "feminist."[9] As cultural theorist Sara Ahmed demonstrates, the image of the feminist killjoy helps orient women away from challenging patriarchal norms.[10]

The term "feminist" has long been controversial and remains so today. Many declared feminism dead in the 1980s after the defeat of the ERA and the election of Ronald Reagan, whose brand of conservatism included championing "American values" hostile to feminism and to other progressive movements.[11] Because of this cultural climate, some posited that the United States had entered a period of backlash.[12] However, a close analysis of texts produced in the 1980s reveals that the failure of the ERA did not end feminist activism, and however hostile Ronald Reagan and his cohort were to progressive activism and social change, they did not eliminate the creativity and dedication of feminist activists and scholars. The death of feminism was more a popular myth than reality, one that described change rather than demise. As early as 1990, political scientist Mary Fainsod Katzenstein declared: "As the 1990s begin, few feminists subscribe to the popular wisdom that the women's movement is dead. Yet we also know that the public face of the feminist movement is not the same."[13] She noted a shift from public demonstrations to institutionalization, providing a complement to sociologist Becky Thompson's analysis of the growth of multiracial feminism in the 1980s.[14] Thompson traces the creation and institutionalization of what we now call "intersectional analysis" during the time period that was previously theorized by pundits and scholars as fallow. If we readjust our lens away from the kind of social movement organizations generally explored in sociological analyses of feminism, we can see growth in the proliferation of anthologies and conferences about women of color feminisms.

Like Thompson, critical theorist Clare Hemmings cautions us to examine how we tell feminist histories. In her examination of narratives feminists create about feminism, she notes a propensity to tell stories about progress that require simplifying earlier feminist ideas and stories about loss that require simplifying current feminist ideas, resulting in competing narratives that either claim that we finally got it right or that we need to return to an idealized past.[15] Neither story effectively addresses the complexity of late twentieth- and early twenty-first-century feminist thinking.

In the years immediately following 9/11, feminists had renewed foci: war and domestic repression of dissent, including feminist critique. Most feminist engagements with war questioned the subsequent wars and the crackdown on civil liberties. Nonetheless, early in the buildup to the 2003 U.S. invasion of Afghanistan, the Feminist Majority provided support for military aggression because of the Taliban's repression of women, resulting in a brief, opportunistic flirtation with feminism by President George W. Bush and his colleagues.[16] Other feminists predicted that war would not translate into substantial changes for Afghani women. They argued that violence generally begets more violence and that war often leads to greater emphasis on traditional gender roles. For example, psychologist Janice Haaken explained some potential traps for feminists responding to the polemical rhetoric about war and terrorism:

> Feminism, no less than other political formations, may engage in forms of splitting and projection in maintaining a sense of goodness and group cohesion. The casting of men as violence prone and women as peace oriented does not take us very far into the complex determinants and dynamics of war. Western feminist campaigns also may inadvertently support neocolonial forms of domination if representations of male "savagery" are stripped of their wider context, including how more remote players are implicated in the suffering. By decontextualizing male violence, the role of U.S. foreign policy and international capital in generating the massive suffering on display remains on the periphery of our vision.[17]

In a militarized climate, the most accessible form of resistance often replicates the dominant, dichotomous mode of thinking. The emphasis on traditional gender roles in the United States, heightened during the buildup to the invasion of

Afghanistan and Iraq, affected how women viewed their own public presence. While this was particularly noticeable for those protesting militarism, women addressing other issues also had to navigate the renewed salience of associations between women and passive domesticity. As Heather's comment above indicates, for some women, deploying normative gender roles provided a relatively safe method for entering the political domain. For others, such as some Dyke March participants I interviewed, an explicit refusal of such norms was key to why and how they claimed public spaces.

There are many ways people can challenge disagreeable public policies and restrictive cultural norms. Public demonstrations are collective, providing a sense of community, and public, making participants' opinions visible. By claiming and holding space, people not only demonstrate their presence and their demands but also transform space in ways that reflect desired social changes and expose current conditions that are often taken for granted. Thus, this affective and physical process intervenes in the present and seeks to shift the future. It is both practical in its immediacy and utopic in its aims. While often mixed with fear, anger, and other emotions, hope is key to these gatherings. This mixture is unsurprising. As José Esteban Muñoz reminds us, "Hope along with its other, fear, are affective structures that can be described as anticipatory."[18] The marches, vigils, and direct actions I analyze in this text anticipate other realities by demonstrating what different ways of being might look and feel like while demonstrating resistance to contemporary oppressive conditions.

Acknowledgments

As a doctoral student at the University of California, Santa Barbara, I enjoyed support from numerous faculty, staff, students, and community members. Dwight Reynolds and Eileen Boris generously directed my research despite its divergence from their own. Beth Schneider and Tom Carlson served as readers and sounding boards. Lou Anne Lockwood and Sally Lombrozo navigated various crises with aplomb. Sharon Hoshida and Elizabeth Robinson made sure the Women's Center and KCSB-FM were welcoming, nurturing spaces. Other faculty and staff, including Marisela Marquez, Leila Rupp, Mireille Miller-Young, Cedric Robinson, and Roger Friedland, nurtured my intellectual and political growth. Fellow students and visiting fellows, including Mark Schuller, Karl Bryant, Tiffany Willoughby-Herard, Jeanne Scheper, Simone Chess, Jessi Quizar, Jessica Caldwell-O'Keefe, William Robert, Melissa Wilcox, Julie Cordero-Lamb, Sylvanna Falcón, Ginny Browne, Alison Kafer, and Matt Richardson, provided stimulating conversation and supportive challenges to my thinking. Community members, including Alena Marie and Tara Uliasz, helped keep me grounded. A Graduate Opportunity Fellowship from the Graduate Division; a Graduate Student Research Fellowship from the Walter A. Capps Center for the Study of Ethics, Religion, and Public Life; and a Student Scholarship from the Santa Barbara Gay and Lesbian Business Association provided financial support. I also held a fellowship at the Five Colleges Women's Studies Research Center, where I had the opportunity to think with Christina Hanhardt, Ninette Rothmüller, and many other wonderful scholars.

While I was teaching at the College of William and Mary in Williamsburg, Virginia, as a visiting assistant professor, numerous people supported my visioning of the current form of this book, including Christy Burns, Leisa Meyer, Jennifer Bickham Mendez, and Kathleen Jenkins. Generous local hospitality provided by

Gul Ozyegin, Nancy Gray, Farhang Rouhani, Tom Linneman, Tracy Citeroni, Mark Lewis, Danielle Currier, and Eric Han made my time in the South nurturing.

Since arriving at Eastern Michigan University, I have enjoyed a vibrant intellectual community comprised of wonderful scholars and artists living near and far. Without Petra Kuppers's support this book would not be finished. The balance she creates between work, play, and art is truly admirable. Eastern Michigan University provided a New Faculty Award, two Faculty Research Fellowships, two Josephine Nevins Keal Development Fund Awards, and a course release from the Center for the Study of Equity and Human Rights. Minnie Chiu, Sharon Doetsch-Kidder, Victoria Quiroz-Beccera, Katie Hendy, and Liz Faier offered invaluable writing support in person and over the phone. Amanda Allen, Christine Neufeld, Nataša Kovačević, Rob Halpern, Stephanie Heit, and Lee Azus have been instrumental to maintaining my mental health and encouraging my intellectual and political life. Incredibly, I've been able to build upon my friendships with Simone Chess and Max Matthies since moving to Michigan. V. Jane Rosser's love and kindness have facilitated the final stages of this process. Eileen Boris continues to serve as a mentor and friend.

No acknowledgment section would be complete without recognizing the lifelong support I've enjoyed from my parents, Phyllis and Jim Currans. Despite not always understanding what I'm doing and sometimes actively disagreeing with my choices and views, they have provided a firm grounding for my intellectual growth. I am deeply grateful.

Earlier versions of two chapters were previously published, and I am grateful for permission from Johns Hopkins University Press and the Feminist Press to reprint. Chapter 3 appeared in a slightly different form as "Claiming Deviance and Honoring Community: Creating Resistant Spaces in U.S. Dyke Marches" in *Feminist Formations* 24, no. 1 in 2012, and chapter 4 overlaps considerably with "Demonstrating Peace Countertopographically: Women in Black's Solidarity at a Distance," which appeared in *Women's Studies Quarterly* 42, no. 3–4, in 2014.

I am also grateful for close reading and feedback from anonymous reviewers of this manuscript, who helped me fine-tune my ideas and think creatively about the book's organization. Larin McLaughlin and Dawn Durante also provided wonderful support and guidance during the editorial process.

Marching Dykes, Liberated Sluts, and Concerned Mothers

Introduction

Regendering Public Spaces

On June 26, 2004, approximately twenty-five hundred people, mostly queer-identified women, assembled along 42nd Street in New York City in order to march in the twelfth annual New York Dyke March. As they began promenading down the street, a multiracial group of about thirty young women drummed and danced behind four participants carrying a large black banner that read "New York Dyke March, Women of Mass Defiance: Lick Bush." The march turned south onto the partially closed Fifth Avenue, passing the New York Public Library before moving past department stores, restaurants, and souvenir shops eager for tourist dollars. Occasionally, the lead group broke into a revised rendition of "When the Saints Go Marching In": "Oh when the dykes, oh when the dykes, oh when the dykes go marching in. I want to be in that number when the dykes go marching in." A crowd comprised primarily of supporters assembled along the sidelines. The march ended at Washington Square Park at the edge of the West Village, the historic center of gay New York.

Outside the New York Public Library, facing the street where partially clad dykes had marched and chanted in defiance of gender and sexual norms the previous month, a small group of women silently protested war, as they had every Wednesday evening since late 2001. On this evening in July 2004, five women gathered, all wearing black, some head to toe, some with bare shoulders and arms. Forming a silent line on the library steps facing rush-hour traffic, they held a large black banner declaring, "Women in Black Against War." Over the course of an hour a few more women joined the silent line. At one point the group numbered eight—all over thirty, most over fifty, and all white, save one black woman who appeared to be in her fifties. Most onlookers were also silent. A few verbally asserted their support or gratefulness for this vigil. Still fewer made disparaging comments.

At first glance, the two demonstrations described above (and explored in more depth in later chapters) seem to have little in common aside from their spatial location and the presumed gender identification of the participants. This contingent of Women in Black is part of a global response to war and military occupations that utilizes culturally recognizable gender roles to draw attention to masculine performances of state power. By embodying the silence often expected of women and publicly demonstrating their grief, vigilers draw power from reworking gender expectations often understood as limiting. New York Dyke March participants, in contrast, explicitly reject gender norms that link femininity to female bodies and sexual norms that privilege heterosexual interactions. They intentionally perform what many see as deviant behaviors in public as a way to claim public space for themselves. Despite these differences, both events and their participants are part of a larger pattern of women bringing seemingly private issues into the public eye, blurring such distinctions in the process. These demonstrations cultivated public cultures that reflect the people involved, their belief systems, and contemporary cultural conversations while reshaping public space to fit their purposes and messages. In the process, they created spaces for resistance where people with shared values could meet to challenge cultural norms and public policies.

Marching Dykes, Liberated Sluts, and Concerned Mothers: Women Transforming Public Space intervenes in feminist analyses of social change and the public and private by examining demonstrations attended and organized primarily by women in the early twenty-first century. Most of my examples occur in North America, but I do incorporate material from one vigil in the U.K. This book seeks to evaluate why and how women utilize public protest for participating in political and cultural dialogues about contemporary events and concerns. The concepts of public and private spheres have long been a focus of feminist theorizing and research due to assumed relationships between women and domestic spaces and activities.[1] While rigid separations between the two spheres were never fully upheld and domestic ideals have changed over time, associations between women and private spaces and men and public spaces still influence how we understand spaces and their users. Accordingly, women have contended with these divides and exploited ideological dissonances created by their public presence while organizing for social change, making public protest a particularly salient form of dissent.

This book uses the framework of holding space as a way to explore how a range of women-dominated groups claim and transform public spaces in service of diverse political goals. These groups respond to cultural ideals of womanhood in numerous ways. Some, such as participants in the Million Mom March, a national gun control organization, largely accept proscribed social roles. Others, such as New York Dyke March marchers, defiantly reject them. Still others, such as Women in Black vigilers and CODEPINK participants, utilize gendered expectations in order to undermine them. Some, such as the participants in Sistahs Steppin' in Pride: An East Bay Dyke March and Celebration, celebrate themselves and their foremothers. Yet despite these different tactics, each of these groups, along with the others discussed in this book, treats public space as an important resource and takes steps to claim it, transform it, and hold onto the resulting space for a period of time.

This introduction provides a preliminary explanation of the framework of holding space followed by an exploration of my approach to studying protest cultures rather than social movements. This leads to a discussion of research methodology. Finally, I provide brief snapshots of the book's chapters.

Holding Space

In my use, the phrase "holding space" seeks to bring together two key aspects of public presence: being physically present in a space and claiming it in a way that transforms it for participants and maintains the transformed state for some time. Thus, holding a space requires physical presence and a sustained, affective transformation. It requires emotional investment, planning, and a willingness to be spontaneous, to respond to whatever unforeseen issues may occur—counterprotesters, inclement weather, unnavigable physical or affective terrain, technological problems, police repression. It requires being present emotionally, intellectually, and physically. In the cases discussed here and other examples of counterpublic engagement in public spaces, the process is, by necessity, tactical rather than strategic.[2] Participants carve out spaces where they can gain a foothold; they exploit openings provided by those with power and struggle to expand the space available for other ways of being.

To hold the space, the group must alter it so that it augments the physical presence of bodies. For example, Raisa Bhuiyan, a SlutWalk Toronto organizer, described what she saw as she looked out on the crowd gathered for the 2012 march:

> Being at the rally . . . was probably the best feeling I've had in a long time, just feeling the energy of support, the energy of excitement, the fierce determination of everybody there to support this cause, to walk in that march. That was fantastic for me. . . . And to hear speakers talk about their really personal accounts of traumatic experiences with sexual assault and rape and to hear the crowd being like "SHAME! SHAME!" The crowd was wonderful. The people who came were wonderful. They were so receptive, they were so intuitive, they were so supportive, and they were so wonderful.

The crowd held the space for her as she spoke from the stage, for other speakers who shared heart-rending experiences, and for other participants. The physical presence of approximately fifteen hundred people was important, but the energy Bhuiyan described was necessary to transform the gathered people into a collective entity and the site into a space for addressing sexual violence and victim blaming.

Space is never neutral. It always carries political and cultural meanings. Overt and subtle clues code spaces with gendered, racialized, sexualized, nationalized, and classed meanings. Multiple practices limit who enters or is comfortable in public spaces and what people are able to do in these spaces. These practices include police presence, the behavior of people who dominate spaces, entrances (in)accessible to people in wheelchairs, availability of public transportation, harassment by other people, benches or lack of benches, and even the presence or lack of shade. Along with cultural assumptions about men, women, and, as queer activist Kate Bornstein writes, "the rest of us," such processes gender spaces, whether public, private, or semipublic, and inscribe them racially and sexually.[3] Women, femininity, and sexuality are often linked with the domestic sphere and considered out of place within a public sphere devoted to economic and political behaviors. As Kath Browne argues, "Gendered embodiments create the very spaces they occur in."[4] In similar processes, sexualized and racialized practices also create sexual and racial spaces.[5] While many, if not most, activities are gendered, the long-standing links between masculinity and public space make explicit (re)gendering of public spaces particularly important for women and people with nonnormative gender expressions.

Streets are ambiguous sites, and as cultural theorist Sally Munt reminds us, they offer "an image of freedom and paradoxically of violence."[6] This observation is particularly salient for women and queer people, given fears and experiences of violence. As such, streets are a particularly fruitful site for reclamation. They are not the only spaces, to be sure, and people should have access to more than the "demarcated moments" of public demonstrations.[7] However, streets can be beginnings, reminders, or brief glimpses of another reality. Thus, the importance of the public demonstrations discussed in this book is not simply their claims to public spaces or their refusal to abide by norms of decorum, but also the alternative value systems they model while claiming and regendering public spaces.

Public spaces are generally seen as masculine and private spaces, in contrast, as feminine. The reality is certainly more complex, but these assumptions might be seen as default settings for spaces that can shift due their use and users. For example, the traditional understanding of the home as a gendered space generally focuses on domestic actions that women are expected or assumed to perform, such as cooking, cleaning, gardening, caring for children, and gossiping.

However, activities traditionally associated with men, such as carpentry, vehicle maintenance and repair, heavy yard work, and consumption of televised sports, also take place in homes alongside subtle and overt practices of male dominance.[8] The home is also a primary site for physical abuse perpetrated primarily by men and experienced primarily by women.[9]

These sedimented meanings and individuals' experiences affect how people interact in public spaces. Consider the following anecdote from Re, a white genderqueer-identified SlutWalk Detroit participant in hir late twenties: "We were hanging around our ending place, and there were some people around who then felt comfortable enough to come up and do inappropriate things. There was this one man who . . . came up and very lingeringly touched this woman's shoulder . . . just very inappropriate contact. Since our numbers had dwindled it seems that fear we have been conditioned to have reappeared."[10] At this march on June 16, 2012, the woman Re describes was dressed as a stereotypical "slut," attire that had been part of the claiming of the streets and the park where the march had just ended. This man was reclaiming Grand Circus Park in the center of downtown Detroit for male-dominated values; however, SlutWalk participants didn't simply let the space go. Despite fear, Re intervened, creating an opportunity for dialogue and solidarity. In doing so, ze held the space for other participants for a little longer despite this man's reassertion of normative values.

> I went up to this man and said, "Excuse me. Did this woman say you could touch her?" What really struck me was how bewildered this man was, absolutely not used to being called out for something like this. And [then he] spouted something really ridiculous like, "She should have told me if she wanted me not to touch her." By that point it seemed like people were feeling more comfortable, [and] I was able to say, "No. That's never somebody else's responsibility. It's your responsibility to get consent for things like that." It felt like a very empowering experience too. Then the woman was like, "You got my back!" and sort of high-fived me, and it opened up another little dialogue among us on how to address that more singly. . . . I know personally I rarely have the wherewithal to address when I'm on my own, and just I felt really as a group we were learning how to address those things more.

Hir intervention established feminist solidarity between hirself and other participants, allowing them to hold onto the physical and rhetorical space the march created for a little longer. It also brought the level of fear down far enough that they were able to dialogue with people attempting to reclaim the space with misogynist, objectifying comments. They held their ground for a short time before relinquishing the space.

Claiming public streets, sidewalks, and parks is empowering, and that empowerment can extend beyond the limited time period of the march, rally, or vigil. These events also provide opportunities for affective encounters among people with similar and different approaches to public space. In the experience Re recounted, ze encountered two strangers, one whom ze felt allied with and one ze felt both intimated by and in conflict with. Emotions, according to Sara Ahmed, "are relational, they involve (re)actions or relations of 'towardness or 'awayness.'"[11] Re's emotions drew hir toward the woman and away from the man. Ze could have translated this awayness into physical movement and left the park. Instead, rather than relinquishing the space, ze transformed the discomforting situation into an opportunity for encounter. The intervention resulted in hir and hir supporters "feeling more comfortable." Notably, the people Re identifies as feeling more comfortable don't include the man who brushed the woman's shoulder. In fact, he became "bewildered," less rather than more comfortable.

His decreased comfort seems reasonable, maybe even laudable, if gender and sexuality are the only analytical foci; however, when race and class are also explored, this response becomes more complicated. While Re never identified anyone's race or class background when explaining this encounter, as a march participant I know that most participants were white. Each time I've visited Grand Circus Park there have been a small number of black men, sometimes accompanied by one or two black women, all of whom appear homeless and hang out in the park. On the day of the march, five or six black men were watching us as we gathered to listen to speakers, marched out of the park, and then returned. The park is theirs most of the time. Thus, while the park is generally a masculine, heterosexual space, it's also a site for black homeless people to gather. Their claim to the space is tentative, given that the park is city owned and they can be removed at any time. The park also has a reputation as a site for protest activity, ranging from short rallies and marches to longer-term demonstrations such as Occupy Detroit, which means that other people frequently claim the space for specific purposes. Nonetheless, these men's use of the park simultaneously reinforced dominant gender and sexual norms and challenged racial and class norms. The Detroit SlutWalk held the space for women and their supporters to contest sexual violence and victim blaming; yet it also affirmed some aspects of dominant spatial norms, given the race and class privilege of most participants. In this encounter, people moved both toward and away from each other.

Thus, holding space is about physical and affective presence, but it is also about power. By holding a space, a group leverages the tactical power of countercultural movement, reinstates hegemonic cultural norms, or, frequently, performs some combination of the two. Michel Foucault suggests that "power is co-extensive with the social body" and that "relations of power are interwoven with other kinds of relations."[12] The social body bestows power based on various relationships, including systems of privilege and oppression. Major social cleavages, including gender, race, class, sexuality, and disability, affect how much power people have in relationship with others similarly and differently positioned within the same systems. Relative power plays out differently in different circumstances, including interactions in public spaces. Much of what I trace in this book are examples of publicly performed resistance to power relations upheld by a combination of cultural and political forces. Foucault reminds us that "there are no relations of power without resistances" and that, "like power, resistance is multiple."[13] The multiplicity of resistance is all the more clear when we take into account how different vectors of power interact.

In Re's story, everyone has access to some kind of power in relation to others. As a genderqueer person often identified by others as a woman, Re occupies a precarious position in a male-dominated society invested in a rigid gender binary, a position further complicated by hir disability, which requires that ze navigate the world using either crutches or a wheelchair, depending on the day. The woman ze stood up for is also marginalized due to her gender. Nonetheless, as people who are presumably white and comparatively economically privileged, they have some power in relationship to the presumably black and homeless man who approached them. In their interaction, power shifts multiple times. During the march, participants held space for themselves and their message, exerting power through numbers and a willingness to use space in ways that observers recognized as claiming informal political power. Once most participants dispersed, the park became a liminal space—no longer the space occupied by marchers and not yet the space of its daily inhabitants. When the man approached and touched the woman, he exerted gendered power as a way to reclaim the space. The web of power relations among these three people means that power is not simply assumed by any of them, and their encounters in this urban space reflect their various attempts to assert and resist power.

How people interact in public reflects social power relations, even when people resist those relations. Public space, like all space, is socially produced, the product of "the energy deployed in it."[14] This energy is multifaceted and arises from numerous historical, political, social, cultural, and interpersonal relationships. Public demonstrations operate primarily within the social, cultural, and interpersonal layers of relationality, although histories certainly affect current interactions, and political power undergirds social, cultural, and interpersonal interactions. The energy that shapes public spaces is multifaceted and multidirectional—the result of state power, social norms, and people's efforts to claim and shape it.

Public space is a site for representation, for visibility, a site so alive that "it speaks."[15] Through claiming publicly recognized sites of representational space, participants seek to shift spatial practice. Debates over who can be seen doing what in public demonstrate how spatial practice ascribes values to people and behavior. The demonstrations I describe in this book are culturally and politically significant precisely because they contest hegemonic spatial norms that govern not only how people are supposed to behave in public but also who should be seen. While there are generally no rigid restrictions on who can appear in public in the cities where these events occurred, social norms continue to dictate who has full access to public space and, by extension, who is represented within society. Thus, claiming and holding space even for a short time intervenes in quotidian processes of oppression and addresses whatever specific issues a demonstration focuses on. Successful holding of space is therefore always multifaceted: it focuses on something specific—war, sexual violence, reproductive freedom—and also addresses existing spatial norms by challenging or reinscribing them or, often, doing both simultaneously.

The women-dominated groups described in this book regendered spaces to draw attention to forms of hegemonic violence, to demonstrate the existence and importance of dyke lives, to contest laws privileging gun manufacturers over the safety of children, and to demand and negotiate the meaning of reproductive rights. They entered places where they "didn't belong," including elite political events, the halls of Congress, and public spaces generally dominated by men and/or masculinist norms. They held vigils, they marched down streets in their own cities and streets in their nation's capital, they visited elected representatives in their offices, they spoke from stages and listened from grass-covered lawns and parks. In the process of showing up physically and affectively, they encountered coparticipants and held space for negotiations across differences. These fierce gatherings mapped new possibilities for social interactions.

Participants in the demonstrations explored in this book claim spaces and hold them as part of participation in specific publics or, to paraphrase social theorist Michael Warner, world-making projects.[16] Publics are, according to Warner, "scenes of self-activity, of historical rather than timeless belonging, and of active participation rather than ascriptive belonging."[17] This active participation in service of a self-generated specific, potentially even fleeting, belonging is what holds the space. Participants' desires and devotion are as important to claiming and re-creating spaces as their physical presence. Holding is accomplished in myriad ways—through coordinated movement; through the production of sounds, including chanting, drumming, and singing; and through cultivation and acknowledgment of collective feelings.

Within these shared spaces, individuals often respond quite differently. What feels like a perfect ending to one person can feel incomplete to another, what leaves one person overwhelmed by a feeling of shared purpose can leave another feeling overwhelmed by the number of people from a dominant racial or gender group. Nonetheless, when a space is held, there is a sense of collectivity that transcends the mere presence of a large number of people in the same space. In each chapter, I explore how participants sought to claim and hold spaces for other participants and in service of a political and/or cultural message. In most cases, they were successful. This embodied and affective collectivity is often tenuous, conflicted, and contested; nonetheless, it is compelling. People stay for the duration of these events and return to others. Protests are, as a participant in the March for Women's Lives explained, "the activists' prom," providing opportunities for social engagement and collective experiences of joy and outrage.

The power of these events is something akin to sociologist Émile Durkheim's notion of collective effervescence. In *The Elementary Forms of the Religious Life* he wrote: "If collective life awakens religious thought on reaching a certain degree of intensity, it is because it brings out a state of effervescence which changes the conditions of psychic activity. Vital energies are over-extended, passions more active, sensations stronger; there are even some which are produced only at this moment. A man does not recognize himself; he feels himself transformed and consequently he transforms the environment."[18] In this passage, Durkheim describes the transformation of a person within a collective religious setting. The process of being with others affects energy, passion, and sensation, transforming the individual, who then, in turn, helps transform the space. While for Durkheim this is a descent into irrationality, for me this transformation isn't about a lack of or loss of reason. It's the experience of being together physically and affectively in service of a political goal.

Given views linking emotions to irrationality, focusing on affective links may risk associating women's demonstrations with irrationality and emotion, yet continuing to maintain binaries that separate emotions from rationality and supposedly private and public issues is also risky. Binaries such as rational/irrational, masculine/feminine, public/private have long served to minimize women's contributions to social and cultural life. Accordingly, my interest is not simply in examining these elements in women-dominated events but rather in exploring processes that defy and, hopefully, explode these binaries.

I am not alone in my interest in moving beyond commonly held binaries. For example, in her study of ACT-UP, sociologist Deborah Gould writes: "I begin from the premise that feelings and emotion are fundamental to political life, not in the sense that they overtake reason and interfere with deliberative processes, as they are sometimes disparagingly construed to do, but in the sense that there is an affective dimension to the processes and practices that make up 'the political,' broadly defined."[19] Refusing the generally accepted binary that pits rational politics against emotional private lives, she emphasizes the ways that organizing is infused with emotions that both propel and stall collective work. She clarifies that emotions are nonrational, although not necessarily irrational: "I see no reason to deny the irrational components of human motivation and action—*all* human beings have the capacity to be irrational if by that term we mean something like engaging in illogical, senseless, and unreasonable behavior that goes against one's interests. But my rendering of affect is agnostic with regard to irrationality. Affect *may* generate irrationality, but it does not necessarily do so. Affect is always *non*rational, however, by which I mean *outside of*—but not necessarily *contrary to*—conscious, cognitive sense-making."[20] Our emotional lives exist outside or alongside of rationality. Emotional responses can drive rational *or* irrational decision making; there is not necessarily a link or disjuncture. Instead, the affective dimensions of political life interact with both rationality and irrationality, undermining the distinction between these concepts in the process.

The framework "holding space" emphasizes the ways that nonrational and cognitive sense making together contribute to collective claiming of public spaces. Shared responses to social policies and cultural norms bring people together. These shared responses are very often clearly reasoned, yet most also originate in the nonrational realm of affect: in feelings of exclusion; anger about policies; desire for visibility; hurt due to sexist, heterosexist, transphobic, racist, or ablist norms. This sharing creates effervescent gatherings that can claim a physical site and transform it into a collective space that can be maintained over a period of time, allowing participants the opportunity to experience a space committed to a common value or concern.

As I emphasized above, my focus on shared responses and collective effervescence is not intended to erase the complexity within groups. Organizing communities, like other segments of our society, are part of what Ash Amin and Nigel Thrift describe as an "imperfectly unified and never unitary world."[21] While often frustrating, this lack of unity keeps activist communities moving toward an always elusive ideal. It also requires flexibility and the will to change and adapt. Like the women of color organizers that Chela Sandoval describes as practicing differential consciousness, people need to be willing to choose from among a variety of modes of organizing and narrative strategies.[22] This is social movement in its truest sense—working for change and willing to be changed in the process.

Projecting new, habitable environments out of long-held and newly emerging concerns is at the heart of any political project. The examples I discuss in this book are attempts to create new worlds in response to a variety of injuries and imaginative visions for the future. The people who organize and attend these demonstrations drew from long traditions of street performances responding to various forms of injustice. In doing so, protesters held space for each other and for those who wished to join them.

Exploring Protest Cultures

This book focuses on public demonstrations organized and attended primarily by women, paying particular attention to participants' and organizers' experiences. My goal is to create an analytical snapshot of what happens during these demonstrations rather than to trace social movement. While the events I explore are certainly part of social movement, the movement as such is not my frame of analysis. Instead, I am interested in the public cultures that are created during rallies, marches, vigils, direct actions, and other forms of public demonstration. Put simply, this is not a social movement history or a linked series of mini–social movement histories, nor is it a study of social movement organizations. Instead, my hope is that this book will work alongside such scholarship to provide complementary but distinct explorations of activist cultures. There is much to learn about how a movement emerges and grows over time, or about changes to policy and law as a result of collective organizing, or about how particular organizations contribute to social change. There is also much to learn about what public demonstrations do and how people experience them. This latter project is the one I take on in this book.

In exploring what public demonstrations do, I do not intend to ignore the all too real conditions that sometimes lead people to protest or the ways that demonstrations can be shut down, often violently. The reclaiming of space that occurs in protests is necessary because oppression is spatial as well as economic, political, emotional, and spiritual. Violent, patriarchal, heteronormative, and racist mappings and remappings occur in cities throughout the United States and the world, affecting how people are able to live. The moments of protest and celebration addressed in this book do not erase these realities, but they can provide temporary antidotes and, sometimes at least, maps for less exploitative futures.

I'm interested in how gender and sexuality affect public events in numerous ways—their foci, the ways that organizers and participants evoke gender and sexuality, and how bystanders and media respond to protests and participants—and the particular events explored in this book reflect this interest. Women's public presence remains interwoven with cultural assumptions about sexual respectability and ascribed gender roles that frequently reduce us to our reproductive functions. Gender and sexuality are also intricately linked to other systems of cultural value, including race, disability, and class. These socially embedded vectors of identity affect the reasons people take to the streets and participants' experiences of these demonstrations. As I explore in more depth in each chapter, people's experiences of these events often reflect their histories of oppression and privilege not only within society but also within feminist and queer spaces. Part of what my focus on protests rather than social movements allows me to do is explore the complexity of people's responses in ways that a more macrolevel approach cannot. This approach allows for a closer exploration of the dynamics of protest cultures, dynamics that affect who participates in movement toward social change and what that movement feels like.

As is hopefully already clear, my research is influenced by intersectional feminist scholarship, which demonstrates that social and cultural life cannot be adequately understood by examining only one aspect of social oppression and privilege.[23]

My entry points for this study are gender and sexuality, which I understand to be racialized and class inflected and to interact in complex ways with disability. The events I examine challenge persistent identifications of public spaces as masculine, heterosexual domain. These spaces and the modes of reclaiming them are, of course, also racialized and classed, and my analysis addresses these processes through the lens of racialized gender and sexualities.[24] These spaces are also marked by disabled people's continuing struggles for access.[25] People of color of all genders and sexual orientations engage in struggles to claim and rework urban, suburban, and rural spaces.[26] In some cases, they engage in these struggles alongside other women or other queer people to regender heterosexual and patriarchal spaces; however, women and queer people are not exempt from racism or investment in financial, political, and urban renewal campaigns that disproportionately affect poor people of color.[27] Similarly, feminist and queer organizing doesn't always make itself accessible to people with disabilities and can replicate the able-bodied and able-minded biases of society at large.[28] The demonstrations discussed in this book often simultaneously transgress accepted norms while reinforcing others. Therefore, in the process of exploring how gender or sexuality works in these demonstrations, I emphasize the ways that other forms of privilege and oppression also affect people's experiences of demonstrating and their interactions with coparticipants.

Methodological Concerns

These simultaneously artful and political, affective and reasoned manifestations, to my mind, warrant a suitably complex interdisciplinary and intersectional approach. Accordingly, I draw inspiration from social and cultural geographers, many of whom are actively engaged with feminist or queer theorizing; sociologists who push beyond narrow understandings of social movement studies; political theorists who question citizenship norms; performance studies scholars who examine relationships between outsider identities, art, and political life; and queer and feminist scholars and theorists who urge us to rethink restrictive norms and binaries. This queer, in J. Jack Halberstam's terms, or scavenger, in Gayatri Gopinath's phrasing, methodology allows me to work among and between traditional disciplines in order to address complex processes not capturable with any one research or theoretical method.[29] Transgressing the simultaneously porous and closely guarded border between the humanities and social sciences has always seemed both intuitively useful and necessary to understand how people make individual and cultural meaning.

This methodological orientation affects how I chose my research methods, as well as how I analyzed the resulting data. My analysis works with qualitative interviews, participant observations, and, when appropriate, media reports, videos, and archival data. It is also layered with frameworks from feminist, queer, critical race, and disability theory. Additionally, my discussions are informed by my participation in numerous protests, including other examples of the demonstrations I explore in depth and unrelated events addressing issues from police brutality to union solidarity. I periodically include a vignette from such experiences in order to expand my analysis.

In each chapter, I provide some history and context to situate the reader. Some of the historical material came from archives, including the Lesbian Herstory Archives in Brooklyn, the GLBT Archives in San Francisco, the June Mazer Lesbian Archives and the ONE Institute in Los Angeles, and the Sallie Bingham Collection at Duke University. Additional information was pulled from published sources, including scholarly texts and newspaper articles. I also collected ephemera at each demonstration, including flyers for the event, information about organizations with representatives present, and local newspapers that discussed the events, to establish context and connections.

I attended most of the events I discuss, with the exception of CODEPINK's creative lobbying efforts. I video recorded these events and reviewed the resulting tapes while writing and revising this book. I also interviewed nearly one hundred participants and organizers I met at these events or via organizational listservs. In most cases, I gathered contact information at the demonstrations and then called or emailed participants in the following weeks to set up an interview. Given the scale of the national demonstrations, as well as the logistical issues associated with a transient participant pool, this wasn't feasible for my final two examples. Therefore, I asked organizations that coordinated march contingents in cities I would be in, including Minneapolis and Atlanta, to send a request for interviews to their listservs. Approximately three-quarters of these interviews occurred face-to-face in cafés, parks, and private homes. The remaining interviews were done over the phone.

Most of the demonstrations I explore transpired in 2004; however, in two chapters I discuss later events. Notably, both of these temporally different events were also geographically distant from the bulk of my examples. I attended a Women in Black vigil in London in June 2005. This example helped me explore the transnational context for these vigils when addressed alongside a New York City vigil (see chapter 4). Then, in 2011, activists in Toronto held a SlutWalk in response to a police officer's victim-blaming comment in front of a group of students. The robust media response to this protest and U.S. demonstrations it inspired provided an opportunity to explore the relationship between the discursive public sphere and on-the-ground organizing. Thus, the second Toronto event, in May 2012, forms the core of chapter 3.

Throughout the book I identify each participant by gender, race, sexual orientation, and approximate age not to essentialize what, for example, a Latina lesbian in her twenties believes but rather to provide additional information regarding each respondent's subject position. Given interlocking social hierarchies, these identity markers are sometimes helpful in understanding divergent perspectives. I use pseudonyms for all respondents.

Book Overview

The body of the book is broken down into three sections that address sexuality, war, and citizenship, respectively. Each section includes multiple related chapters after an introduction that provides a brief overview of the issue. These overviews provide contextual links between the chapters in each section. Each section introduction explores historical precedents for the demonstrations addressed, as well as feminist analyses of the primary issues addressed by the protests in each section. I chose this structure as a way to provide historical grounding and examine points of connection between demonstrations while still allowing my explorations of individual events to stand on their own. While most of the demonstrations explored in this book address more than one of these three key issues, I've grouped the chapters in this way in order to highlight long-standing feminist activism and theorizing about sexuality, war and violence, and political participation. Accordingly, the part introductions also address the ways that the three main issues overlap and influence each other. For example, debates about women's sexuality are deeply tied to ideas about who can and should be granted rights. Similarly, controversies about reproductive autonomy are as much about sexuality as about citizenship. Military campaigns are also interwoven with assumptions about sexual mores and citizenship practices domestically and internationally. The part introductions enable some analysis of these contexts and interactions while allowing each chapter to focus on particular examples of women transforming public space.

The first part, "Responding to Danger, Demanding Pleasure: Sexualities in the Streets," addresses a particularly salient yet contested issue within feminist organizing. The part introduction explores debates among feminists about sexuality over the past four decades and explores some of the ways that sexuality is addressed in feminist and queer protests. The first chapter in this section, "Safe Space? Encountering Difference at Take Back the Night," uses the example of a Minneapolis Take Back the Night march to explore divergent understandings of safety in public demonstrations and the ways people with distinct expectations encounter and, hopefully, engage each other. The next chapter, "Enacting Spiritual Connection and Performing Deviance: Celebrating Dyke Communities," examines how two dyke marches enact alternative models of social relation. While the white-dominated New York Dyke March fits easily within existing rubrics for understanding LGBT activism's transformative potential, the black-led Sistahs Steppin' in Pride: An East Bay Dyke March and Celebration emphasized communal- and self-care, presenting an equally robust challenge to normative understandings of social interaction. The final chapter in this section, "SlutWalks: Engaging Virtual and Topographic Public Spaces," explores a recent formation of gendered and sexualized protest, SlutWalks, by examining how the public sphere of online debate and discussion affected on-the-ground organizing.

Part II, "Gendered Responses to War: Deploying Femininities," focuses on two of the myriad post-9/11 antiwar protests. The part introduction examines women's protests against war, beginning in the early twentieth century, and grapples with the easily refutable yet frequent assumption that women are more peaceful than men. The first chapter, "Demonstrating Peace: Women in Black's Witness Space," discusses silent vigils that mourn victims of war as a way to explore the transformation of public space into witness space. Participants at events in New York City and London used their immobile bodies and silent presence to draw attention to ongoing wars. By reworking expectations that women remain silent about political issues, they offered embodied commentary and demonstrated an alternative to militarism. The following chapter, "Uncivil Disobedience: CODE-PINK's Unruly Democratic Practice," analyzes one organization's self-conscious and playful use of stereotypical sexualized femininities in two kinds of spaces: semipublic political and legislative spaces, and public spaces utilized for collaborative antiwar mobilizations. Participants disturbed official legislative hearings and presidential nominations, lobbied Congress, and claimed space in large demonstrations through attention-grabbing feminine costuming.

The final part, "Engendering Citizenship Practices: Women March on Washington," examines how women-dominated groups claimed national public spaces while marching on Washington. The part introduction explores women's participation in the now-iconic tradition of marching on Washington. The first chapter, "Embodied Affective Citizenship: Negotiating Complex Terrain in the March for Women's Lives," examines how different constituencies navigated the ideological and physical terrain at a national reproductive rights march. The second and final chapter in this section, "Participatory Maternal Citizenship: The Million Mom March and Challenges to Gender and Spatial Norms," examines enactments of political mothering at a gun control demonstration. These events claimed citizenship rights through bringing issues coded as private, including emotions such as grief and rage, into national public spaces.

The conclusion explores the affective purposes of public demonstration. I examine the ways that group boundaries are navigated, local and national movement direction is negotiated, and copresence is facilitated in protests using my experiences at the 2015 New York Dyke March as inspiration. This recent example provides an opportunity to revisit and synthesize the events I analyze throughout *Marching Dykes, Liberated Sluts, and Concerned Mothers.*

PART I

Responding to Danger, Demanding Pleasure

Sexualities in the Streets

Introduction

Part I addresses sexuality, long an important aspect of feminist organizing and of intrafeminist disagreements. A 1984 volume, edited by Carole Vance, bears the simple yet illuminating title *Pleasure and Danger*. These two terms, either together or separate, frame most feminist responses to sexuality. The focus on danger seemed more prominent in the 1980s when I first encountered feminist writing about sexual violence and images of women in the media. Vance's anthology grew out of one attempt to broaden this focus, a conference that also became one of the key events in what is often called the feminist sex wars. On April 24, 1982, Barnard College hosted "Towards a Politics of Sexuality," a conference exploring the pleasures and dangers of women's sexualities. Organizers and participants wanted to challenge cultural assumptions that women's sexuality was passive and oriented toward male sexual assertiveness; however, they believed that discourses focused on the exploitation of women only presented a small slice of the broader context of women's sexuality. Attention to race and class, as well as inclusion of butch/femme lesbian sexuality and S/M practitioners, were central to their mission. The latter two foci angered feminists associated with the antipornography movement. This other group of feminists responded with direct actions, including phone calls to the university and to speakers' employers and a protest outside the conference. Demonstrators wearing T-shirts declaring "For a Feminist Sexuality" also handed out leaflets critiquing the conference and invited speakers. (Vance's epilogue to *Pleasure and Danger* discusses these protests in some depth.) This conflict over how feminists should approach women's sexuality led to the confiscation of conference agendas and greater surveillance by Barnard authorities of the center sponsoring the event; it also contributed to an already long-standing division among feminists over how best to address sexuality in a misogynist and erotophobic society.

In recent years, more feminist thinking has emphasized women exploring their sexuality and making choices about whom they have sex with, how often they have sex, and what kind of sex they enjoy. Some of these latter perspectives developed in conversation with LGBT and queer studies. Yet the most commonly recognized feminist view of sexuality remains focused on sexual dangers rather than pleasures. For example, I recently visited a used bookstore with a substantial collection of older academic texts. In their LGBT studies section, I found a volume of the journal *Social Text* from 1993 devoted to the sex trade that included numerous contributions by feminist scholars, including Anne McClintock (the guest editor), Nancy Fraser, Janice Irvine, Judith (now Jack) Halberstam, and Linda Williams. In the women's studies section, I found a 1981 edition of *Pornography: Men Possessing Women* by Andrea Dworkin. While the placement of a cultural studies journal devoted to sexuality in one section over another might well have been arbitrary, it also represents a common split. Critical explorations of sexuality are generally seen as lining up with queer analysis, while discussions of the negative aspects of sexuality are seen as part of feminist analysis, even though numerous writers in both camps address both dimensions (and often see their work as being part of both arenas of knowledge production). Notably, the articles in the *Social Text* volume do not simplistically celebrate sexuality, nor do they focus exclusively on nonheterosexual behaviors.

Public demonstrations also reflect this view of queer approaches to sexuality as focused on pleasure and feminist approaches as focused on danger. After the 1969 Stonewall rebellion, people started coming together on the last Saturday in June to remember this iconic example of LGBT resistance to police violence. In their early years, these events were protests. Over time, the tone has shifted toward joyful play rather than dissent. In the United States, the iconic annual feminist protest is Take Back the Night, which now occurs primarily on college campuses but originated in communities where women came together to protest sexual violence and social norms that blamed women for the violence they experienced. Many of these events provided opportunities for participants to share their experiences with others as a way to destigmatize experiences of violence and transform an isolating experience into a collective one. Both events originated in resistance to social norms and violence; however, current versions of each have distinct and divergent tones. These two events are but a small percentage of public demonstrations addressing sexuality, but their iconic status demonstrates the frameworks that are most recognizable as either queer or feminist.

The demonstrations addressed in this section fit somewhere on this spectrum between queer expressions of pleasure and feminist responses to danger. In the first chapter, I examine the 2004 Minneapolis Take Back the Night march, an event that closely fits normative understandings of a feminist approach to sexuality by using urban space to spread awareness about sexual violence primarily affecting women and advocate for better prevention and support for survivors. The next chapter explores an explicit blend of queer and feminist approaches to sexuality using two distinct Dyke Marches in different communities, focusing primarily on the pleasures of nonheteronormative sexuality. The New York Dyke March embraced the supposed deviance of lesbian sexuality as a way to defy social norms. Oakland, California's Sistahs Steppin' in Pride: An East Bay Dyke March and Celebration focused on building community among queer women and their allies. The final chapter in this section focuses on an event that fits somewhere between Take Back the Night and a Dyke March in tone and focus. SlutWalks were a short-lived and distinctly early twenty-first-century feminist phenomenon that sought to address both the dangers and pleasures of women's sexuality. Participants claimed urban streets as "sluts" in order to embrace the potential pleasures of self-directed sexuality and contest the victim blaming that frequently occurs when women encounter sexual dangers. Together these chapters demonstrate the fecundity of sexuality as a site of public, gendered engagement, as well as a diversity of ways that an emotionally fraught issue can inspire fierce public gatherings.

The variety of goals in these events translated into diverse approaches to claiming and holding space. The Take Back the Night march transformed urban parks and streets into sites for protest, education, and remembering violence. The New York Dyke March converted city parks and streets into a demonstration of playful deviance that intentionally defied cultural norms. Sistahs Steppin' in Pride: An East Bay Dyke March turned parks and streets into celebrations of a community often marginalized due to members' gender, sexual, and racial backgrounds. The Toronto SlutWalk combined elements of all of these events by protesting and remembering violence, refuting restrictive sexual norms, and celebrating participants. Streets and open spaces were temporarily transformed into sites that celebrated consensual sexuality and contested sexual violence.

Advocating for a world free from sexual violence and cultural values that limit women's sexual expression requires resisting beliefs that sexuality is a private rather than a public issue, as well as refusing the masculine and heterosexual defaults of public space. Thus, not only do these demonstrations address specific aspects of women's experiences of sexuality, they also actively contest masculine, heterosexual spatial norms and demonstrate alternative ways of being in public.

1

Safe Space?

Encountering Difference at Take Back the Night

Near dusk on April 8, 2004, a crowd comprised primarily of women enrolled at local colleges and universities milled around tables set up by local organizations in Boom Island Park in downtown Minneapolis. The emcee, a white lesbian-identified local radio personality, reminded attendees that the gathering would remember sexual violence that primarily affected women and identified a microphone available for anyone interested in speaking. While a woman spoke, the emcee encouraged people to line up. An organizer raised her megaphone and quickly explained that the front of the march was reserved for women desiring "safe space"; she then started a chant of "we have the power, we have the right, the streets belong to us tonight." Two white women holding a cloth banner reading "Take Back the Night" led the march, followed by three large, grandmotherly puppets.

As they walked toward downtown, marchers carried handwritten signs emphasizing the importance of speaking ("Stop the Violence, Break the Silence") and claiming the streets ("The Streets Belong to Us Tonight"). Others focused on sexual violence ("No Means No"), while a few explicitly addressed gender ("We Are Women, We Are Strong"), pornography ("Pornography Is Woman Hate"), or social justice ("Ain't No Power Like the Power of the People"). Still other placards recast older feminist mottos ("People Unite, Take Back the Night" instead of "Women Unite, Take Back the Night"). One placard connected violence against women to cultural and environmental destruction ("Stop Rape of Lands, People, Culture"). Within ten minutes a young white man carrying a sign reading "Men Can Stop Harassment" was marching directly behind the puppets. Once the assembly entered Hennepin Avenue, a city thoroughfare, marshals wearing red armbands held hands across intersections in order to keep the march together, resulting in angry honks from vehicle drivers. Soon police officers in patrol cars began following the group of about two hundred.

Downtown was nearly deserted; however, a few bystanders looked on, many smiling supportively. Under a sign reading "Hot Hot Hot Hot Topless Girls Beer/ Cocktails," three male employees of a club blew soap bubbles at marchers. Two young Latino men stopped their bikes in the middle of the street and watched, seeming amused. At one point a sport utility vehicle drove by, and four young white male inhabitants booed the crowd. Just after sunset, marchers entered Loring Park, a popular city center venue. The event ended with a talk by a white woman professor from the University of Minnesota, a reading by a young black male poet, and music from local bands. Shuttles returned participants to Boom Island Park and college campuses.

Different visions for how to address sexual violence were apparent in the rally and march. The event included elements traditional to Take Back the Night events—the open microphone, the safe space for women at the beginning of the march—along with other modes of engagement—a mixed-gender organizing committee, the emcee hurrying people along before the only speaker had finished, the young man marching in the area supposed to be reserved for women. Different methods for addressing sexual violence, one focused on supporting women who had already experienced trauma, the other focused on how to change society beginning at the current moment, encountered each other. These meetings of different agendas demonstrate the potential of Take Back the Night and all public demonstrations: interacting with and learning from others with different ways of approaching a similar goal. The march, rife with a diversity of views, then moved through the city, encountering other responses—support, bewilderment, and hostility. The past and the present came together as different ideologies worked to unify. Feminism met multi-issue politics, antipornography slogans moved through bubbles blown by strip club employees. The city, a quintessential site of encounter, facilitated the exchanges among marchers.

Public protests provide opportunities to be among like-minded people. Yet these spaces of encounter can also provide opportunities to engage people with vastly different experiences. What safety meant for different attendees provided a key point of encounter at this demonstration. Much discussion and critique of the concept of safe space occurs in pedagogical literature.[1] In exploring the limits of safe classroom spaces, education scholar Jeannie Ludlow attempts to create contested spaces to enable a variety of voices to be heard, including those that feel shut down by the sometimes rigid guidelines created to make spaces "safe." For her this framework allows disagreements to occur and, simultaneously, for students "to affirm another's witnessing, to testify together," a concept that draws from the Latin root of contest, "con, which means together, and testari, which means to bear witness or testify."[2] In this chapter, I explore something similar, focusing on the ways that this Take Back the Night event allowed or didn't allow people to testify together, to encounter each other, to come together in a space that endorsed a variety of forms of copresence.

Participants' and organizers' discussions of safe space predominantly addressed gender inclusions and exclusions; however, concerns about race and class also surfaced in interviews, demonstrating the multifaceted social coding of safety, security, and comfort. This chapter explores this complex terrain, arguing that simplistic understandings of safety can shut down rather than open up opportunities for social change. Accordingly, public events such as Take Back the Night marches may be better imagined as sites of encounter.

I begin with a brief exploration of the national and local history of Take Back the Night events. Then, before working closely with interview material from the 2004 Minneapolis gathering, I provide additional examples of the complexity of discussions of safety within feminist and antiviolence organizing. Finally, I offer suggestions about how spaces created at Take Back the Night marches and similar events can work as sites of productive discomfort where people can engage each other in more liberatory ways.

National and Local History

The first documented organizing to address violence against women in the United States was a January 24, 1971, Speak-Out arranged by the New York Radical Feminists and attended by three hundred women. They held a conference about rape a few months later. In 1972 the Bay Area Women Against Rape formed, and a rape crisis center began operating in Washington, D.C.[3] These activists confronted the police and hospital staff for treating the women who reported assaults disparagingly.[4] Rape crisis centers continue to be a mainstay of organizing to end sexual violence; however, their relationship to the state has changed dramatically, and some question whether they remain feminist.[5] Public protests, including Take Back the Night marches, have been part of organizing to end sexual assault since the 1970s, drawing attention to continuing brutality and inadequate responses by institutions.

Maria Bevacqua traces "the concept, if not the name" of Take Back the Night to a pamphlet titled *Stop Rape* published in 1971 by Women Against Rape (WAR) in Detroit.[6] In 1978 Women Against Violence in Pornography and the Media (WAVPM) sponsored a conference called "Feminist Perspectives on Pornography" in San Francisco that included a Take Back the Night march. A press release describes marches held in Boston, Denver, Philadelphia, and London prior to the one WAVPM planned for that November.[7] A few years later an anthology entitled

Take Back the Night, dedicated to "the thousands of women in this country and abroad who recognize the hatefulness and harmfulness of pornography, and who are organizing to stop it," emerged, chronicling the movement.[8] For the editor, Laura Lederer, and many other seventies organizers, taking back the night meant demanding that women be safe not only from sexual assault but also from sex work and pornography, which they linked to violence against women. Feminists never universally linked sexual violence to pornography; however, in the 1970s and 1980s the perspectives articulated in this anthology were widely shared.

Like other events stemming from the women's liberation movement, including consciousness-raising groups, music festivals, rape crisis centers, and feminist bookstores, Take Back the Night was designed to provide a place for women to speak their truths in a culture that privileges men's perspectives and experiences. Take Back the Night marches frequently include a nighttime procession that temporarily reclaims streets, time for survivors to testify about experiences of violence, invited speakers and musicians, information about services, and on-site support for those in need. The time that is generally provided for survivors to testify, often called a speak-out, is a unique feature of these demonstrations and allows the audience to hear about traumatic intimate experiences. Survivor interpretations of their experiences are not challenged, but the telling of and listening to stories facilitate a discursive engagement with survivor experiences. April is sexual assault awareness month for many universities and organizations, and marches often occur as part of the month's programming.[9] Minneapolis's event is among a small number of community-organized marches remaining in the United States.

The Midwest has a vibrant feminist history.[10] The Twin Cities of Minneapolis and Saint Paul, Minnesota, are particularly associated with organizing against sexual assault and pornography. In 1983 Minneapolis held hearings led by prominent feminists Andrea Dworkin and Catharine MacKinnon that attempted to declare pornography a form of discrimination against women.[11] Minneapolis was the only U.S. city that passed such an ordinance. (The law was ultimately vetoed by the mayor.) Minneapolis's Take Back the Night march is heir to this history.

Unlike many similar events, Minneapolis's Take Back the Night has always included men. Historically, men marched in the back. This spatial arrangement of marchers allowed two approaches to ending sexual violence to coexist. Women were able to claim the streets without male chaperones, and men were able to demonstrate their support for ending sexual violence, which is primarily perpetrated by men. In recent years, this spatial segregation was abandoned in favor of a gender-integrated march.

The 2004 demonstration was the seventh Take Back the Night march organized by Minnesota Public Research Interest Group (MPIRG), a multi-issue campus-based organization that took over the march in 1997, when the local chapter of the National Organization for Women (NOW) stopped organizing the march. This shift in leadership provided opportunities for younger organizers to address sexual violence, but it also disrupted the continuity of organizing. Leah, a white Jewish lesbian professor in her fifties, was one of the keynote speakers after the march. She worried that the leadership change sidelined feminist history:

> When I moved here in 1985 there was a huge antipornography, Take Back the Night community because in 1984, right before I came, Andrea Dworkin and Catharine MacKinnon taught in women's studies. They did a year visiting professorship, and they did their antipornography course. . . . So when I came here the first two or three years there were really huge community-based Take Back the Night marches, and we did eventually close some porn movie theaters in town. . . . The most recent Take Back the Night march . . . was not connected to really any community, it was pretty much student-based, small, not a sense of history.

In an attempt to narrow this gap between history and present, she contextualized the march and rally during her postmarch comments.

As Leah's statement demonstrates, people came to the event with vastly divergent expectations. Some expected the march to replicate events held in the 1980s; others knew little about feminist organizing; still others worked with survivors of sexual violence every day and thus brought expertise and expectations from that work.

Safety: Competing Discourses

Discussions of safety are endemic to anti–sexual violence organizing and resonated with many Take Back the Night participants. For example, Suzanne, a white woman in her fifties, described the purpose of Take Back the Night as "to affirm the rights of women to feel safe." Similarly, Wendy, a white graduate student in her late twenties, explained that she attended Take Back the Night because she believed in "taking back the streets and feeling safe." Other marchers responded in similar ways, demonstrating not only the expectations they brought to the event but also the broader discourse about safety in organizing to address sexual violence.

This discourse about safety was not unique to the 2004 Minneapolis march. Below I describe issues that arose at another Take Back the Night march I attended in 1998. That spring I volunteered to help organize a Take Back the Night march in Eugene, Oregon. Two issues came up during this process that demonstrate how differing understandings of safety affect organizing to address sexual violence. The first was a conversation that haunted me for many years, the other was a series of events that dramatically shifted how the event unfolded.

One evening, the lead organizer came to our weekly meeting exhausted. She had spent the night before in conversations among employees at the domestic violence shelter where she worked about how to respond to a transgender woman seeking shelter. Other women already at the shelter indicated that they wouldn't feel safe if this woman was given shelter. Organizers were torn between offering refuge to all women and offering refuge to the most women. I never learned what their decision was, but the conversation left me, as someone still learning about transgender experiences, confused. Such debates continue to influence how shelters operate.[12]

The day of the demonstration, May 21, 1998, the city and the nation were shocked by one of the first high school shootings to draw national attention. For people in Eugene and Springfield, Oregon, two small cities separated by a river, the shootings at Thurston High School in Springfield, which left two students dead the morning after the shooter killed his parents, were particularly heartbreaking. At the final meeting about the event, volunteers learned that the march focus had shifted to address violence more generally, and the deceased students' families and other members of the Thurston High School community would attend the march.

That evening, the coalitional group marched from the University of Oregon to a small downtown plaza where a stage was set up. Organizers introduced the march as an event that usually focused on sexual violence and explained that it had been broadened on this occasion to address violence in many forms. The principal of Thurston High School spoke, followed by the father of one of the murdered children. Then women began stepping up to the microphone to testify about their experiences of violence. Part of the crowd grew uncomfortable with the topical shift from gun violence to sexual violence. Some of the people from Thurston High School began complaining to each other and to organizers about what they saw as these women's selfishness. In our debrief session afterward, the on-site counselors reported that women had approached them explaining that they didn't feel safe telling their stories because of the crowd's negative responses.

In both of these examples, people with different understandings of safety and comfort encountered each other. The security of a transgender woman was pitted against the comfort of other women who believed that transwomen were threats, physically or ideologically. Personal stories of sexual violence made people focused on gun violence uncomfortable, and their discomfort undermined the comfort of women who wanted to share their experiences.

Discussions of safety abound in activist spaces and political debates. Yet the meaning of the terms "safety," "security," "comfort," and "threat" varies widely. In her research about gay and lesbian campaigns addressing street violence, historian Christina Hanhardt explores some of these connotations:

> Safety is commonly imagined as a condition of no challenge or stakes, a state of being that might be best described as projectionist (or, perhaps, isolationist). This is not to say that the ideal of finding or developing environments in which one might be free from violence should not be a goal. . . . Ultimately, I argue that the quest for safety that is collective rather than individualized requires an analysis of who or what constitutes a threat and why, and a recognition that those forces maintain their might by being in flux. And among the most transformative visions are those driven less by a fixed goal of safety than by the admittedly abstract concept of freedom.[13]

Key to her exploration are the complex relationships socially marginalized groups have to the state and the ways that these relationships are leveraged, sometimes to the detriment of other groups differently situated in relationship to the state.

Hanhardt's concerns about how safety is understood and mobilized overlap with those of scholar and creative writer Samuel Delany. He emphasizes what is lost when interactions among strangers are coded as dangerous:

> As, in the name of "safety," society dismantles the various institutions that promote interclass communication, attempts to critique the way such institutions functioned in the past to promote their happier sides are often seen as, at best, nostalgia for an outmoded past and, at worst, a pernicious glorification of everything dangerous: unsafe sex, neighborhoods filled with undesirables (read "unsafe characters"), promiscuity, an attack on the family and the stable social structure, and dangerous, noncommitted, "unsafe" relationships—that is, psychologically "dangerous" relations, though the danger is rarely specified in any way other than to suggest its failure to conform to the ideal bourgeois marriage.[14]

For him, overemphasizing safety limits contact among people from different communities and demonizes nonheteronormative ways of relating. "Safety," therefore, constrains movement and limits encounters.

Feminist concerns with safety often draw from the discourses and policies Delany critiques. These same discourses and policies frequently, as Hanhardt points out, collude with state regulation of impoverished people and communities of color. While most feminist campaigns to address sexual and domestic violence in the 1960s and 1970s were critical of state agencies, organizing to address gendered violence has increasingly become entangled with the state. This is what political scientist Kristin Bumiller describes as the appropriation of feminist organizing against sexual violence, which, in addition to bolstering the mass incarceration of men of color and poor white men, has done little to help alleviate sexual violence against women. In fact, she argues, it has allowed for greater state control of women and marginalized men.[15] Through this transformation of grassroots collective responses into a problem to be solved by law enforcement and medical and therapeutic institutions, the "safety" of women justifies controlling them and the people perceived as threats to them.

Bumiller emphasizes the loss of feminist control of organizing to end sexual violence and feminist complicity in state-sponsored responses that reinforce social hierarchies. While neither the 1998 Eugene nor the 2004 Minneapolis Take Back the Night marches directly advocated for state intervention, organizers also didn't challenge it. Minimal participation by people not affiliated with local universities, including communities of color, raises questions about perceptions of Take Back the Night's relationship to the state. If contemporary responses to sexual violence reinforce race and class divides and frequently advocate for increased incarceration, then organizing to address it, even if not immediately affiliated with the state, might seem unfriendly to communities that are targeted for surveillance and state control.

Creating Safe Spaces

Creating space that feels comfortable to a diversity of people isn't easy. People bring experiences of violence and rejection. Gender-exclusive spaces may have granted refuge or been sites of exclusion. Mixed-gender organizing may have created opportunities for greater understanding or been unproductive. Particularly fraught issues for participants in the Minneapolis 2004 Take Back the Night march were the amount of space allowed for testimony, gender inclusions and exclusions, and race and class diversity.

TESTIMONY

Some find publicly testifying about experiencing sexual violence healing in a culture where sexual violence is seen as a private rather than a public topic, women's perspectives are regularly discounted, and survivors of all genders are habitually blamed for the violence they experience. In light of this, Take Back the Night has historically been a hybrid space that blends protest with support, a space where people could tell their stories, hopefully purging the self-hatred that often accompanies violence. Putting into words the seemingly unspeakable knot of memory and feelings is therapeutic for many people. Hearing others speak can demonstrate that one's experiences and feelings are not isolated or aberrant. It can help demonstrate the collective trauma of sexual violence.[16]

These disclosures risk other kinds of reception. Audiences can tire of disclosures. The details can become overwhelming, blending into each other.[17] Feelings of frustration and anger after hearing stories can seem too much to bear. A clear path to resolve the problems identified can seem elusive. There's also the risk that audience members' investment is prurient. Despite these perils, within feminist organizing, testimony has long served as a way to demonstrate the ways that personal experiences are part of political organizing.

In 2004 Suzanne was finally ready to speak about her experiences with sexual violence, which had occurred two decades before. She attended and helped organize Take Back the Night because she was invested in telling her story and creating a space for others to do so as well. At a prerally before the Minneapolis event, she testified. For her, sharing was healing in ways she struggled to explain:

> I can tell you that spiritually and emotionally and mentally it cleared me to be public. I don't know all the words to say to explain this . . . but it's because publicly I could do it. . . . My huge issue in life where I almost didn't end up being here and choosing not to be here on this planet anymore is because I felt so invisible, because I did not have a voice, because I did not have a voice I was so invisible. I felt so much that way for so many decades that being public is absolutely key.

Sharing her experiences with violence and self-hatred in a small public forum was one of the most moving things she'd ever done. Suzanne viewed testimony as an opportunity to connect with other survivors, creating something like a public support group. The anonymity of the crowd was important, as was the potential for testimony to overcome it. Her testimony broke down barriers between her and some traditionally aged students: "Those young students, who actually would have been my daughter's age, just one at a time buried their heads into my chest. They just sobbed. . . . I was so happy I could be there and be present to them at that moment and that they could be present."

She wanted to tell her story again that evening but claimed that the Minneapolis gathering "wasn't safe." The emcee hurrying people along, marchers lining up, and the safe space at the beginning being announced but not explained diminished her comfort. She encountered a protest culture that emphasized the march over the rallies before and after, as well as a sense of weariness about long speak-out sessions. (While we were setting up our interview, the emcee explained that she was glad that the speak-out session was short in comparison to those she found tediously long at events in the 1980s.)

Some women who had been to other Take Back the Night marches also found the minimal space for survivors to share their experience disconcerting. Wendy connected the lack of space for testimony to what she described as the unfriendliness of the crowd:

> But it wasn't really a welcoming crowd—only one person did a speak-out, and I've never been to a Take Back the Night march where only one person did a speak-out. And I felt like it must have been because people didn't feel comfortable. . . . And then when we did the march itself, I didn't really feel like there were people

> who, if you would be having flashbacks or something, that you could go talk to. I felt like they said there were people with armbands you could talk to if you got lost or something, but who were you supposed to talk to if you were having issues of some sort?

She felt isolated, describing the event as lacking "warmth." She also expected more infrastructure to support people who'd experienced violence, including trained advocates and more space for testimony.

Some of these expectations came from Wendy's experiences organizing other marches and, as I discuss in more depth below, her discomfort with the presence of openly queer speakers. Her description of another Take Back the Night event she attended and helped organize is quite different from her lukewarm response to the 2004 Minneapolis march and rally:

> We never had a very big turnout—it was probably even a third of what we had [in Minneapolis]. So it's small, but we would make the paper—not only the school paper but the paper in town. . . . I was one of the advocates. . . . We wore these shirts that made us stick out from the crowd, and we had to be in the front of the march and at the back of the march and at the sides—like the marshals. . . . People would often just grab you and say I need to talk to you.

Wendy seemed nostalgic for another time in her life when she was part of a closer-knit community and an organizer rather than a participant.

Other participants also referenced other events they'd attended previously as counterpoints to the 2004 Minneapolis march and rally. Juana, a queer Latina in her midtwenties, described a Take Back the Night event she attended at another university: "After the march is done whoever wants to can go in this room, and they tell their stories, and you can hear people's stories being an ally or whatever. It is really interesting, and it's more personable or something, and you feel like it's shared, even though you may have not ever gone through any of these experiences. Whereas in Minneapolis you don't really get that at all." For her, testimony provided an opportunity to connect to other people through engaging with their experiences. Notably, the speak-out sessions she attended were optional. Those who wanted to march but not share or listen could do so, leaving a more intimate group to testify and listen.

Jin, an Asian American queer woman in her midtwenties, also described a previous demonstration as "more community-based. . . . It was a smaller march . . . with personal testimony." She remembered a particular woman who spoke: "They led the march to a department at the university, and at that moment this girl talked about her sexual harassment case that she hadn't talked about at all with anybody, and it was with a prominent professor at the university, and the professor was there at the march. . . . She was very emotional because she was coming out of the dark and telling her story." The emotional intensity created an opportunity for people to engage with the realities of the issue they came together to address. Jin used this other march as a counterexample: "That Take Back the Night was people from the crowd coming up and testifying for the first time, whereas for this Take Back the Night rally it was artistic, it was statistics." At the other event, the crowd formed a collective support structure that enabled survivors to speak, transforming the space into an opportunity for encounter. In Minneapolis in 2004 the focus was on the abstract political aspects of violence rather than on traumatic experiences. These distinct emphases created different kinds of spaces.

GENDER INCLUSION AND EXCLUSION

The organizing framework at the 2004 Minneapolis march was explicitly gender inclusive, although the march was women dominated. This reflected not only Minneapolis's history of including men but also an activist orientation that emphasized the importance of men's participation and a growing awareness of transgender people. For most participants, this emphasis was welcome; however, a few people believed that gender inclusion was linked to lack of attention to women survivors' needs.

Organizers understood that planning a Take Back the Night march involved issues that were different from those of other kinds of marches. Mandy, a white woman in her midtwenties who had led the organizing the year before, explained the difficulty of creating a space where everyone feels safe:

> We debated a lot about how to work with the safe space and how to make it good, because when we were thinking about it, it seemed like it would take a lot of courage for women to even want to be in the safe space. . . . It's basically separating yourself from the rest of the group and saying "There is some reason why I need to be in this space," . . . and we didn't really know how to create the right mood where people would feel comfortable doing that.

She worried that attempting to create an gathering that did the work of a gender-exclusive event and of a gender-inclusive event could backfire, leaving women feeling uncomfortably exposed.

Christine, a white heterosexual woman in her early twenties and the lead organizer for the 2004 march, described the planning process on a more macro level, emphasizing the delicate balance required for a successful event: "Take Back the Night is such a balance that you have to strike because sexual and domestic violence is such a hard issue to deal with because . . . the transformation from someone that has been a victim to becoming a survivor is so intense and so delicate that there's such a space that you have to create at Take Back the Night, like a feeling of safety and openness for people to come." The difficulty of addressing trauma along with event logistics, while common in feminist organizing, was new to these organizers. In other campaigns, they had primarily focused on getting people to events and ensuring adequate technical support and transportation.

Some participants questioned whether organizers achieved the right blend of logistical and affective success. For example, Suzanne linked her sense of safety to how the space was organized and who attended the event. Because a man raped her a few decades prior, men in the audience and on the organizing team were disarming:

> Ideally men, women, [and] children would all be supporting this. But this is not an ideal world. . . . I real quietly freaked out at my first MPIRG meeting when I walked in there and realized it was co-ed. . . . It wasn't like I thought they were going to hurt me, but I did not want them there because it wasn't safe with all the issues and the history I was bringing. . . . That's the whole reason I didn't come years ago. . . . If there was a man there, there would have been no way I would have done a speak-out; actually, I wouldn't have even wanted to march. . . . I loved meeting all the young men that helped at the MPIRG chapter after I was with them for a number of weeks, but still I think it should be women only.

She saw great promise in men's participation but wasn't ready to work with men to address sexual violence. Despite her misgivings, she worked alongside other organizers to make the event as welcoming for survivors as possible. In particular, she pushed other organizers to think about how to create a space where survivors would feel safe. She didn't think that her efforts worked, though, since the "safe space closed up within a matter of seconds on the parade route." The failure of this small gesture was a big deal for her. "There was no safe space," she declared. "It wasn't made to be safe in any sense, coming from the history I come with."

Suzanne seemed to mourn an opportunity she hadn't taken earlier in her life, as well as the lack of space for her to speak once she was finally ready. Once she was prepared to tell her story, organizing to address sexual violence had changed. She was a woman out of time and place who still needed to establish for herself that her story was valid and who encountered younger people who took for "granted that misogynist violence is a legitimate political issue."[18] Her discomfort discussing her experiences in a mixed-gender setting ran counter to many other people's understandings of how to best address an ongoing social problem.

Despite the similarity of their critiques of the march's organization, Wendy didn't share Suzanne's investment in women-only spaces: "I agree that there needs to be a safe space, but just because men are there I don't think it precludes a safe space from forming. And that's what I like about Take Back the Night is that it's possible to have this safe space with people that you wouldn't have necessarily thought you could." Gender diversity didn't undermine the safety of the space, since, for her, people's intentions rather than their identities shape the space.

For two of the women of color I interviewed, women-only spaces were linked to people-of-color-only spaces. Rebecca, an African American–identified mixed-race lesbian and one of the few people not affiliated with any of the local colleges that I spoke to, described making events limited to a certain demographic as complicated yet sometimes necessary. "I think there's an absolute reason for a-lot-of-things-only events. But that doesn't mean it's not going to turn people away," she said. In light of this, she believed that "it's crucial for women, especially women who have been abused or attacked or in unsafe situations ever, to have a space where they feel safe and to be able to build their voice and to be able to build their strength and their identities and then go back out into the world, into the unsafe world." Making an event such as Take Back the Night one of these spaces would be complicated. "I could see it looking like it's a march against men. I could see many people taking it that way, and also because it very often has a lot of dykes in it I think that straight women are going to look at it like 'they hate men, I love men, I can't be part of that.'" Thus, for her making something exclusive is risky yet important.

In discussing women's baths in Sydney, Australia, Kurt Iveson claims that "some kinds of exclusion might be justified on the grounds that they facilitate the exploration of forms of co-presence and sociability which are not possible in other public spaces."[19] Arguments for women-only spaces seek copresence that some believe is impossible in mixed-gender settings due to the male dominance of most aspects of social life. Unlike the copresence Wendy advocated for, which brings people together based on their investments rather than their identities, the solidarity sought by Suzanne and Rebecca is based on shared experiences of oppression.

Jin also believed that the benefits of exclusive spaces outweighed the risks. She wanted there to be a gender-exclusive space within Take Back the Night; however, she thought that men who wanted to support women should also have a space within the event. "I think there should be a safe space for women to talk about those types of violations or abuses that have happened within an all-woman's space and for men to have a teach-in space." This middle-ground approach, similar to Juana's example above, allows men to be part of the event while still creating a space for women to speak to other women about their experiences. Yet it doesn't address Wendy's view that integrated events enable learning experiences that can lead to greater change. As these perspectives demonstrate, "safe space" has many potentially conflicting meanings.

Some who believed that women-only spaces are beneficial weren't sure that Take Back the Night was the kind of space that needed to be gender exclusive.

Andy explained that as someone who had recently begun taking testosterone as part of a gender transition, he was figuring out which spaces he'd been part of in the past were still appropriate for him: "I don't think that there's many transmen who want to go into a women's space, because that would be really uncomfortable, and you would definitely feel the same thing I feel in my AA [Alcoholics Anonymous] meeting, where it's a women's AA meeting and I'm like 'At some point obviously I can't be here. Once I'm on higher doses of hormones, it's going to be really uncomfortable for everybody in this room, including me. . . . It's going to suck.'" Regardless of his belief that he would need to find a different AA group, he was invested in attending Take Back the Night as a man, just as he was as a girl marching in the front of the march with his mother while his dad and brother marched in the back. While he understood the need for women-only spaces and had benefited from them in the past, he saw Take Back the Night and the Dyke March, which he also attended in 2004, as spaces for people with a variety of gender identities.

Different approaches to violence address distinct facets of social experience. Jin, Rebecca, and Suzanne primarily focused on addressing past and current issues. In contrast, Wendy posited that experiences at an event such as Take Back the Night can have lasting effects, allowing people to be better able to talk about their experiences or hear about others' experiences in private settings. This ripple effect is one of the key arguments for creating temporary spaces that demonstrate other modes of interaction. Jin, Suzanne, and Rebecca emphasized a different kind of extension beyond the event. In their vision, the comfort people find in exclusive spaces provides strength to face the difficulties marginalized people encounter. In both views, events allow people to practice modes of interaction that can become part of their everyday lives.

Concerns about men's participation are tied, in complex ways, to discussions about transgender inclusion in gender-exclusive spaces. The legacy of transgender-exclusive interpretations of women-only spaces, such as those employed at the Michigan Womyn's Music Festival through their womyn-born-womyn-only policy, have influenced interpretations of gender-exclusive spaces.[20] Some participants framed their support for men's participation as responses to trans-exclusive interpretations of women's space. For example, Mandy explained that for her, all forms of gender exclusion are connected: "I feel really passionate about transgender issues, and I feel like by saying that anyone is excluded, then like you have to define what 'woman' means and what 'man' means. . . . I just don't want to be defining what other people are . . . and so I think it's really important to be like 'everyone is included because this is a problem in everyone's lives.'" Her statement demonstrates familiarity with trans-exclusive radical feminist views and an understanding of gender as self-defined rather than biologically or socially determined. As she emphasizes, exclusion requires defining people's gender for them.

March participants demonstrated two ways of approaching transgender inclusion. One focuses on self-definition but tends to still view people as either men or women. For example, Rebecca asserted, "I personally feel like it's for transgender people to choose where they feel most comfortable, whether it's in transgender-only spaces or women's spaces or male spaces only or a bunch of different people spaces." For her, gender-exclusive spaces can be transgender friendly as long as people are allowed to decide for themselves which spaces are appropriate for them. The other position questions the binary itself. Erica explained that people "think of sex in men and women, and it's really hard for people to break those [habits]." Thus for her, exclusion of men assumes a gender binary and ignores the range of gender expressions people might have.

Most people in our society are not well equipped to address people who don't identify with a binary gender system that ties birth sex to adult gender identity. Yet because some transgender people identify as men or women and others do not, paths for inclusion are sometimes confusing. Inviting all women-identified people to women-only events rejects transgender-exclusive practices, but it may not address the experiences of men such as Andy who were raised as girls and still have ties to women's spaces or people who find both labels limiting. The Minneapolis Take Back the Night march's policy of being open to everybody allowed for self-definition for participants but didn't address the modes of sociality enabled or disabled by social hierarchies.

Many people I interviewed had not thought much about transgender inclusion or remained unsure of how to include transgender people. A few were very uncomfortable even discussing transgender inclusion, describing such conversations as "controversial," in Jin's words. Wendy expressed the most discomfort with transgender issues: "And of course it would be good to see everyone included, right? People doing personal narratives of gays, lesbians, transgenders, straight people—whoever. But it does need to be balanced. We do need to realize that it's an including event for everyone and not just these particular populations. . . . If someone wants to get up and talk about a transgender who was abused in some way, that would be fine. They should be welcome just the same as anyone else." Wendy struggled to respond to my question. She had already described the event as focusing too much on gay and lesbian people because one bisexually identified speaker was from an LGBT advocacy group, the emcee was a local lesbian celebrity, and an out lesbian professor spoke at the after-march rally. This left Wendy uncomfortable, defensive. She didn't want to appear homophobic or transphobic, but she also wanted the comfort of a group dominated by heterosexual cisgender people.

Her statement that transgender people "should be welcome just like anybody else" is often described as a liberal inclusion model. Saying that everybody is welcome isn't the same as working to create a space where people know that they'll be recognized and affirmed. Such approaches to inclusion are generally nonperformative, not creating the conditions necessary for inclusion.[21] Given histories of transgender exclusion in some feminist communities, welcome needs to be explicit. She also never advocated for transgender people to speak about their own lives; instead, she grudgingly granted that others could speak for them. Transgender people are clearly outside of her vision of a feminist community.

Wendy's discomfort is particularly complicated in light of Andy's comment that the 2004 march was the first time that transgender people had been mentioned from the stage, a reference he found affirming. This small welcome was meaningful for him, yet it contributed to Wendy's uneasiness. It also demonstrates that comfort may not be the ideal goal. Change often requires discomfort. A robust understanding of inclusivity involves those who are already included risking becoming uncomfortable in order to create new practices and spaces that affirm those who aren't already embraced.

SAFETY AND CROSS-RACE, CROSS-CLASS ENCOUNTERS

The 2004 Minneapolis Take Back the Night march was, like many public demonstrations, white dominated. Participants provided a variety of explanations for this dynamic, including police brutality, the specific history of Minneapolis organizing, the legacy of white-dominated feminism, and limited outreach by organizers. Those I interviewed who were familiar with local communities of color described the event as either unwelcoming or of low priority. Andy explained that people of color he knew were reticent about attending protests because of the legacy of violence against people of color. He also described one person who didn't want to attend without other people of color. Similarly, Suzanne explained that when she began volunteering for MPIRG she called a number of organizations that worked closely with communities of color. "I couldn't hardly get past the second or third sentence of what I was calling about, and I knew I was being shut down. . . . I don't know if they'd experienced times before where they weren't heard or their critiques weren't received." Without more research, it's impossible to know what that history was, but critiques of similar events may provide clues.

Some Take Back the Night events (as well as their British counterparts, Reclaim the Night marches) have downplayed police violence against communities of color and have sometimes focused their reclamation of space on working-class areas dominated by people of color. Consider this description from Kum-Kum Bhavnani and Margaret Coulson:

> Reclaim the Night marches, held in the mid- to late 1970s, often went through black areas while demanding that the streets be made safe for women, sometimes with an accompanying slogan for "better" policing. Despite the arguments and protests of black women then, and since, Reclaim the Night marches (e.g., one held in Cambridge in 1984) often still carry slogans for "better" policing. Not only is it racist to march through black areas with demands for safer streets for women (which women?), but also, to understate it, we don't know of many black women who see police protection as any way of doing this.[22]

In this example, racially privileged groups of women claimed black-dominated spaces in order to challenge gendered spatial norms and simultaneously reinforced white racial dominance of urban spaces. While their analysis focuses on the U.K., Take Back the Night events in the United States have often ignored the ways that state institutions replicate a variety of social hierarchies based in sexist, racist, heterosexist, and classist norms.

There are hints that the Minneapolis march replicated at least part of this legacy. Andy explained that in earlier eras, when NOW organized the march, "they always changed the marching pattern and sometimes it seemed like they marched through South Minneapolis . . . where there were higher incidents of police responding to domestic violence calls and other things like that. They would march down those areas." This practice didn't take into account patterns of police response that focus on working-class communities and communities of color. Similarly, the Minneapolis antipornography movement's work with the state also advocated for increased state surveillance. Organizers were hoping to leverage state power to address gender issues without addressing how state power is also used to enforce race and class hierarchies. As Bumiller argues, the neoliberal state has appropriated feminist organizing against sexual violence, resulting in criminalization and surveillance of marginalized communities. While practices that emphasize the supposedly inherent criminality of men of color do not originate in feminist organizing, "the movement framed the issue of rape without regard to its historical legacy as a tool to control black men."[23] As a result, women of color feminists have been among the most vocal feminist critics of moves to focus on individual victims and locate responses within various apparatuses of the state.[24]

Some organizers and participants in Minneapolis's Take Back the Night were aware of similar critiques of feminist organizing from women of color and their allies. A number of participants thought that the march drew mostly white people because feminism is generally associated with white women. For example, Mandy attributed it to "the long history of women of color being left out of women's rights issues." She explained that "violence is a really huge issue everywhere. I don't think that it really discriminates as far as class or race or gender or anything.

But I think . . . a lot of people when they just say woman it sounds like they mean white woman."

Additionally, some participants thought that organizers hadn't done enough outreach in communities of color or working-class communities. Rebecca said, "I don't think it's advertised in communities of color. And I think because it's especially advertised in colleges and little coffee shops and a lot of communities of color don't hang out at those places. So along with the racial thing it's kind of a class thing." Jin described the event as "university focused," and Andy noted the dominance of participants from local universities. Considering that the organizers worked for an explicitly university-oriented organization, this isn't that surprising. Yet, given the difficulties in creating a space that welcomes people with different experiences with violence, outreach alone probably wouldn't have dramatically shifted the racial composition of the march. Racialized distrust generally has deep roots that require long-term organizing to eradicate.

Creating Spaces of Encounter

The 2004 Minneapolis Take Back the Night march and rally brought people predominantly associated with local universities together to raise awareness about sexual violence. While it's not clear that everyone felt comfortable at the event or that it successfully pulled together the desired audience, people came together to express solidarity with survivors of violence and to demonstrate investment in ending sexual violence. Accordingly, the focus of Take Back the Night might be better understood as encounter instead of safety.

By encounter I refer to something akin to, yet broader than what Samuel Delany theorizes as contact. For Delany, contact is what happens when people from different communities and classes coexist in urban spaces. Contact happens in bookstores, in grocery stores, in spaces designed for casual sex. It is the happenstance, one-on-one interactions that occur when people are in proximity to each other.[25] Encounter, in the way I'm using it, is more collective and more structured than happenstance contact. Encounter is coexisting for a period of time. It requires some kind of recognition of another person's experiences or needs. Thus, spaces of encounter include possibilities for one-on-one contact, as well as being part of an audience to someone else's story, engaging collectively around an idea, and responding to a threat. Public events create possibilities for encounter by bringing people together around a shared theme or goal.

Contact does not necessarily lead to encounter. Geographer Gill Valentine raises important questions about the way that many urban theorists romanticize what happens when people are in proximity to each other.[26] Valentine demonstrates the degree to which people who regularly came into contact with each other harbored prejudicial views of each other. Similarly, geographer Helga Leitner explored the overwhelmingly negative responses when increased numbers of nonwhite immigrants moved into a white-dominant small town.[27] In each case, contact resulted in some changes to existing views, but on the whole people retained or, in Leitner's example, deepened discriminatory beliefs.

How, then, can encounters become opportunities for transformation? In particular, how can public events such as Take Back the Night that bring people together around a common goal create opportunities for engagement across difference? By difference, I refer not only to forms of social stratifications such as gender and race but also to differences based on experience, including histories of violence. As a way to begin exploring what a space of encounter can look like, I return to Suzanne's narrative.

Despite feeling too psychologically unsafe to share her story with the mixed-gender group gathered in Minneapolis, Suzanne found other ways to make the march comfortable for herself and others.

> When I got in the middle of downtown Minneapolis I just challenged myself physically to take on that space, and I tried out different points in the parade route not on purpose at first but when I realized what I was seeing after I'd moved from the front for a reason, to the middle for a reason. I was just there to help people. All of a sudden I'm in the back, and I'm watching this gentleman who couldn't keep up with the crowd, and all of a sudden I got behind him, and then I started moving a little bit farther behind him to protect that space, and something changed in me. And I realized that I was watching it from a totally different point of view, and that's when I remembered to use my body and to see if I could use my voice in a whole new way.

This group of people transformed the streets through claiming them but also created a mobile space dedicated to addressing sexual violence. Suzanne worked to maintain the space she cocreated by moving through it, assessing the tone at different points in the assembly, and protecting the rear so that all participants could remain within the bounded yet permeable space of the march. She helped hold the space with her body, her voice, and her intention.

In the process, Suzanne claimed a new role for herself, shedding her victimized status and assuming agency, becoming fully present and assessing others' needs. In her official role as a volunteer, she worked to make the march an inclusive space. Helping maintain the space transformed her as much as speaking in front of an audience had. Rather than testifying, she spoke to others, emphasized that they belonged, and shouted to other organizers to help keep the group together. The somatic and affective shifts occurred through encountering others in a public space that she helped create and maintain. While not comfortable enough to testify about her experiences, she was still able to work to ensure the group's cohesion. By encountering others and their vulnerabilities, she found strength and an alternative way to meet her own needs.

This is just one person's experience and doesn't address all of the issues raised in this chapter. Yet it offers an example of how people can allow the discomfort of encountering other people and other ideals to move them in ways that can be transformative. This example also doesn't clarify how an event such as Take Back the Night could become an opportunity for cross-racial and cross-class engagement. As Valentine's and Leitner's writings remind us, this is a problem that goes far beyond any individual demonstration. Nonetheless, Suzanne's story can provide a map for moving beyond compartmentalized ways of being. If events such as Take Back the Night were advertised as places to encounter others with a common goal, then maybe people could come together to help define a shared agenda for addressing violence and supporting survivors. The end result could mean that Take Back the Night in its current form would change in ways that current participants and organizers cannot envision. True engagement means being open to such possibilities.

Conclusion

The 2004 Minneapolis Take Back the Night march and rally was a space of encounter. People encountered each other and ideas that challenged their own. Suzanne encountered men organizers. Andy encountered the first trans-inclusive gesture at an event he'd been attending his whole life. Jin encountered an event without the emotional depth she sought. Wendy encountered openly queer people. Rebecca encountered a community that didn't reach out to people like her. Christine encountered critiques of her organizing. Leah encountered young people who didn't know her feminist history. The young women who cried in Suzanne's arms encountered her story. These encounters resulted in a diversity of responses: discomfort, relief, loss, confusion. Yet they all took something away from the event.

Rather than imagining Take Back the Night or any other public event as a safe space, reframing it as a space of encounter, of learning, would allow for a wider range of engagements. Such a framing would require patience. Those weary of public testimony might need to listen to more testimony. Those desiring deep emotional engagement might have to tolerate more statistical or artistic responses. Women wanting gender-exclusive spaces might have to confront people of other genders. Men might need to hear why some women are uncomfortable with their presence. People used to white-dominated spaces might have to hear critiques from people of color. People of color might have to be patient with uncomfortable white people. Marking such an event as a space of encounter would require openness to a variety of encounters, risking disappointment and discomfort. Change requires willingness to be moved.

2

Enacting Spiritual Connection and Performing Deviance

Celebrating Dyke Communities

On August 28, 2004, approximately 250 people, primarily adult women and predominantly black, assembled at the edge of Oakland's Lake Merritt. Spirit Drumz, a local women's drumming collective, initiated an upbeat, relaxed rhythm.[1] Four women holding a large black banner with the text "Sistahs Steppin' in Pride: An East Bay Dyke March and Celebration" in bright lettering stepped in time to the beat, leading the march onto the sidewalk along Grand Avenue followed by two women holding Spirit Drumz' red-and-white banner. Walking backward, a black woman clad in a flowing red blouse and a loose white skirt, with beads braided into her hair, led the drummers, all dressed in red shirts and white pants and skirts. The leader kept the beat with a tall staff adorned with red strips of cloth. Two black men wearing white and carrying crystal-adorned walking sticks strolled alongside her, adding to the ceremonial feel of the contingent. Shaking rattles, tapping on hand-held drums, and holding signs covered in slogans and photographs of local figures and community institutions, the assembled group followed the drummers and proceeded past the weekly farmers' market and Oakland's landmark Grand Theater to briefly occupy Grand Avenue. Children danced along to the rhythm as the group moved down the street. When marchers arrived on the edge of the lake near the entrance to Lakeside Park, a Native American woman wearing red paused to make an offering over the water. The group then proceeded along the perimeter of the lake before crossing Lakeside Drive to enter Snow Park, a small grassy space on the edge of the downtown financial district.

After entering the park, the group slowly walked up a small hill and circled a large tree. At the Ma Ajuba Tree of Joy Sanctuary rugs and cloth laid on the ground formed a path to a small incense pot at the base of the tree. Ajuba, a Lukumí term, means "I salute" or "we salute you" depending on the context; thus, this arboreal sanctuary explicitly honored participants and the ancestors who were soon evoked.[2] Altars decorated with brightly patterned cloth holding candles, photographs, a pair of antlers, and other objects surrounded the path to the tree. A joyous wail accompanied a sudden elevation in the drum beat. A black woman joined the drummers, fanned herself with the incense smoke, and began chanting: "Close your eyes for a few minutes and allow your inner self to feel the energy, the vibrations, the healing we have created. . . . Give thanks to all the ancestors who are with us on this journey in the air, the water, and the earth. . . . Sistahs Steppin' with every step we are creating medicine. With every step we are healing a nation. With every step we are creating community. With every step we are erasing racism and all the isms." Another expression of joy came from the crowd, and most of the group chanted along as the leader moved to the rhythm of her own voice and repeated: "We are erasing separation." In closing, she emphasized women's participation in social change and a clear connection with feminist explorations of spirituality: "We are resurrecting feminine energy to bring balance on this planet. Our steps give back what the ancestors give to us."

Participants dispersed and relaxed on the sloping lawn facing a stage. Another black woman stepped up to the microphone and called to the crowd, "You are fully invited to participate in song, dance, emotion, heart, and spirit," before introducing Spirit Drumz and their collaborators for the opening stage performance, Native American drummers and singers from the Hummingbird Lodge, a pantribal group that travels up and down the West Coast. A woman from the Hummingbird Lodge holding a condor feather and an abalone shell filled with ceremonial herbs moved to the front of the stage and invited people forward. "Prayer is not a spectator sport. Come forward, sisters, so we can start this prayer," she requested. After honoring the waters, earth, wind, air, and the four directions, she acknowledged the strength it takes to walk as "two-spirit" and finished with the hope that the "man who shall not be named" will have the courage to "move out of the way."[3] It was just over a month before George W. Bush would be elected for a second term, at the third annual Sistahs Steppin' in Pride celebration and Dyke March in Oakland, California. For the next three hours the stage hosted musicians and performers, including poets, blues singers, and drag kings, while people reclined and danced on the grassy expanse.

This group claimed space in a variety of ways. Their physical presence in parks and along city streets and pathways established their claim to these spaces. Drumming, chanting, and singing shifted the tone of these spaces, creating a collective sense of ownership. Ritual established a shared understanding about the meaning of the group's presence and movement through urban spaces. Presence and movement were ascribed communal and spiritual meaning, transforming the everyday processes of moving between locations and talking with friends and loved ones into political and spiritual acts. Ritual leaders, organizers, and participants held these spaces for each other, for memories of women who came before them, and for queer women and their allies who will seek their legacy in the future.

This chapter examines two distinct although related responses to the devaluation of queer women's lives: Sistahs Steppin' in Pride and the New York Dyke March. Each gathering presented a viable paradigm for social interaction that contests heterosexual norms. Both events addressed societal norms and oppressions in multiple ways, and there were clear overlaps between the groups' strategies; however, the differences between their approaches provide an entry point for analyzing the complexity of each march and help establish something of a cultural dominant, to borrow from Fredric Jameson, for each event that is attentive to the "forms of affective life that have not been solidified into institutions" that Ann Cvetkovich describes.[4] Participants held space for distinct yet complementary visions of dyke solidarity and in the process created two unique public cultures.

By examining Sistahs Steppin' in Pride alongside the New York Dyke March, I explore how queer women create geographically specific spaces for resistance. I began with a description of Sistahs Steppin' in Pride in order to shift how we imagine Dyke Marches and dyke public presence more broadly. Those who are familiar with Dyke Marches have likely encountered, in person or through media or word of mouth, the San Francisco or New York Dyke March. These intentionally rebellious events, which emerged in the 1990s, demonstrate a different variety of urban dyke presence, one more informed by direct-action organizing and punk aesthetics than race-conscious feminism or spirituality. I argue that each version models a form of social relation that explicitly contests dominant value systems privileging consumption over self-care and abstract moral standards over the well-being of women, queer people, and people of color. In the process, both gatherings created spaces to resist homophobia, heterosexism, misogyny, and, at Sistahs Steppin' in Pride, racism.

In the years following the 1969 Stonewall Rebellion, public Gay Pride celebrations became vital parts of the growing movement for lesbian, gay, bisexual, transgendered, and queer (LGBTQ) rights. This annual politicized celebration is, in many ways, a demonstration of unity among various constituencies within LGBTQ communities; however, support for Gay Pride events is not universal among LGBTQ people. In addition to different political strategies advocated by individuals and organizations, fault lines within the broader LGBTQ movement emerged along race, class, and gender axes. For example, some LGBTQ-identified people, including many people of color, have critiqued the singular focus on sexual identity.[5] Beginning in 1970 as a "protest against discrimination, police bar raids, and anti-gay violence," Gay Pride events have taken on a more celebratory and, some claim, depoliticized nature over time.[6] Dyke Marches occurring alongside many Gay Pride celebrations since 1993 were envisioned as defiant responses to this depoliticization, societal misogyny and homophobia, and the male-focused nature of many recent Gay Pride events.[7]

Queering public space through demonstrating dyke pride creates public cultures modeling alternative visions of social relations. As I explore below, the New York Dyke March favors a politics of deviance intended to push back against social norms by reveling in gender and sexual expressions deemed outside the norm. Critiquing norms rather than the ascription of deviance to particular bodies and identities provides another way of being in public. Overt displays of denigrated behaviors create a space of openness and acceptance that values exploration over conformity.

Sistahs Steppin' in Pride provides a different model by focusing on community building and emotional sustenance. The lack of explicit engagement with narratives of sexual deviance in favor of modeling self-care evinces negotiation with a politics of sexual respectability identified as pivotal for black women by many black feminists due to long-standing stereotypes of black women as sexually deviant.[8] While centering racially diverse lesbian experiences is, by definition, outside of sexual norms, Sistahs Steppin' in Pride avoids the overt politics of deviance apparent at its New York counterpart. Celebration is also part of the New York Dyke March; however, the public performance of desires deemed aberrant by dominant moral standards takes precedence. Participants perform for other marchers and for supportive, unwitting, and, occasionally, hostile onlookers.

The playful embrace of deviancy coupled with a demand for public recognition presented by the New York Dyke March fits easily within a binary understanding of queer politics that divides resistance and assimilation, a rubric often used for evaluating the potential for social change of different forms of organizing for LGBTQ rights.[9] The women marching in New York aren't interested in proving that they are like everybody else, a framework for political engagement often described as assimilationist. Instead, they refute such expectations by demonstrating their rejection of cultural norms. Participants in Sistahs Steppin' in Pride, however, provide another vision for intimate and communal relationships. They too challenge dominant value systems that privilege moral ideals over the physical and emotional safety of people deemed sexually suspect; however, this challenge demonstrates an alternative form of communal engagement rather than an overt rejection of social norms.

In what follows, I provide some historical context, then explore the New York Dyke March in some depth before returning to Sistahs Steppin' in Pride. I subsequently wrap up the chapter by exploring how demonstration participants claim and hold public spaces for queer women.

Beginnings and Contexts

While there may have been some Dyke Marches in Los Angeles in the 1970s, and some claim that the first official march occurred in 1991, most people identify the Dyke March at the 1993 National March for Lesbian, Gay, and Bi Equal Rights and Liberation in Washington, D.C., as the first.[10] Who organized the national Dyke March also remains contentious. The Lesbian Avengers take credit for planning it, as have a group of women from San Francisco, Los Angeles, Chicago, and Seattle who returned to their respective cities to plan local events.[11] All of these women were involved in some way in the march of approximately twenty thousand dykes the night before the 1993 National March. This event created a visible and defiant lesbian presence in response to what participants saw as a conservative platform for the March on Washington and male-dominated and increasingly commercial Gay Pride events nationwide.[12] By not getting a march permit, they articulated a radical position regarding the use of public space that many contemporary Dyke Marches still maintain.

A primary concern of early Dyke Marches was visibility in a heteronormative society. While media attention and representation, legal battles, and acknowledged representation in the workforce achieved some aspects of visibility, proponents of public demonstration insist that using public spaces is central to the production of queer and dyke counterpublics. In the process they enter broader cultural conversations about the nature of public and private behaviors. Participants repeatedly emphasized the importance of being themselves in a society that rewards heterosexuality and expects homosexual behaviors, if they are to occur at all, to remain out of public view. As Helga, an Austrian lesbian in her early forties who attended the 2004 New York Dyke March, declared: "For me it's important to be seen because I think that . . . lesbians in general are not so visible in society." This emphasis on public presence remains central to most Dyke Marches.

The first New York and San Francisco Dyke Marches occurred in June 1993 during their respective Gay Pride weekends and were subject to intracommunity debates. Approximately ten thousand women attended the first San Francisco march. Like the Gay Pride parade it precedes each year, the San Francisco Dyke March is the largest gathering of its kind in the nation. While many gay men were supportive of early marches, some felt "truly disgusted" by the national march because it allegedly separated the community and would therefore diminish the collective response to homophobia.[13] Others, including many Dyke March participants, asserted that the so-called gay community often remained focused on white wealthy men's experiences and that the annual parade had lost its political edge.[14] Dyke Marches responded, at least partially, to these silences by centering queer women's experiences and emphasizing protest over celebration. New York's first Dyke March drew between six hundred and one thousand participants and continues to be smaller than San Francisco's event. Numerous other cities, including Atlanta, Chicago, Minneapolis, Philadelphia, Los Angeles, and Oakland, host their own marches each year, often on the same day in June.

Racial inclusion remains elusive.[15] The Lesbian Avengers, who initiated the New York march, began their organizational life in conflict with black and Latino/a parents over diverse public school curriculum in New York City.[16] The lesbians of color involved in the New York Lesbian Avengers also walked out in protest of racism in the organization in May 1995.[17] While many women of color participate in the annual New York march, it remains disproportionately white in comparison to the racial demographics of the area. The organization in 2002 of a racially diverse, black-dominated East Bay counterpart to the San Francisco march also demonstrates a continued need for geographically specific ways of addressing sexism and homophobia that take into account different relationships to racially charged narratives of sexual deviancy.

The two events discussed in this chapter transpired in unique urban areas. The East Bay's history as site for feminist, lesbian, and queer life has yet to receive concerted scholarly attention; however, as part of the larger San Francisco Bay Area, it is both an extension of San Francisco's queer environment and an alternative to the emphasis on youthfulness and men's experiences. While historian Nan Alamilla Boyd has demonstrated that lesbians did contribute to the creation of queer urban communities in San Francisco despite claims to the contrary, focusing solely on the fabled "city of desire" obscures nearby queer spaces, including the East Bay's queer women's communities.[18] Just as the Park Slope neighborhood of Brooklyn provides an alternative to Manhattan's West Village, Oakland and Berkeley serve as more family-friendly, economical alternatives to San Francisco's Castro and Mission Districts. Lesbians in all of these locations also participate in gentrification.[19] Cities east of the bay, especially Oakland, also draw a more racially diverse group of LGBTQ people than San Francisco. Oakland's importance as a site for internal migration and relocation for black and Native American communities and international immigration for Asian communities is well documented.[20] Thus, Sistahs Steppin' in Pride provides an alternative to San Francisco's Dyke March in a location more welcoming to women of all races and people of color of all genders, and one that is known within queer communities as a racially diverse and woman-focused queer scene.

New York City is also an important national site for queer women's communities. Vibrant queer organizing has animated the city for over a century; however, while three scholarly histories of queer San Francisco extending into the 1990s

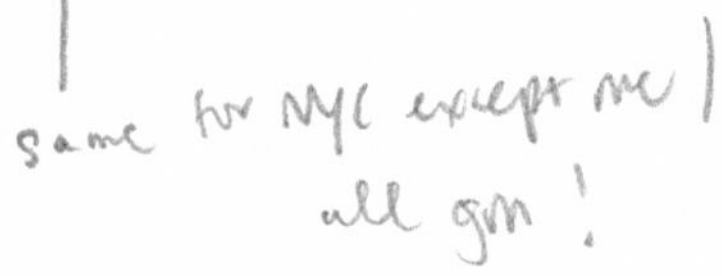

exist, the only exhaustive chronicle of New York's queer history ends in 1940 and focuses exclusively on men.[21] Scholars that include Martin Duberman, Christina B. Hanhardt, Martin F. Manalansan IV, and David Valentine address specific LGBTQ events and social processes in New York City in the late twentieth and early twenty-first centuries.[22] Home of the frequently hailed Stonewall uprising and birthplace of Gay Pride celebrations, the city also witnessed the birth of important direct action groups such as ACT-UP and the Lesbian Avengers, as well as gay liberation and HIV/AIDS research and advocacy groups. Like San Francisco, Manhattan has a vibrant community advocating for political, legal, and cultural shifts for LGBTQ people; however, while these are important moves toward greater social inclusion of LGBTQ people into mainstream U.S. society, racist and classist policies often reinforce social exclusion of poor LGBTQ people, including many people of color. The piers along the Hudson River at the edge of the West Village are particularly fraught sites where queer space is contested, pitting gender-transgressive youth of color against older, wealthier, predominantly white and male residents.[23]

The spaces where these demonstrations occur reflect the desired affective experience and audience. The New York Dyke March's confrontational celebration of deviant desire transpires along the concrete-lined elite shopping and business district of midtown Manhattan's Fifth Avenue. This internationally known location for consumption and accumulation of wealth provides the backdrop for marchers' appeal to cultural norms. For them, as for many queer geographers, the "streets represent both the dominance of heterosexuality as an institution and the persistent possibility of subversion and contestation."[24] These dykes are tired of consumer culture and worn-out sexual morality. They defiantly embrace each other and their often-denigrated identities, refusing to conceal their desires despite heteronormative spatial norms and risks of violence. Participants in the New York Dyke March overtly refuse the self-policing expected of them and proudly demonstrate their nonconformist desires despite risk of moral disapproval and violence either during the march or later, if participants are recognized without the safety of numbers. Drawing from New York's history as the site of gay liberation activism, these women combine the rebellious political energy of early Gay Pride celebrations with a celebration and performance of dyke desire.

Contrastingly, Sistahs Steppin' in Pride: An East Bay Dyke March and Festival begins with a march but continues with a ritual and an afternoon of entertainment. Participants celebrate themselves and their legacy in a small grassy oasis tucked between the popular Lake Merritt and downtown Oakland's business district, evoking a transhistorical community of queer women of color and their allies. Thus, while Sistahs Steppin' in Pride utilizes the framework of the Dyke March, it also reflects an ethics of care that centers the experiences of queer women of color. Their presence may well subvert sexual and gender spatial norms, but subversion is not the focus. These distinct histories and spatial orientations set unique stages for events celebrating queer women, influencing each demonstration's engagement with sexual politics and ideals of public presence. Dyke Marches, as gendered, sexualized, and racialized enactments, create the spaces they occur in, transforming them into dyke spaces for the time they hold them.

Queer women's bodies are central to this claiming and reworking of space; however, these marches and celebrations don't simply present embodiment as the locus of identity. J. Jack Halberstam argues that within "queer renderings of postmodern geography, the notion of a body-centered identity gives way to a model that locates sexual subjectivities within and between embodiment, place, and practice."[25] Dyke Marches provide opportunities for participants to enact sexual subjectivities and provide alternative visions for social interaction while claiming public space.

Pride and Deviant Desire: Visibility and Alternative Safety Frameworks

The 2004 New York Dyke March began as a gathering in Bryant Park, where people picked up signs to carry, finalized outfits, and then assembled along 42nd Street before marching south down the partially closed Fifth Avenue, passing the New York Public Library's regal lion statues and towering columns before moving past the Empire State Building and elaborate stone architecture holding boutiques, restaurants, and souvenir shops eager for tourist dollars. Most of the twenty-five hundred or so marchers appeared to be in their twenties or thirties and white. Many wore revealing outfits; a few were topless despite the chilly afternoon. A multiracial group of about thirty women drummed and danced behind four women carrying a large black banner reading "New York Dyke March, Women of Mass Defiance: Lick Bush." Occasionally, the lead group broke into a revised rendition of "When the Saints Go Marching In": "Oh when the dykes, oh when the dykes, oh when the dykes go marching in. I want to be in that number when the dykes go marching in." The signs marchers carried included commentary about contemporary global and national politics: "Iranian Lesbian with Weapons of Mass Seduction," "Hersband and Wife," "Cream Bush," and "We're Queer. We're Asian. Get Used to It." A series of signs explicitly evoked defiance of cultural norms: "I Defy the Closet," "I Defy George W. Bush," and "I Defy Misrecognition of My Family" were among the most notable. A crowd comprised primarily of supporters assembled along the sidelines. The Church Ladies for Choice, a drag performance troupe, sang "God Is a Lesbian" from the sidewalk in front of Marble Collegiate Church on the corner of Fifth Avenue and 29th Street, and a group of

Asian and Pacific Islander men ventured into the streets to hand paper cups of water to thirsty marchers about halfway through the thirty-five-block march.[26] Two young white-appearing women prayed for participants' souls while signaling disapproval by adamantly pointing their thumbs toward the ground.

About forty-five minutes after entering the streets, the march snaked around the arch at the north side of Washington Square Park to end at the park's central fountain. Here at the edge of the West Village, the historic center of gay New York, where Gay Pride festivities would take place the following day, a few drummers and dancers continued their revelry. Most of the crowd dispersed within thirty minutes. This conclusion to the unpermitted but subdued march was disappointing for some. Bobby, a thirty-something black queer who requested that no pronouns be used,[27] declared: "The taking up of space really needed to continue beyond the march," appealing to the activist legacy of the Stonewall uprising and the birth of Gay Pride celebrations, located just blocks away. In contrast, Veronica, a black lesbian in her forties, stated: "At the end of the march when you get to Washington Square there are no speeches, no rallies, the drummers and percussionists get together in the middle of the fountain and everybody dances. Then it takes on a very spiritual feel." These divergent perspectives are only two examples of the range of meanings participants attributed to the demonstration. Some wanted to take over public space. Others sought a festive energy. Most wanted to celebrate queerness and meet other dykes.

This spectrum of responses reflects the march's history. For some participants, taking over the streets without asking permission is still a primary goal.[28] Others question the effectiveness of this tactic. For example, Bobby mourned the loss of spontaneity: "After awhile that's not enough of a statement. . . . There is something that happens with repetition that makes it no longer a radical act in and of itself." Karen, a white Jewish lesbian in her sixties, concurred: "It's kind of boiled down to 'ho, hum, here come the dykes.'" Similarly, Sandra, a white lesbian in her thirties, noted that the event felt "rote." Like Bobby and Karen, Sandra was initially attracted by the Dyke March's political energy. Their engagement has waned along with the defiant affect; however, an erotic charge has replaced the outrage for many participants.

The New York Dyke March carves out time and space each year for dykes to publicly perform their desires. It's fitting that this erotically charged performance occurs along Fifth Avenue, a well-known shopping district. As Virginia Blum claims, "Consumption has outstripped sex as the preeminent contemporary libidinal experience."[29] Rather than purchasing goods, dykes use this space to find dates, publicly exhibit their desire for current lovers, or both. For Alana, a white Jewish lesbian in her thirties, the Dyke March is a place to be "on exhibit and be powerful in a group of people and to express deviance very publicly in a very safe way." Other participants may not crave exhibition in the same way; however, concerns with gaining "recognition for a particular subset of women," in Karen's words, or showing "solidarity with other queer women," as Greta, a white Jewish immigrant from Eastern Europe in her early twenties, articulated, still focus on performing publicly as dykes. These investments in public, collective recognition require contesting heteronormative morality.

Responding to the erasure of queer lives from dominant political and cultural representations, virtually all of the people I spoke to named visibility within a culture invested in the devaluation and erasure of LGBTQ lives as a motivation for marching. Sandra described recognition as "the biggest purpose" of the march. The Dyke March is "a Take Back the Life march. . . . It takes so much to be out to the point where you're not hiding," she declared. A public event like a march is one way to "take back" the meanings of queer lives from people describing queers as deviant and/or expendable. Sandra's comment also demonstrates her familiarity with feminist organizing, specifically Take Back the Night marches, which address sexual assault and street harassment of women. Slogans on signs also demonstrated this reclamation of space: these dykes explicitly defied stereotypes, misrecognition, and patriarchy and publicly claimed their queerness.

For Alana, public perception is linked to sexualized interactions with other queer women. She described the Dyke March as a performance with three audiences: the "girls" at the march, the police, and bystanders. "If I'm getting dressed in the morning for the Dyke March, I'm going to figure out a way to look cute for the other girls. But . . . part of the performance is people seeing us flirting for each other and kissing each other." In addition to the audiences Alana identifies, bystanders provide another set of performances for marchers to observe. Luisa, a multiracial Jewish Latina lesbian in her twenties, reluctantly admitted that her primary motivation for attending the Dyke March was to "watch as a bunch of shirtless women hold hands to block traffic down Fifth Avenue and the people in their cars being awestruck." Dykes hold the space for each other and so that others can witness their performances.

Alana suggests that deviance from accepted norms of social interaction is inherent in the relationship between performer and audience. "I think there are people who don't want to be on display," she asserted, "precisely because they think that there is something unsavory about that relationship, that it's prurient or something at some level. To me prurience is beautiful." Film studies scholar Celine Parreñas Shimizu describes the relationship Alana identifies as perverse authorship and spectatorship, which together provide an avenue for critique of normative structures of sexual value.[30] While not all of the participants in the New York Dyke March describe the event as prurient, many participants performed lesbian desire. The woman holding the sign reading "Iranian Lesbian with Weapons of Mass Seduction" combined an olive-green military-style hat and jacket with fishnet stockings and short, tight, black shorts reminiscent of the tuxedo Marlene Dietrich famously wore in *Morocco* (Josef von Sternberg, 1930). Her playful engagement with global discourses about terrorism and imperialism within a sexualized public culture rewrites scripts about desire, danger, and ethnic identity. Another striking example of perverse authorship was one participant's "casual study on women and public sexuality." Virginia, who is white and forty-something and who described her gender as "effeminate uncle, more or less," explained: "Something I've done [for] several years was to just go up to people I found hot and say 'I'm doing a casual study on women and sexuality, so can I feel you up?'" This script provides a method for approaching other participants that, depending on whom she approaches, may be perceived as flattering or harassing. Another woman wore a dog harness, presumably signaling participation in sadomasochistic sexual cultures, and others were topless in defiance of public nudity laws. Through embracing deviance these marchers turn the equation of difference with abnormality into a form of empowerment rather than aberration. Public embodiment of nonnormative sexual desires through costuming, flirtation, and displays of affection affirms denigrated behaviors and the people practicing them, highlighting performers' status as what Shimizu terms "creative subjects" rather than passive recipients of social sanction.[31]

According to Alana, perverse performance of dyke life, love, and desire "raise[s] the general level of deviance the city can tolerate. I feel like if we stopped doing it every year, New York would become a little more normal and therefore a little less safe for us." This revelry and resistance to normative constructions of proper behavior is central to U.S. queer history from gay liberation to the Lesbian Avengers and Gay Shame.[32] Alana presents an "alternative safety framework" in which freedom from violence for people deemed sexually aberrant by dominant cultural standards is valued over preserving moral ideals.[33] By claiming and celebrating deviant identities rather than refuting homophobic claims that queer people are deviant, marchers attempt to take the power away from value judgments that privilege monogamous heterosexual experiences. These moral judgments often have institutional legitimacy and therefore organize state control over bodies deemed sexually deviant. This alternative understanding of social life explicitly contests neoliberal models of citizenship focused on heterosexual family-based consumerism.[34] For Alana, performing deviance with other queer women in the Dyke March every year makes New York City safer because it demonstrates that deviance exists in the city, draining some of the power out of systems that privilege heterosexual lives and behaviors. The power of the short-lived event extends beyond the time and space in which participants march.

Johnna, a white Jewish woman in her early twenties, described the Dyke March as a fun and confrontational form of public presence. "It's kind of a 'fuck you' in some ways. 'Who are you to say that we can't be visible?'" This rhetorical question, aimed at an often-overwhelming heteronormative culture, taps into the protest energy of early Dyke Marches. While Greta described recognition as demonstrating the normality of lesbian life, and Karen bemoaned the fact that lesbians are often portrayed purely in terms of their sexuality, participants primarily discussed visibility in terms of being seen by other queer people, especially those still "in the closet." Accordingly, the march is a forum for so-called deviants to recognize each other.

Queer frameworks of visibility and safety do not always entirely diverge from conventional security discourses. Christina B. Hanhardt argues that in the late 1970s, neighborhoods and populations in San Francisco and New York deemed in need of protection from antigay violence were predominantly white, relatively wealthy, and generally male.[35] Much of the community organizing and police response focused on disenfranchised populations supposedly responsible for the violence, especially youth of color. Such engagements are backdrops for Alana's claims that "when gays and lesbians became a consumer demographic the world got a lot safer for us. It also got less interesting and more exploitative, but it's less dangerous—except at the very edge, where it's become even more dangerous." Alana emphasizes a distinction between exploitation and danger. Danger, in her analysis, references violence and harassment from citizens and authorities, while exploitation indicates economic vulnerabilities. These two forms of insecurity can, and often do, intersect; however, economic oppression is not generally recognized as a form of violence that can be wielded and experienced by people who are culturally disadvantaged in other ways.

While a politics of visibility has achieved greater recognition for some LGBTQ people, Alana identifies crucial questions about who benefits from forms of public presence geared toward corporate-based consumerism. For example, immigration status may influence whether or not public attention is advantageous.[36] In addition, recognition as an LGBTQ person in the sense articulated by many U.S. activists in the late twentieth and early twenty-first centuries may be advantageous principally for those who focus their identificatory energy primarily on their LGBTQ identity. A simplistic binary between visibility and closetedness does not address the complex negotiations regarding privacy and disclosure that some individuals with same-sex desires and behaviors perform in relationship to their families, ethnic and racial communities, religious beliefs, and jobs. The political recognition promised by dominant understandings of visibility also imagines state, legal, and dominant cultural institutions as the primary status-granting entities. Such forms of public readability are crucial for legal and political rights; however, community or familial recognition may hold equal or greater importance for many people, especially those for whom state recognition is elusive or undesirable due to racial, ethnic, or immigration status.

New York Dyke March participants' desires for visibility and safety are contextualized within a passionate embrace of sexual behaviors and identities often considered deviant. Celebrating deviance is part of an affective culture that emphasizes public demonstration of sexual desire and refusal of dominant standards of propriety. This disidentificatory stance fits easily on one side of the common binary drawn between resistance and assimilation to dominant norms of gendered and sexual comportment despite the potential slippage between the cultural politics of safety articulated by Alana and the neoliberal politics of safety described by Hanhardt.

Sistahs Steppin' in Pride, however, resists easy categorization within such binaries. Participants in the Oakland festival cultivate a joyous celebration of themselves that reflects their position as sexual and, often, racial outsiders. Thus, the recognition they seek is not from legal or political institutions; rather, the march and celebration serve to solidify participants' presence within a transhistorical collective of queer women of color and their allies. They claim and hold public spaces to honor those who created space for them and to help keep spaces open for those who will need them in the future.

Enacting Spiritual Connection: Affirming Communal Care

While many women of color activists focus their activism on more explicitly political goals,[37] Sistahs Steppin' in Pride participants focus their energy on communal and self-care, a project that often takes on spiritual dimensions and responds to the devaluation and ascribed deviancy of queer women's lives. Pioneering black feminist essayist and poet Audre Lorde, whose image was carried during the march, described self-care as explicitly political in a racist, homophobic, and sexist world: "Caring for myself is not self-indulgence, it is self-preservation, and that is an act of political warfare."[38] The march and festival also demonstrated queer women's presence in the city, but visibility was an added bonus rather than a primary motivation for gathering. Instead, communal preservation was the primary focus.

Drawing from feminist spirituality, participants connected the spiritual and the political through focusing on the work self-empowerment does "when set loose on the world."[39] While the women's spirituality movement is often described as focused on white women's experiences, the inclusion of a ritual at Sistahs Steppin' in Pride shows a geographically specific linking of women's spiritual development to social change led by women of color. The geographic specificity may have had particular resonance for the Native women participating, given ongoing struggles for tribal land sovereignty.[40] The overt spirituality of the ceremony that welcomed participants to Snow Park tied the public presence of queer women to a community of women, living and ancestral, through ritual. By seeking to "resurrect feminine energy to bring balance on this planet," women's contributions to a male-dominated culture were given spiritual, emotional, and political value. Rather than having an overtly political theme such as "Uprooting Racism" or "Women of Mass Defiance: Lick Bush," themes of the 2004 San Francisco and New York Dyke Marches, respectively, leaders focused on "erasing separation" among participants.

Sistahs Steppin' in Pride: An East Bay Dyke March and Festival began in August 2002 as a march along the footpaths surrounding Lake Merritt in central Oakland. After the first year, organizers added a postmarch festival in Snow Park, which had evolved by the third year to include the ritual described above, vendors, a healing circle, an elders' space, and a children's activity area. The primary organizer, Peggy Moore, and most of the organizing committee were part of the large black lesbian population in Oakland. Oakland has the largest number of lesbian households and one of the largest black lesbian populations in the nation.[41] The Lake Merritt area is known for its vibrant queer women's community.[42] Sistahs Steppin' draws heavily from the black lesbian community; however, people from many other backgrounds also participate. The march happened each August from 2002 to 2011, when Moore decided she didn't have the energy to keep organizing, and nobody else was willing to take over.[43]

The site-specific nature of this event is clear in its origin stories. Charlene, a black lesbian in her early forties, recalls:

> One morning after the Dyke March in San Francisco, that Monday after Pride, [Peggy Moore] came in, and . . . she's like, "The East Bay should have that." And I'm like, "Well, you should do it." . . . The East Bay has a really strong history, particularly lesbian history. . . . So [we] just really started to brainstorm on that at Peet's Coffee on Lakeshore, and then we'd head across the street to ABC Café and have breakfast, and all these different people would kind of rotate in and put their two cents in.

While she attributes the founding of the event to Moore, Charlene places herself and others who "put their two cents in" at the center of envisioning an Oakland march that would ultimately draw on and diverge from the San Francisco model. Moore's description of the event origin in a published account is quite similar. A few days after the San Francisco Dyke March, she was having coffee with friends, and "I was like, 'Dang, y'all went to the dyke march? There was a lot of people from Oakland, right? What do y'all think, should we start a dyke march of our own?' They said, 'Yeah, do it. We got your back.'"[44] The march originated in a group of friends committed to their city and the queer women who live there.

Charlene described this community-focused event as an experience East Bay lesbians craved. In particular, the second annual festival elicited an overwhelmingly positive response to the new postmarch celebration. "We had to kick people out of the park," she recalls. "It felt like it was something people had been waiting for." Teresa, who attended the second year, described Sistahs Steppin' as "the first time here in Oakland that I had experienced women energy in an all-day event." A recent transplant and veteran of the Michigan Womyn's Music Festival, the longest-standing women-only summer festival in the United States and the most salient example of tensions between lesbian feminist separatists and people invested in transgender inclusion, her organizational involvement stemmed from feelings of comfort and joy.[45] For Teresa, the point of Sistahs Steppin' is to "bring people together and to have some fun. We will work on some common causes, definitely, but that is not what is pulling us together at this point in time." Creating this kind of collective energy also motivated Barbara Price's commitment. A longtime producer of the Michigan Womyn's Music Festival and the only white woman on the core organizing committee in 2004, she mused, "I call myself a producer, but all my work is really community building." While she often produces events on her own, the communal effort of Sistahs Steppin' was rewarding. By bringing women together with the intention of celebrating and honoring themselves and those who paved the path for a racially diverse group of queer women to live openly, these organizers nurture their contemporary queer women's community. This community includes people of many genders and racial backgrounds but is centered on the experiences of lesbians of color.

Bonding is a distinct feature of rituals, according to Robert Bellah, wherein "members of the group, through their shared experience, feel a sense of membership, however fleeting," accompanied by a "boundary between those sharing the experience and those outside of it."[46] Through the ceremony at the Ma Ajuba Tree of Joy Sanctuary, participants identified a reciprocal connection to each other, the earth, and their ancestors maintained through collective marching and celebrating. Using what Kevin Ladd and Bernard Spilka call radical, outward prayer, which demands social change, along with a ritual that blends spiritual and political impulses created an event focused on connections among participants.[47] Building and maintaining affective ties through this annual festival was the gift offered to the women who fostered a women's community in the East Bay. This same impetus was reflected in some signs carried by marchers. For example, one woman held a sign that declared, "♀Proud, Walking in Spirit, Steppin' in Pride" next to a figure reminiscent of a heart with two spirals at the top. This West African symbol, Sankofa, emphasizes the importance of learning from the past.[48]

Sistahs Steppin' employed spirituality as "a tool for combating racism and injustice," a practice Akasha (Gloria) Hull describes as central to some strains of black women's organizing since the 1980s.[49] This intertwining of spirituality and politics taps into a long history of merging religion and activism in African American communities. Some strands of Native American feminism also draw from spiritual traditions to empower women.[50] The references to ancestors, the honoring of the lake, the ritual under the tree in Snow Park, and the drumming that opened the entertainment in the park blended these lines of thinking, creating a panethnic, women-centered, spiritual approach to contemporary political issues. These activities transformed these urban places into spaces for spiritual and political healing.

This embrace of the spiritual reveals a distinct understanding of social change. In her exploration of the erotic, Audre Lorde emphasizes that our culture's attempt "to separate the spiritual and the erotic" relegates "the spiritual to a world of flattened affect, a world of the ascetic who aspires to feel nothing," and feeds into a false dichotomy "between the spiritual and the political."[51] Participants at Sistahs Steppin' in Pride refuse these binaries. During their gathering, spirituality was intertwined with the political project of honoring and sustaining a community that lives outside of dominant cultural norms. The erotic was present in numerous ways—in their gathering as dykes, in the drumming and chanting, in the coordinated movement through the streets, in the naming of themselves as a community. Overt sexuality was part of a broader erotic of relationships among participants and between the natural world, the city streets, and people no longer living.

The ritual leader evoked spiritual power as she chanted, something Leela Fernandes describes as the only form of power that "can transform and transcend all forms of hierarchy, injustice and repression."[52] It's also the power described on a sign carried by a marcher that invited people to "Follow the Powah of the Drum" on one side and proclaimed "Sistah Powah" on the other. Power, spelled powah in reference to black colloquial English, is located in relationships among women and collective movements coordinated by the beat of a drum. This power seeks to transcend hierarchy and injustice, paving the way for continued community building. Sistahs Steppin' in Pride brought the erotic, the spiritual, and the political into a coherent whole. In the process, they claimed space, held that space for each other, and articulated an understanding of communal care as a political project.

Ritual links individual experiences to collective work for change. During the opening evocation, the leader highlighted the ritual efficacy of the march: "With every step we are creating community. With every step we are erasing racism and all the isms. With every step we are erasing separation," she emphasized. By speaking the words "with every step we are creating community," the leader drew on the power of performative language to acknowledge and reinforce connections among marchers. By ascribing meaning and efficacy to marchers' steps, the ritual leader described moving through space as a performative ritual. Ritual enables change through transforming the people involved. By marching in unison, divisions among queer women would hopefully disappear and bonds would ideally develop.

The march, blessing, and festival addressed contemporary problems by cultivating a caring collectivity and by emphasizing both spiritual and social change. A sign carried by a participant during the march asserted, "I am Alive. I am Creative. I am Beautiful. I can do Anything" in bright rainbow colors, affirming the marcher's potential. A white woman pulled her young female child in a wagon decorated with a sign reading "Imagine" on one side and "Liberty and Justice for All" on the other. Both of these signs appeal to the imagination as central to cultural change. Collectively, the group enacted a way of being in the world that acknowledged social hierarchies while simultaneously coming together to celebrate.

The festival also remembered what Charlene described as the East Bay's "women's history," a legacy that motivated her and other organizers to continue creating new institutions such as Sistahs Steppin' in Pride by including large photographs of local activists and institutions on signs carried by marchers. The contributions of Margaret Sloan-Hunter (a writer who founded the National Black Feminist Organization), Coleen Gragen (the founder of Hand to Hand Kajekendo Self Defense Center, a women-led marital arts school), Louse Merrill (the publisher of the short-lived newspaper the *Feminist*), and Carol Wilson and Alice Malloy (the owners of the now-defunct Mama Bears Bookstore) are not included in official histories of the East Bay. A Woman's Place Bookstore, open from 1971 to 1984, has all but disappeared from discussions of women's organizing, even if its successor, Mama Bears, open from 1983 to 2003, remains firmly in the minds of women living in the area. These institutions and figures are among the racially diverse, feminist, and queer ancestors who paved the way for Sistahs Steppin' in Pride. Through including them, the march served as a mobile archive, commemorating the history of the nationally influential East Bay dyke culture and contributing to the performative enactment of community. While marches and other public demonstrations function primarily as what Diana Taylor refers to as repertoire or "embodied practice," they can also draw upon elements of the archive of "enduring materials," as the use of photos in this example makes clear.[53]

The festival leaders' evocation of connection had a political edge. Following the performative articulation of community, the ritual leader highlighted specific issues, "racism and all the isms," indicating awareness of societal prejudices and exclusions, as well as the primary barrier to community building for the women present. This proclamation, which participants responded to with a rousing cheer, helped create a physical and affective space dedicated to working together across differences. "We're very strategic in what is represented in the celebration itself," Charlene asserts. "The march itself has a lot of different organizations that use the march in ways, like signs, to promote certain things like antiwar [views]." Some marchers did emphasize overtly political messages. A T-shirt worn by a marcher read, "No Bush, No Dick," and a sign carried by another declared, "No War! Dykes for Peace in the Middle East," demonstrating engagement with national political figures and global politics. As these signs indicate, focus on communal care did not mean that participants were apolitical or disconnected from national or international issues. Instead, the primary focus was on supporting themselves rather than on external issues and conflicts. Teresa emphasizes, "We're conscious of what's going on, but celebrating, just bringing us together to celebrate, that's a good step in the right direction." Affirming themselves was a key aspect of addressing social inequities. She describes Sistahs Steppin' in Pride as "a solidarity of just showing that we're here and we're enjoying ourselves." In a society that devalues queer people, people of color, and women, this solidarity is both necessary and inherently political.

In the process, participants also challenged normative understandings of activism. In a discussion of South Asian LGBTQ organizations, Monisha Das Gupta critiques common binaries, including "social/political, identity/issues, assimilation/resistance," to which we might add spiritual/political.[54] These categories divide queer responses to political and cultural exclusion into mutually exclusive categories based on the organizing practices of white-dominated groups. Like the organizations Das Gupta discusses, Sistahs Steppin' in Pride responded to homophobia, racism, and sexism but did so in ways not always recognized as political. Accordingly, Teresa contrasts Sistahs Steppin' with the 2004 San Francisco Dyke March's theme "Uprooting Racism": "It's not to say that we don't all have work to do, but . . . racism, it's a white institution," she emphasized. "Instead, we are starting at a good point, which is celebrating the empowerment of who we are." Insisting that collective enjoyment is both deserved and necessary counteracts the everyday demands of a culture concerned primarily with power and money. Social change requires an ethics of caring for self and consciously created community. Fernandes describes this process as spiritualized feminism, which affirms the body, mind, and spirit of participants.[55]

Through providing an alternative to dominant value systems that devalue queer women's lives, Sistahs Steppin' in Pride: An East Bay Dyke March and Celebration critiqued mainstream values using methods drawn from their community's legacy and needs. Instead of the overt sense of protest or investment in political visibility apparent in the New York event, participants in Sistahs Steppin' in Pride emphasized their commitment and contribution to a community that nurtures queer women of all races and includes allies and ancestors. The space they created affirmed this multifaceted collective. Maybe Moore's and other organizers' images will adorn signs at a future celebration of the East Bay queer women's community.

Conclusion

The two examples I explore in this chapter demonstrate that different groups of people have different needs; therefore, how public spaces are claimed and transformed needs to reflect those divergent investments. For some, claiming the streets without official permission is an essential part of demonstrating dyke self-determination in a misogynist and homophobic world. For them, holding space means transforming the city into a site for celebrating women's love for women rather than for elite consumption of consumer goods. This requires not only being a public presence but also halting the usual flow of vehicles, bodies, and dollars. For others, being able to hold hands, touch each other, and appreciate each other's bodies is what transforms urban spaces generally unsafe for open expression of queer sexuality into sites for freedom. Still others seek an opportunity to gather to affirm their community in a culture that values men over women, heterosexual people over queer people, and white people over people of color. Holding space to honor a multiracial community of women and their allies may seem not only more important but also more emancipatory than creating a space to enact sexual deviance. The Dyke March as a framework for public claiming of space has enabled all of these avenues for emancipation.

Dyke Marches have occurred for two decades and will likely continue, even if in different forms with more or less emphasis on protest, celebration, and community building. The flexibility of this framework for queer women's public presence has enabled people to hold space for each other in diverse geographical locations and toward a range of goals. Just as Dyke Marches built on and diverged from Gay Pride events, an annual Transgender March has emerged in San Francisco and other locations, and Disability Pride events occur in many cities.[56] The potent combination of pride and protest enables people to claim and hold space for each other and therefore can be deployed to address diverse needs within and beyond dyke communities.

3

SlutWalks

Engaging Virtual and Topographic Public Spaces

Just before 5:00 p.m. on May 26, 2012, participants began arriving in Nathan Phillips Square in downtown Toronto. Located along Queen Street West, in front of City Hall, and amid towering skyscrapers, the square bustled as people left work for the weekend. The woman-dominated crowd gathered for SlutWalk Toronto 2012 was remarkable not only for its gendered composition but also for the range of attire. People clad in hot-pink striped tights, cut-off shorts, corsets, garters, and electrical tape pasties mingled with others wearing jeans, T-shirts, knee-length skirts, and sleeveless flannel button-down shirts. Police officers on bicycles began circling the periphery of the crowd as a black truck with purple accents pulled up.

Organizers standing on the back of the truck announced the assembly time, and the crowd began spilling into Queen Street West. Directly behind the truck, two stilt-wearing marchers—a woman of South Asian descent wearing a bright-yellow bikini with matching stilt covers and a white-appearing man in a yellow shirt and hat with yellow pants covering his stilts—danced to the music flowing from the truck's speakers. A sign hanging from her neck exclaimed, "I Only Fuck Feminists!" His sign declared, "Patriarchy Sucks for Everyone!" The crowd followed the dancing, stilted pair east to University Avenue and then north toward Queen's Park. Marchers carried signs emphasizing women's subjectivity ("My Body Is Not Your Object") and consent ("A Ho Can Say No!" and "My Silence Did Not Make It Consensual"). Some participants marched with slogans painted on their bare thighs, chests, bellies, and backs. One woman linked misogyny and the containment of women: her back exclaimed, "End Patriarchy," while her chest and belly declared, "Set Your Wild Woman Free." Popular chants included Take Back the Night stalwarts such as "whatever I wear, wherever I go, yes means yes and no means no" and the anarchist-inspired "I shake my ass to smash the state, not to make you salivate." The chant "yes means fuck me, no means fuck you" best encapsulated the tone and message of the march, which emphasized women's right to claim sexual agency *and* refuse unwanted advances.

There was a wide range of gender expressions among the women-dominated crowd. The wizard in his purple hat seemed perfectly at home alongside topless young women and a woman who had a handwritten sign reading "Senior Slut" pinned to her green T-shirt. A three-nun contingent of the Sisters of Perpetual Indulgence in full makeup and habits marched comfortably next to a contingent from the Bad Date Coalition, an organization seeking safe working conditions for sex workers. While the crowd of approximately three thousand was dominated by white women, it included a substantial number of women of color and a handful of men of various racial backgrounds. Among the women marching were a few who appeared to be transgendered and a handful of butches. Most participants appeared feminine in comportment and under thirty.

Once the group arrived at Queen's Park in front of the Ontario Parliamentary Building, the truck became a stage for invited speakers, including Crystal Melin, a First Nations woman who addressed sexual violence in Canada's First Nations communities; white transfeminist activist Morgan Page, who discussed transgender people's experiences of violence; Kim Crosby, a Caribbean-born mixed-race artist and educator who described the intersections of gender, race, and sexual orientation for women of color; and South Asian Canadian feminist activist and scholar Tara Atluri, who explored recent issues faced by Canadian Muslim women. Other speakers discussed the importance of comprehensive sexual education and the dangers of slut bashing for teenage women. Participants held the space for these speakers and each other despite being observed by police officers and onlookers, including a man quoting biblical passages and describing participants as sinful.

This gathering took place eight years after most of the demonstrations discussed in this book. This temporal shift, which accompanies a geographic shift, enables me to address how some of the key issues explored in my discussions of Dyke Marches and Take Back the Night remain relevant. The first SlutWalk occurred in April 2011 in Toronto. This new form of feminist public presence quickly spread across Canada and the United States and throughout the Americas, Europe, and the world, eventually appearing in locations as geographically and culturally diverse as India, Argentina, South Africa, New Zealand, and Kyrgyzstan. These marches elicited strong responses of a variety of tenors and depths. Some responses were as blatantly misogynist as the victim-blaming discourses SlutWalks contested. Others rejoiced in the renewed presence of feminist public protest. Still others questioned whether this tactic could successfully challenge sexual violence or sufficiently address the experiences of women from a variety of racial, economic, and national backgrounds. These marches set the stage for electronic discussions about gender, sexuality, race, and appropriate responses to violence. In other words, engagements in topographically public spaces facilitated conversations in the digital public sphere. These often polemical engagements, in turn, influenced organizing on the ground.

In this chapter, I draw from commentary published in newspapers and blogs, participant observation of SlutWalk Toronto in 2012, and interviews with SlutWalk Toronto organizers to explore the relationship between local activism and transnational internet conversations. While I attended the 2012 Detroit SlutWalk and interviewed participants, online debates about SlutWalks led me to focus on Toronto. The vitality of the mostly online debates about the word "slut," appropriate attire, racial and cultural difference, and the role of sexuality in organizing to address sexual violence that occurred in the wake of the first SlutWalk warrants such a movement across geopolitical borders, especially since online discussions among North American feminists affected Toronto's second SlutWalk in 2012. These debates provide a window into ongoing activist debates about tactics and the complex world of feminist disputes about whether there is or should be a singular feminist message. In a sense, SlutWalks became a barometer for twenty-first-century feminist organizing and discussion. Thus, while the center of this chapter remains a particular demonstration—the 2012 Toronto SlutWalk—the context for the event requires materials different from those examined in previous and succeeding chapters.

The feminist discussions of SlutWalks posted on blogs and other internet forums demonstrate a range of approaches to critique and dialogue. Broadly speaking, there were three forms of feminist critique. The first, similar to what Eve Kosofsky Sedgwick describes as paranoid criticism, declared SlutWalk organizers and participants to be irredeemably misguided. These condemnatory criticisms labeled SlutWalkers as illegitimate feminists, hopelessly racist, or simply deluded. The second set of commentaries, which I describe as supportively critical, critiqued SlutWalks while acknowledging that participants and organizers had legitimate complaints and/or honest intentions. The third, and smallest, group of critiques was similar to the second, with one small difference. This group offered critical analysis, acknowledged SlutWalkers' reasons for marching, *and* sought dialogue with organizers and marchers. Accordingly, I refer to these as dialogic critiques. This final form of critique is similar to Sedgwick's model of reparative reading or what Sharon Doetsch-Kidder describes as loving criticism.[1] These critiques were not simplistically celebratory; instead, they addressed concerns with SlutWalk tactics while also acknowledging legitimate intentions and the possibility of transformation through dialogue.

As I demonstrate below, these forms of critique interacted in distinct ways with the two dominant topics of concern. The first topic, focused on sexuality and sexual violence, included critiques of frameworks for organizing and cultural critique variously referred to as prosex, third-wave, and queer feminisms. For many of these critics, the overtly sexualized attire of some participants and the irredeemability of the word "slut" were key issues. A good number of these commentators defined themselves as radical feminists. The second dominant topic emphasized intersectional feminist analysis concerned in particular with the whiteness of most organizers and many participants and the lack of racial analysis in the march's messaging. Like commentators concerned with sexual norms, these critics were uncomfortable with the word "slut." They focused on the racial specificity of the term and their perception that the framework for mobilization resulted from a racially privileged subject position rather than an inherent irremediability of the term. While some critiques from each of these categories utilized the condemnatory and supportively critical modes of critique, most feminists concerned with sexual norms were condemnatory, and most intersectional feminists were supportively critical. Only two interconnected commentaries called for dialogue; both were intersectional analyses.

These debates, which took place, for the most part, in virtual space, affected organizing on the ground. The interplay between events in topographically public spaces and counterpublic conversations demonstrates how deeply these seemingly separate realms are intertwined. Thus, people's experience of the space claimed and held during the march reflected their responses to the emotionally charged conversations that occurred prior to people arriving in downtown Toronto to march, chant, and listen to each other's experiences. The space was held not only in defiance of cultural norms that blame women for the violence they experience and of feminists who deemed marching under the mantle of sluthood counterproductive. Participants at the second and final Toronto SlutWalk demonstrated solidarity with each other and an investment in ongoing dialogue.

Beginnings

In January 2011, during a public safety forum at York University, Toronto police officer Michael Sanguinetti stated, "I've been told I shouldn't say this, but women should stop dressing like sluts to avoid being victimized."[2] The student newspaper reported the comment, which quickly spread via print and electronic forums. Heather Jarvis, a white queer-identified woman in her late twenties, learned about the incident after a friend shared the newspaper article on Facebook. She explained:

> I re-shared it, saying, "This makes me want to go down to Toronto Police Headquarters and bang on their door and tell them to do better," and one of my friends, Sonya J. F. Barnett, said, "I think that's a good idea. I think you should do it." Later that day, we were texting back and forth . . . and she said, "I can help you." So we were just tossing around ideas, and . . . she was talking to a colleague [who asked], . . . "What are you going to call it? A SlutWalk?" She said to me, "What do you think about SlutWalk?" and I said, "Done. Let's do this."

They began organizing along with two York University students, Alyssa Teekah and Erica Jane Scholtz, and three months later hosted the first SlutWalk. This strategy addressed Sanguinetti's message, as well as Canadian culture more broadly, and claimed public space to affirm and value women. In the process, they sought, in geographers Gavin Brown and Jenny Pickerill's words, "to change the emotional resonance of certain places and political messages."[3] The idea caught on, and soon there were hundreds of similarly named protests from Bhopal to Buenos Aires, London to Cape Town.

While the incident at York was the immediate impetus, it represented a larger pattern. "This is not just one officer," Jarvis insisted. "This is too many occasions of too many people, especially people in power, blaming the victim and completely degrading women survivors." As Barnett, who was in her late thirties and of Argentinian descent, explained, "I was reading articles about all the bullshit that was happening in Canada and in the U.S. about the war on women's reproductive rights and taking away certain privileges from women in terms of healthcare, and then there was a judge in Manitoba that had given a rapist a slap on the wrist because his victim had been wearing a tube top and no bra, and so she was 'asking for it.'" Within a cultural climate of continued denigration of women, Sanguinetti's comment was, for Barnett, "the straw that broke the camel's back." As educational scholars Jessica Ringrose and Emma Renold explain, "One of the goals [of SlutWalks] is to push the gaze off the dress and behaviour of the victim of sexual violence back onto the perpetrator, questioning the normalisation and legitimization of male sexual aggression."[4] Barnett, Jarvis, and their collaborators claimed the streets to question sexual norms that blame women for the violence they experience.

The media responded immediately. The *Toronto Star* reported that it was planning to provide coverage. Suddenly, news outlets across North America were requesting interviews with the organizing team. Barnett recalls, "I would go to bed with my phone, wake up with my phone, see all the messages, see what other organizational stuff that we had to deal with, what interviews we had to answer, and it just exploded. It was extremely overwhelming, and we thought, 'Okay, it's going to end, all we have to do is get to April 3rd.'" However, after the march on

April 3, 2011, the calls didn't stop, and criticism multiplied along with the marches themselves.

The Blogosphere: Feminist Publics, Critique, and Dialogue

Critiques were diverse and multifaceted. Jarvis explained that "we've had criticisms of any variety you can imagine, including threats of rape and death and stoning, and also people I would want to ally with and stand next to in solidarity calling me out." Feminist assessments were similarly wide-ranging, although they fell into two broad camps, which Jarvis defined as radical and racialized feminist critiques and I describe as sexual norm–based and intersectional analyses. Notably, most of these commentaries originated in the United States, which has a distinct cultural context, even though the United States and Canada share a border and a dominant language.

Competing feminist approaches to sex and sexuality are long-standing and cross-generational. These debates, often referred to as the sex wars in the United States, date back to at least the 1970s.[5] Different approaches to pornography, sex work, and BDSM are key facets of these intrafeminist disputes. Some of the most prominent contemporary antipornography feminists, Gail Dines and Kathy Miriam, were also among the most vocal critics of SlutWalks. In contrast to their overwhelmingly critical view of sexuality, another approach, sometimes referred to as prosex feminism, treats sexuality as a site of both empowerment and oppression, emphasizes women's sexual agency, and views "the body as a site of openly challenging social and sexual norms."[6] Critics of this latter approach accuse adherents of capitulating to patriarchal sexual norms and, sometimes, describe them as unfeminist. Debates about how to approach sexuality have become so reified that each side describes the other as little more than a stereotype: radical or antisex feminists as antiquated and doctrinaire, and prosex feminists as frivolous and inattentive to structural power. Like most binaries, this polarized and often polemical debate erases complexities and ignores positions that don't firmly adhere to either pole.

SlutWalk organizers quickly distanced themselves from sexual norm–based critiques from radical feminists. These appraisals generally described SlutWalks as, at best, a waste of feminist energy. For Jarvis, the condescending and, at points, cruel treatment of sex workers, as well as the denigrating descriptions of her and her fellow organizers by some radical feminists, led her to question her own commitment to the term "feminism." "Feminism is such a broad politic in and of itself, and in the last year, for the first time ever, I've actually started to become, at times, uncomfortable with the label 'feminist' because I see some of the really,

really oppressive, horrible things that parts of feminism do, and I think, 'If that's what this is, I don't want it,'" she explained.

Ultimately, Jarvis remained committed to the term "feminist" and SlutWalk's critique of patriarchal views of women's sexuality. In the process, she formulated a strong critique of feminist views that provide little room for other varieties of feminism. Barnett, in contrast, had a more distant relationship to feminism. She explained that she "retreated from the word over the years, due to its reputation of 'man-hating, hairy-legged, birkenstock-wearing' descriptions that appeared around the term."[7] This statement became fodder for some dismissals of SlutWalk. For example, Meghan Murphy, a Canadian blogger, in a post that assumed that all SlutWalk Toronto organizers shared Barnett's view, asserted:

> Rejecting the word feminist but embracing the word slut sounds, to me, a lot like we've all drank the systematic kool-aid. I feel a little bit like all those patriarchal powers-that-be are snickering, witnessing the success of their hard work, having scared women away from labeling themselves feminist and instead taking on the oppressive language used to keep us down, to insult us, to objectify us, and to rape us. Hoping that they'll stop. That maybe they'll like us, respect us, and join us, so long as we don't make them feel too uncomfortable. So long as we look sexy while we march.[8]

While Barnett's statement certainly replicated some stereotypical images of feminists, what Murphy either missed or dismissed was Barnett's explanation of why she embraced sluthood after being slut-bashed as a teenager: "When *The Ethical Slut* finally landed on my bookshelf, I felt vindicated. I could finally dump the learned shame of enjoying sex. I've seen people do way worse to others and never get labeled with such a harsh word originally meant to inflict a serious sting. So, to hell with those who thought I was a bad person for enjoying sex, who thought I was less deserving of respect."[9] This was not a simple taking on of the oppressor's language.

The way organizers and some participants use the term "slut" is intended to be a critical reclaiming. As legal scholar Ratna Kapur asserts, "It is about the politics of power, which produces the meaning with which the term is imbued."[10] This tactic is similar to what José Esteban Muñoz describes as disidentification, "a strategy that works on and against dominant ideology" and "tries to transform a cultural logic from within."[11] Rather than identifying with or risking reifying an image by counteridentifying with it, the performers and visual artists he describes embrace stereotypical images and transform them by using them differently. In contemporary use, the term "slut" judges actual or presumed sexual behavior based on moral codes that link sexual purity to self-worth, assume that appropriate sexual agency belongs only to men, and justify violence against women who violate sexual and gender norms. According to the *Oxford English Dictionary*, the word "slut" refers to a woman who either has "dirty, slovenly, or untidy habits or appearance; a foul slattern" or is "of a low or loose character; a bold or impudent girl; a hussy, jade." The shift to associating the term solely with sexuality connects illicit pleasure and filth, women's bodies and contamination. Contemporary ascriptions of sluthood are often based on appearance, assuming that one's attire, adornment, and comportment are directly linked to sexual behaviors. Rather than refusing the label, SlutWalkers respond with a "so what?" in hopes of rendering the moniker powerless. SlutWalks create temporary spaces in which the term "slut" is reworked from the inside to become positive rather than negative.

Marchers claimed and revalued a term intended to devalue women in order to strip it of its oppressive power. They were, in Judith Butler's terms, "reworking the force of the speech act against the force of injury" that the appellation "slut" has traditionally held.[12] Such appropriations are always partial and always contested; however, some attempts to resignify everyday usage of hurtful words have enjoyed some success. The revaluation of the term "queer" is one example of a relatively successful claiming of an insulting term, even if other monikers, most notably, ni**er, are widely viewed as irredeemable. While some people find "queer" hurtful, and it continues to be used as a slur in some circumstances, organizations, academic programs, and entire fields of study utilize the term in a positive way. Queer is now much more than an insult, even if it hasn't entirely shed its negative connotations. The success of this revision lies, at least in part, in exposing the sexual and gender norms that describe deviance from idealized behaviors as unethical or even sinful. The potential for claiming the term "slut" depends on a similar politicized rhetorical strategy: critiquing social norms that view sexually liberated women as shameful rather than sexually liberated women. Like the New York Dyke March participants described in the last chapter, rather than refute denigrating stereotypes, SlutWalk participants revel in sexualized genders deemed deviant by societal standards in order to undermine the disciplinary intent of labeling people as sluts (or dykes).

For many commentators, such an effort is a losing battle that drains energy away from other, more worthy endeavors. On a BBC call-in webradio show, antipornography crusader Gail Dines declared, "You can't reclaim slut. It was never ours. We never, as women, decided that was how we wanted to be defined."[13] For her, resignification is impossible. In a related written commentary, Dines and coauthor Wendy Murphy lambasted SlutWalks as a waste of feminist energy because "the term slut is so deeply rooted in the patriarchal 'madonna/whore' view of women's sexuality that it is beyond redemption. The word is so saturated with the ideology that female sexual energy deserves punishment that trying to change its meaning is a waste of precious feminist resources."[14] They saw SlutWalk participants' claiming sluthood as a futile waste of time.

Many feminist critiques focused on sexual norms share Sanguinetti's obsession with women's attire. For example, Rebecca Traister opined, "To object to these ugly characterizations is right and righteous. But to do so while dressed in what look like sexy stewardess Halloween costumes seems less like victory than capitulation (linguistic and sartorial) to what society already expects of its young women."[15] Both Traister's and Murphy's descriptions depict participants as dupes of the system rather than political actors, people who "drank the systemic kool-aid" rather than people rejecting misogynist values. Not only do they replicate misogynist judgments of women based on their appearance, they don't fully address what people wear to these demonstrations. While some don lingerie and short skirts, others wear sweatshirts, jeans, and business attire. Few SlutWalk participants dress as stereotypical sluts. Thus, both Traister and Murphy provide a simplistic vision of these events that reifies the exact sensationalist coverage to which they object.

Many of the feminist critiques focusing on sexual norms employ what Clare Hemmings has described as loss and/or return narratives that treat forms of feminism they don't agree with as illegitimate.[16] In surveying feminist theorizing, Hemmings noted three primary narratives about recent feminist history. First, progress narratives describe the feminist past as a time of intolerance that was addressed by postmodern approaches to gender and a deeper understanding of race. Second, loss narratives reverse this, claiming that, due to the influence of postmodernism, feminism was depoliticized and lost its early radicalism and structural analysis. Finally, return narratives, a subset of loss narratives, articulate a desire to return to prepostmodern feminism.

For many radical feminist commentators, the sense of loss was palpable as they berated SlutWalk participants and organizers. These commentators' descriptions of SlutWalk participants, which depict them as capitulating to patriarchal norms, wasting feminist outrage, being duped by the system, and even parodying feminism, were also overwhelmingly ungenerous. The specter haunting these descriptions was a romanticized past when women came together as women, identified problems, and worked together to address them. That SlutWalks might be doing exactly that didn't seem to matter, because commentators so strongly rejected marchers' approaches to sexuality and their attempt to revalue a sexist slur. Instead of honoring the feminist impulse within these demonstrations, these commentators sought a return to earlier frameworks that approached sexuality differently. Simultaneously, their inflammatory comments shut down conversations rather than facilitating dialogue among different groups of feminists equally concerned with victim-blaming rhetoric.

Kathy Miriam's critique of SlutWalks is the clearest example of a condemnatory critique focused on sexual norms. It's also an excellent illustration of a feminist loss narrative. In her blog post, she ridiculed Jaclyn Friedman's speech at SlutWalk Philadelphia: "The feminist outrage spurred by the comment was fierce and a terrible thing to waste—which is precisely what happened when outrage against victim-blaming in a rape culture was (and is) redirected and de-fused into shallow and bubble-headed libertarian credo: 'If you've ever been called a slut, stand up now and say together—I am a slut. . . . Stand up and say it with me: I am a slut. I am a slut. I am a slut.'" She went on to wonder whether or not leftist feminist commentator Katha Pollitt had been brainwashed into supporting SlutWalk before declaring that "the only thing that's parodic about Slutwalk, albeit inadvertently, is the event's appropriation of *feminism*."[17] According to Miriam, not only are SlutWalks not feminist, but those who support them are misguided.

Some feminists who were active in the 1970s supported SlutWalks organizers rather than lambasting them. Pollitt wasn't the only feminist over forty who wrote in support of these women collectively taking to the streets.[18] Alice Walker identified with women's efforts to control their sexual lives. "I've always understood the word 'slut' to mean a woman who freely enjoys her own sexuality in any way she wants to; undisturbed by other people's wishes for her behavior. Sexual desire originates in her and is directed by her. In that sense it is a word well worth retaining," she claimed.[19] Germaine Greer's support for SlutWalks also complicates depictions of SlutWalks as appealing only to younger women: "It's difficult, probably impossible, to reclaim a word that has always been an insult. And yet here are women spontaneously deciding to adopt it. Before we decide that thousands of our sisters are simply stupid or misguided, an attempt must be made to understand what's going on." Focusing on etymological links between sluts and dirty homes, she concluded: "The rejection by women of compulsory cleansing of mind, body and soul is a necessary pre-condition of liberation."[20] Miriam emphasized differences between generations, while these other feminists of similar age highlighted connections and the potential of street activism to bring people together.

Marches are, by their very nature, collective responses. While some have argued that public demonstration alone, without the backbone of strong organizing, is inherently limited, public demonstrations nonetheless require concerted, communal energy to organize and demonstrate a collectively held, if not simplistically unitary, belief. Radical feminist dismissal of these events as lacking a sense of collectivity, thus, also requires ignoring some of the exact dynamics that made SlutWalks newsworthy.

Along with the radical feminist critiques, a number of feminists wrote what Jarvis described as racialized critiques. I prefer to describe them as intersectional analyses because they address gender and sexuality along with race, class, and, sometimes, immigration status. These commentaries emphasize that all perspectives, including those of white participants and organizers, are racialized. For Raisa Bhuiyan, a heterosexual-identified South Asian antiracist and antipoverty activist who joined the 2012 organizing team because she "wanted to . . . find ways that SlutWalk could be accountable to its critiques and build a lot of bridges and move forward with accountability to Toronto communities," these critiques underscored "institutions of power, the functioning of white supremacy, and the lived experiences of women of color." For these writers, racial privilege and oppression among feminists provided a window into the larger workings of societies structured around interlocking hierarchies.

In contrast to assessments from commentators concerned with sexual norms, Jarvis explained that critiques addressing the racial valences of the term "slut," which were primarily written by U.S.-based black women, were "really important for us to listen to." While intersectional commentators share other analysts' concern with the use of the word "slut," they do not describe people involved with SlutWalks as illegitimate feminists, focusing instead on white and, sometimes, class privilege and occasionally describing the marches themselves or specific participants as overtly racist. While generally not invitations to dialogue, these critiques, with one exception, acknowledged the intent of organizers and the liberatory potential of gathering to collectively respond to victim blaming.

The racial valences of "slut" were key concerns for most of these critics. Harsha Walia, a Canadian blogger and migrant rights activist, penned one of the first critiques, claiming: "I find that the term ["slut"] disproportionately impacts women of colour and poor women in order to reinforce their status as inherently dirty and second-class, and hence more rape-able. The history of genocide against Indigenous women, the enslavement of Black women, and the forced sterilization of poor women goes beyond their attire."[21] Nonetheless, she did march. She explained: "Even though I did not march under the banner of 'sluthood,' I marched to mark the unceded territory of women's bodies. I marched because language is a weapon yielded against the powerless. I marched because rapists cause rape and sexual assault can never be justified. I marched to end the policing of women by other women." While she saw the framework of SlutWalk as potentially reifying an image of feminism as solely for white women invested in Western beauty standards, the pressing issues of violence and victim blaming took her to the Vancouver, British Columbia, march. Her description of women's bodies as unceded territory asserts women's rights to control their bodies in language commonly used to describe indigenous land claims. This emphasized links between contemporary and historical resistance to Eurocentric heteropatriarchal violence. Her blend of critique and support was rare among feminist commentators.

Most intersectional critiques originated in the United States and focused on black women's experiences. For example, Crunktastic, a member of the Crunk Feminist Collective, explained that "Black women's histories are different, in that Black female sexuality has always been understood from without to be deviant, hyper, and excessive. Therefore, the word slut has not been used to discipline (shame) us into chaste moral categories, as we have largely been understood to be unable to practice 'normal' and 'chaste' sexuality anyway." Redefining "slut" is valuable, she asserted, but only from a specific subject position: "I'd prefer that white women acknowledge that they are in fact organizing around a problematic use of terminology *endemic to white communities and cultures*. In doing so, this would force an acknowledgement that the experience of womanhood being defended here—that of white women—is not universal, but is under attack and worthy of being defended, all the same."[22] This description of a limited but still valuable subject position enabled critique while simultaneously acknowledging a worthwhile intent.

Another black woman blogger, Tamura Lomax, provided similar analysis and conclusions. While she presented a nuanced understanding of why people would march under the mantle of sluthood, she nonetheless feared that risks of negative consequences for some women, especially women of color, were too great. She asked, "How does one truly reclaim such profoundly cross-pollinated terminology already present within our individual, social, cultural, political, institutional, and even economic landscapes, especially when one is raced, classed, and/or sexualized in the pejorative?" The temporariness of each SlutWalk's claim to the streets carried too much risk. "Claiming slut-hood for ourselves," she explained, "when we [as black women] are already thrust into a Jezebelian context—will likely only make the sexual terror that too often goes hand and hand with such a reality, worse."[23] For her, disidentification with the term "slut" not only didn't seem fitting, it also didn't appear productive, given the hypersexualization of black women.[24] Due to what Celine Parreñas Shimizu calls "racialized hypersexuality," the black women referenced by these bloggers, along with Latinas and Native women, as well as the Asian American women addressed by Shimizu, are always assumed to be sluts, hos, prostitutes, and mail-order brides.[25] Nonetheless, in response to another blogger whom I discuss in depth below, Lomax wrote, "I have problems with how Blogando reduces SlutWalk to white supremacy while overlooking the positive benefits of a heightened national conversation about rape and victim blaming." Like Walia and Crunktastic, Lomax modeled a form of critique that addressed problems without dismissing the beneficial aspects of these marches.

These appraisals emphasized that the framework for the march stemmed from a racially privileged position and an assumption that white women's issues were universal. In October 2012 this undercurrent became more overt when a young white woman at SlutWalk New York City carried a sign with a quote from John Lennon and Yoko Ono declaring that "Woman is the Nigger of the World." In response, Crunktastic expressed frustration with white feminists who defended those who carried the sign and described black women as "hyper-sensitive and divisive."[26] After these exchanges, her message became more pointed: "To organize a movement around the reclamation of a term is in and of itself an act of white privilege. To not make explicit and clear the privilege and power inherent in such an act is to invite less-informed folks with privilege (in other words, folks who know just enough to be dangerous) to assume that reclamation can be applied universally."[27] This specific incident exemplified the concerns she and other bloggers had with an event that didn't include racial consciousness at the core of its mission and strategy and shifted her critique toward complete condemnation.

Not all women of color bloggers shared Crunktastic and Lomax's decisions not to support SlutWalks, although all voiced similar concerns with events that did not explicitly address the racialization of gender and sexuality. For example, while Andrea Plaid initially "felt the word 'slut' didn't speak to [her and] found the word 'ho' more damaging," she ultimately decided that because of the ways words such as "slut" and "ho" have been used against women of color specifically she would not only attend but also speak at the New York City SlutWalk.[28] In explaining her decision, Plaid identified the ways that women of color and poor women are particularly vulnerable to accusations that their sexuality is excessive or deviant.

A collaboratively authored post published on the *Feminist Wire* was among the most poignant responses to SlutWalks and provided a range of views. One author, Donika Ross, had read other black women's critiques but didn't completely identify with them: "While I understand and support the arguments that these women are making about black women's relationship to the word slut, as an individual I feel somewhat isolated from the finer terms of the debate," she explained. "See, as far as I know, no one has ever called me a slut or ho or chickenhead or hoochie or anything to that effect. If anything, I was asexualized as a teen and adult black woman, which is, I think a category left under-discussed when we focus on the hypersexualization of black women."[29] By focusing on a different aspect of the racialized, gendered terrain of black women's sexuality, her response highlights the multiplicity of ways that race, gender, and sexuality can intersect for black women. She responded to what is often referred to as a politics of respectability, something Janell Hobson referenced in her contribution to the ongoing conversation about black women's relationships to the SlutWalk.[30] Respectability, as historian E. Frances White explains, "is one of a number of strategies African Americans have developed to create unity." Such efforts, she notes, "depend on the demonization of too many people."[31] Political theorist Cathy J. Cohen similarly describes respectability as "a process of policing, sanitizing, and hiding the nonconformist and some would argue deviant behavior of certain members of African American communities."[32] This politic has disproportionately affected people considered to be gender and sexual outsiders, including unmarried women, gay men, lesbians, transgender people, and sex workers.

These varied comments reveal the diverse range of black women's responses to SlutWalks. All commentators referenced the interlocking nature of gender, race, and sexuality, but how those simultaneous experiences worked together and their impact on critics' views of SlutWalk was far from monolithic.

While most of the women of color bloggers who discussed SlutWalks were of African descent, the first woman of color to respond in an online forum was Aura Blogando, an Argentinian-born Latina. Her post, "SlutWalk: A Stroll Through White Supremacy," was also the most damning. Like others, she questioned whether reclaiming the word "slut" would be successful and emphasized organizers' privilege. Key among her critiques was SlutWalk Toronto's relationship with the police, most notably organizers' investment in getting the police to address their misogynist practices, which was, as I explain below, also an issue for some communities in Toronto.

Seeking police accountability was central to the 2011 Toronto platform. For example, in an interview with the *Excalibur*, York University's community paper, Alyssa Teekah, who is of South Asian descent and was part of the 2011 organizing team, stated, "One of our main aims is to reappropriate the word 'slut.' We are also looking for increased transparency, accountability and greater anti-oppression training for police."[33] Teekah's comments demonstrated one of Blogando's points while simultaneously disproving her and other blogger's depiction of the organizers as all white. The march framework and strategy may have reflected dominant racial values, but there was always at least one woman of color on SlutWalk Toronto's organizing committee. The shorthand way that racial privilege is frequently discussed often conflates privilege with race in ways that can either erase the presence of women of color in white-dominant organizations or depict them as disconnected from their communities of origin.

Despite her astute analysis of the racial valences of working with the police, Blogando's critique became simplistically inflammatory at points, replicating the dialogue-stopping rhetoric of some commentaries focused on sexual norms. For example, she wrote that "the event is slated to be reproduced in Argentina sometime this year. It's the country I was born and raised in . . . and I can assure you that the word 'slut' is not used by anyone there. . . . I do not want white English-speaking Global North women telling Spanish-speaking Global South women to 'reclaim' a word that is foreign to our own vocabulary."[34] She then suggested that organizers focus their effort on transwomen in hurricane-ravaged New Orleans.

There is no evidence that organizers from Toronto or anywhere else in North America told Argentinian (or any other) women to hold a SlutWalk. This piece, like Meghan Murphy's and Miriam's, condemned SlutWalks without exploring any positive potential or intentions. It left no room for dialogue.

After Blogando published her piece, the 2011 organizers had strong and, ultimately, divergent reactions. Blogando's discussion was particularly hurtful to Barnett. "My parents were both born in Córdoba in Argentina," she explained. "It almost felt like a personal affront to me that she was saying this, and how dare she assume that I am just one of those supremely privileged white university students." In response, "what I wanted to say was kind of like a big 'fuck you, this is not what we are and who we are.'" While Jarvis was also affected by Blogando's comments, her flashpoints of frustration were less personal. Jarvis asserted, "I feel like we would have gotten a whole different set of critiques if we made it about a city that we are not in, that we do not know, and we shouldn't be speaking for." For her, SlutWalk Toronto was about Toronto. She welcomed the global response of groups around the world wanting to host demonstrations with the same name, but she emphasized that SlutWalk Toronto's focus was on dynamics in Toronto.

After critiques began streaming in, disagreements arose regarding the best method for and tenor of response. "We couldn't drop everything and spend a week meeting together and discussing these criticisms and what they meant to us and where to go," Jarvis said. Barnett was clearer about what she thought they should do, particularly in response to Blogando. "I wanted to deal with it directly with her and open a proper conversation. If she was going to attack us, I was going to be defensive, but at the same time, I didn't want to shut her [down]," she explained. Other organizers wanted to think through their response, which took more time than Barnett thought was appropriate. "At that point I made the decision to veer off and to leave SlutWalk as an organizer because I didn't want to say anything that would harm them, because I understood that they felt that they had to be accountable to a larger community," she explained.

Jarvis and other organizers did want to be accountable to communities in Toronto and beyond; however, they also wanted to stay true to the original mission of the march. A balance between these goals was hard to strike. Figuring out how to be direct without seeming defensive was one difficulty; appropriate tactics were another. In the end, they posted collaboratively written responses on their website, held an open forum in Toronto, and had phone conferences with at least one set of critics. As time went on, the stress of finding this balance led to all except Jarvis leaving the organizing team. She found new organizers to help respond to critiques, organize the forum, and plan the 2012 march.

The energy-intensive work of organizing not only a march but also a community response was overwhelming. This labor was intensified by the ferocity of some of the online commentaries and by the way that online posts made dialogue difficult. The public sphere of blog posts and newspaper and magazine articles disseminated electronically allows for an exchange of ideas. Similar to the print culture conversations explored by Jürgen Habermas and Michael Warner, this form of counterpublic engagement builds knowledge through creating a delayed conversation.[35] In contrast to verbal dialogues, internet exchanges generally begin with one person writing something in a home, office, or other location, editing it on her computer, and then posting it. Others then respond in kind. Additional conversations can develop in comments that are posted below the initial posts. Commentators frequently reference each other and often build upon or refute other perspectives. SlutWalk Toronto organizers participated in these exchanges on their own and others' websites. Hallie, a twenty-year-old undergraduate student who became the volunteer coordinator a month before the 2012 march, explained that organizers allowed critics to post on their website and engaged "in a way that is confrontational, but it's not aggressive." Organizers found this form of engagement productive but limited. While the internet facilitated a conversation of sorts, there was rarely dialogue between critics and organizers.

Feminists have long valued dialogue as a form of knowledge building. In a coauthored piece written in four distinct voices, Maria Lugones and Elizabeth Spelman described friendship as the basis of feminist theorizing attentive to difference.[36] Other theorists have similarly demonstrated the significance of engaging multiple voices by producing collectively authored and edited volumes.[37] They have also thought through how to include the voices of others in their work.[38] Activists have also engaged in the difficult work of dialogue and coalition building.[39]

One collaboratively written critique offered an opportunity for dialogue. An open letter from Black Women's Blueprint, a New York–based civil and human rights organization focused on black women's specific needs through "progressive research, historical documentation, support[ing] movement building and organiz[ing] on social justice issues steeped in the struggles of Black women within their communities and within dominant culture," became the most well-known critique of SlutWalks in general and SlutWalk Toronto in particular.[40] Their September 23, 2011, letter echoed points raised by Walia, Lomax, Crunktastic, and Plaid, citing concerns about black women's "bodies as sexualized objects of property, as spectacles of sexuality and deviant sexual desire," and "as unable to be raped whether on the auction block, in the fields or on living room television screens." Explicitly framing their letter as part of a dialogue, they asserted, "We know the SlutWalk is a call to action and we have heard you. Yet we struggle with the decision to answer this call by joining with or supporting something that even in name exemplifies the ways in which mainstream women's movements have repeatedly excluded Black women." They requested that organizers address women's diverse experiences, which are grounded in racial and class backgrounds, and that organizers rebrand the movement and do the work to make it a movement rather than just a march. They also explicitly sought ongoing dialogue:

> We would welcome a meeting with the organizers of SlutWalk to discuss the intrinsic potential in its global reach and the sheer number of followers it has energized. We'd welcome the opportunity to engage in critical conversation with the organizers of SlutWalk about strategies for remaining accountable to the thousands of women and men, marchers it left behind in Brazil, in New Delhi, South Korea and elsewhere—marchers who continue to need safety and resources, marchers who went back home to their communities and their lives. We would welcome a conversation about the work ahead and how this can be done together with groups across various boundaries, to end sexual assault beyond the marches.[41]

According to Jarvis and Bhuiyan, this interest in dialogue was unique among SlutWalk's feminist critics. The only other invitation to dialogue I found was a blog post by Andreana Clay, one of the letter's signatories.[42]

Notably, Black Women's Blueprint's letter also demonstrated the U.S. centrism of most U.S.-based commentators. In their letter, SlutWalk is depicted as U.S. based: "We are still struggling with the how, why and when and ask at what impasse should the SlutWalk have included substantial representation of Black women in the building and branding of this U.S. based movement to challenge rape culture?"[43] Thus, despite their astute analysis of black women's relationships to the word "slut," they depicted the movement as originating in the United States, thereby simultaneously held Canadian activists accountable and erased their national context.

SlutWalk Toronto organizers responded to Black Women's Blueprint in a number of ways. After posting an initial statement a few days later, indicating their intent to "thoughtfully respond," organizers met and decided how to react in a way that honored the critique, the invitation to dialogue, and their own investments.[44] Then, on October 17, they posted a longer response on their website, which began by emphasizing their gratefulness: "The small group of us in SlutWalk Toronto are very thankful these organizations and many voices have connected with us. We are appreciative of the support, concerns, requests and the openness to engagement in dialogue with us." They subsequently outlined their commitments, referencing specific issues raised by Black Women's Blueprint, as well as other critics:

> SlutWalk Toronto has endeavoured from the beginning to not operate outside of our knowledge and experience, which for us has meant doing our best to not cross geo-political boundaries or speak for communities and SlutWalks outside of

> our home city of Toronto. . . . While SlutWalk Toronto as the inaugural SlutWalk is often looked to as the "head" of SlutWalk, we are not involved with organizing other SlutWalks and we are not structured to oversee and determine what all of SlutWalk will look like. We do not envision our activism as a hierarchical dictation of our ideas upon others, whether across Canada or across the world. In recognition of this, SlutWalk Toronto is committed to engaging with our community here in Toronto for direct feedback. . . . We've been having many conversations and exchanges to better understand the experiences and criticisms of people within our own city and outside of Canada and now we would like to turn these conversations into actions to make SlutWalk Toronto better, more anti-oppressive and more inclusive.[45]

Their emphasis on not speaking for communities and refusing to engage in a "hierarchical dictation" of ideas seemingly alludes to Blogando's comments about New Orleans and Argentina. The focus on Toronto also highlights key points that came up in the interviews I did with organizers: Toronto is a unique location, and, importantly, Canada is not the United States.

Organizers' attentiveness to Toronto's specificity continued in subsequent responses to Black Women's Blueprint and other critics. In "Racism and Anti-racism: Why They Matter to SlutWalks," a response to the racist slogan at the New York march, they wrote, "Grassroots organizing means that we need to start in our own backyard and work from the ground up." Accordingly, they organized an open forum in November 2011 to discuss race, racism, and privilege. Different organizers described the forum's success very differently. For Jarvis, it was an enlightening conversation. For Bhuiyan, it was sparsely attended and white dominated.

Organizers also engaged in the transnational conversation about the racial valences of SlutWalks: "SlutWalk Toronto does not support the actions or language of this SlutWalk participant." This post demonstrated their attempt to navigate local organizing needs and their role as initiators of what became transnational protests: "SlutWalk was an idea that began in Toronto and has spread across the world at lightning speed, which has and does limit our reach and influence over other SlutWalks. . . . However . . . what happens under the SlutWalk label or idea connects us all."[46] Being accountable to these two communities, one local and another global, required multifaceted messaging.

Finally, SlutWalk Toronto organizers and representatives from Black Women's Blueprint spoke over the phone. Bhuiyan explained:

> It was an uncomfortable conversation . . . but . . . we all talked about it a little bit more, and they were so patient with us. They're a big organization, so even for them to take two hours to speak to us was huge. We worked a lot of things out. . . . [W]e asked them if they wanted to be an ally. Black Women's Blueprint said

"no." They don't want to be our ally because they don't agree with our messaging, and that's fair. But they would like to stay in dialogue with us.

SlutWalk organizers were grateful for the dialogue with Black Women's Blueprint. Dialogue didn't lead to consensus; nonetheless, it allowed organizers from each group to explain their positions and to better understand each other's perspectives. Bhuiyan explained further that the "phone call and that letter really . . . triggered the accountability actions and strategies that we took on later," which included greater engagement with a variety of feminist, queer, and racial and ethnic communities in Toronto. The conversation helped Toronto organizers to clarify their commitments, to begin sorting out how to best be accountable to people in Toronto, and to figure out their role in addressing issues that came up at other SlutWalks.

The dialogue was particularly important for Bhuiyan, who received support from other women of color in the process. She explained that "a lot of what I'm going through I feel like Black Women's Blueprint has been able to address a bit more than SlutWalk has. . . . So much psychic support, so much emotional support . . . and it's been really great." As the only woman of color on the 2012 organizing team, she frequently felt that her opinions were undervalued or even ignored by other organizers: "It's almost like I have to convince them of how things impact me differently to a really tiring degree," she explained. She was also under special scrutiny from outsiders because she was working from the inside to make the second march attentive to a wider set of issues. Finding camaraderie among other women of color organizers was, therefore, essential for her continued presence on the organizing team.

Engaging in this dialogue took time, something Bhuiyan believed was important. Presenting a perspective almost diametrically opposed to Barnett's, she emphasized the importance of process in community work:

> I feel like a really big difficulty this year was negotiating how much attention we would give to the process of being accountable in forming an action, versus the product. . . . I felt like the rally often came before the uncomfortable talking about our messaging. We literally did our messaging in one Skype call that was an hour. That totally was not enough, I think. I think that's a lot of the reason why after the march we received critiques from local communities in Toronto and local organizations, being like "what was the messaging of SlutWalk this year? Why wasn't it a stronger stance?" Even accusations of us almost tiptoeing around the issue, which was the police, right?

As someone with a community organizing background, she valued the role of dialogue, of listening and being listened to, in developing an ethical response. The style of organizing favored by her co-organizers, which minimized face-to-face meetings, was expedient in getting tasks done but not in fostering connections or understanding across differences in opinion, experience, or analysis.

Jarvis also described her gratefulness that Black Women's Blueprint took the time and effort to engage SlutWalk Toronto organizers in dialogue. She'd desired dialogue with other critics but found others unwilling; however, her strategy for initiating conversations was to invite others to come to SlutWalk Toronto, which left the impetus on them to engage SlutWalk organizers on their turf. She, as the cofounder and dominant media presence for the group, didn't offer to go the distance herself. According to Bhuiyan, saying to "groups who are angry with us that we would like to invite you to come to our space and have a discussion with us" recentered SlutWalk organizers, leaving critics marginalized. Accordingly, the conversation with Black Women's Blueprint was rare for two reasons. First, internet posts generally don't facilitate dialogue. Additionally, other organizations weren't willing to do the requisite work. Not only did other organizations have their own agendas, SlutWalk Toronto organizers expected people to come to them. Dialogue might have been more common if SlutWalk organizers had been willing to meet other groups on their own turf, literally and figuratively.

Black Women's Blueprint's critique of the white-centric framework of SlutWalks stemmed from signatories' experiences living in the United States. Thus, the letter both identified the privilege of most SlutWalk Toronto organizers and ignored their specific national location. For Jarvis, the conversation with Black Women's Blueprint exemplified U.S.-based critics' difficulties understanding the differences between the United States and Canada. "I remember saying to Black Women's Blueprint, 'This is what we heard from Toronto, and it doesn't feel good for us to root our efforts and make changes based on what we're hearing from Brooklyn while ignoring what we're hearing from Toronto,'" she explained. The open forum revealed that for many Canadians, the primary critique was SlutWalk's engagement with Toronto Police Services. Jarvis explained:

> A lot of the criticisms, especially from women of color, who are frequently . . . migrants and immigrants, as well as people of color, . . . came down to [this:] . . . by us engaging in a dialogue [with the police], we were recognizing that system as a valid one, and any changes that would be made would only be available to people that could currently access the police, and there's this huge amount of people who still see the police as violent in and of themselves, who cannot access the system, who do not want to access the system because of what it'll do to them.

Race was an issue in Toronto, just not in the same way as it was for most U.S.-based commentators. SlutWalk Toronto's relationship with the police rather than their use of the word "slut" was the biggest concern for many people and communities of color. Blogando, herself an immigrant, identified this issue in her post.

Differing relationships to the police divided the 2012 organizers. Bhuiyan explained that she was "more reluctant to want to talk to the police, to engage them in anything just because of [my] collective history and knowledge about the police." As a Bangladeshi immigrant, she had a relationship to state power that was distinctly different from that of the other 2012 organizers, Jarvis, Hallie, and Colleen Westendorf, another white woman. While I was unable to interview Westendorf, the description she posted on SlutWalk Toronto's website describes Michael Sanguinetti, whose comment sparked the first march, as well intentioned.[47] For people who have experienced police repression of their communities, this description might seem ignorant of their treatment by the police. Jarvis landed somewhere in the middle, describing her understanding of police brutality as evolving over the course of organizing SlutWalk Toronto.

While the 2012 march didn't focus as much on reforming the police as the first march did, one of the messages from the stage emphasized, in Bhuiyan's words, that "despite the horrible institution that the police is in Toronto, there are good officers." Not only was this messaging problematic for her, but responses from communities frequently targeted by the police were sometimes addressed directly to her. "People have messaged me in particular and been like, 'We wish you would have taken a stronger stance on the Toronto police rather than presenting them as a benevolent force that just needs antioppression [training] to do better,'" she explained. This put her in an awkward position, because she supported SlutWalk's critique of victim blaming but understood why people were uncomfortable with the organization's unwillingness to put forward a stronger, more multifaceted critique of the Toronto police.

On the Ground

At the rally after the march one of the organizers and a few of the speakers addressed the letter from Black Women's Blueprint. This explicit engagement, with over a year of blog posts, newspaper op-eds, open letters, and one conference call, was only the tip of the iceberg of organizers' responses to other people's reactions to prior SlutWalks. The interaction with Black Women's Blueprint, in particular, moved SlutWalk organizers. The dialogue helped them clarify their own commitments and find ways to balance their investment in being accountable to people providing constructive criticism with the original intent of the march. According to Bhuiyan, "It's proof of how many paces being in dialogue with great people can move you. I think we've come such a long way since that phone call and that letter." A conversation that began in the blogosphere led to dialogue between organizers and critics that shifted how these organizers engaged with people in their hometown and, ultimately, how the 2012 SlutWalk Toronto unfolded.

The dialogue with a U.S.-based organization facilitated the accountability practices organizers undertook. The open forum created opportunities for dialogue, and so did the 2012 march. Bhuiyan continued:

> I felt like, by having the rally and having the speakers, we were able to symbolically build a lot of bridges, to make it easier to talk to us. . . . A lot of communities have felt a lot of hostility towards us, and by having speakers like Kim Crosby talk about the systematic structural violence that black women and black girls face and then having Tara Atluri speak about nationalism and colonialism and how those forces work in concert on Muslim women's bodies and having people like Morgan Page talk about transphobic violence was probably one of the best decisions that we have made.

Organizers also worked to engage a wide range of communities within the city, which affected who showed up to the march. "This year, the thing that was very different, I think, was that we had many, many more organizations come out . . . to support us," Jarvis explained. "There were at least fifteen, so that was different. Everything from the White Ribbon Campaign [men working to end sexual violence against women]; YWCA; Planned Parenthood; the Bad Date Coalition, which is a sex worker–run advocacy group; No One Is Illegal, which is a Canadian-based organization." The effort organizers had made between the two marches changed who attended and who was represented on the stage. The 2012 march wasn't flawless, as Bhuiyan's comments about community response make clear; however, organizers responded to critiques and worked with community groups to better address multiple perspectives. At some points, critiques left organizers feeling defensive; however, in the midst of all the criticisms and stress, organizers engaged in dialogue with some critics and created relationships with other local organizers. They grew as a result of both the critiques and the support they received.

Despite changes in response to critique and dialogue, the 2012 march maintained many elements of the first march. The mixture of anger and playfulness in the crowd remained. The emphasis on women's control over their sexuality—the message that no means no *and* yes means yes—continued. Some women still wore fishnets and lingerie, despite judgments from misogynists and feminists alike. Others wore less sensational attire, just as they had the year before. White women still dominated the march, although Bhuiyan thought there were more women of color than in 2011, and the views expressed from the stage highlighted a greater array of perspectives about gender, sexuality, and violence.

Thus, people held space for forms of copresence that reflected the debates and discussions of the year prior. People brought their relationships to these conversations, as well as their investments in the demonstration's message to the streets and park. They held the space for each other despite varying relationships with the word "slut," with the organizing team's choices, and with perspectives about the best method for organizing to end sexual violence. Their presence contributed to the ongoing dialogue about sexuality, gender, race, and privilege that emerged in response to the first SlutWalk.

Conclusion: Contesting Virtual and Public Space

Kapur describes SlutWalks and related campaigns in India as forms of cultural critique and "analytical space clearing."[48] While her use of the term "space" is metaphorical, her observation is useful for thinking about physical and cyberspaces. In the process of claiming topographical and rhetorical space, public demonstrations seek to clear out other less welcoming and often damaging cultural and spatial associations. In their use of the term "slut," SlutWalk organizers and many participants wanted to create new associations for the term and, by doing so in city streets and squares, to cleanse these public spaces of patriarchal assumptions.

In their street and virtual presence, SlutWalks also provided an opportunity to revisit and update the feminist sex wars and conversations about racialized gender and sexuality. These debates about the ideal feminist public presence are themselves claims to rhetorical and physical spaces. The online commentary about SlutWalks offered an opportunity to explore connections between demonstrations happening in public spaces and counterpublic conversations about gender, sexuality, race, and the ethics of organizing. Each affected the other in a dynamic dialectical process. Constituents engaged online, in person, or both, negotiating the dimensions and style of feminist public presence in the process. This included some boundary policing regarding what kinds of claims, rhetoric, and actions would be recognized as feminist. Accordingly, the style of debate was frequently contentious, only shifting into dialogue on a few occasions.

Despite the often vitriolic nature of some of the commentary, SlutWalk Toronto organizers parsed the critiques, responded to those that reflected their vision, and ignored those that didn't. While the second march didn't entirely address the concerns of either Toronto community members or the feminist blogosphere, the speakers organizers gathered addressed the concerns of a wide range of people, and the assembled crowd claimed the streets and Queen's Park, a symbolically important space in front of parliament. For a few hours, participants held these spaces for each other and demonstrated what a victim-supportive society would look and feel like.

The chapters in this part of the book have explored responses to sexuality, a uniquely vexed site in heteropatriarchal and erotophobic societies. These events demonstrate a variety of approaches to bringing sexuality into the public sphere in ways that address women's experiences with the pleasures and dangers of sexual subjectivity. By creating spaces for encounter, refuting cultural norms, celebrating community, and addressing intrafeminist debates, each event approached the multifaceted nature of women's sexuality in a patriarchal culture from a different vantage point that reflected the cultural and geographical positions of participants. Attendees held these sites for each other in defiance of cultural values that marginalize them as women and, sometimes, as dykes and people of color. As the discussions about the viability of SlutWalks as a framework demonstrate, women's differing experiences with racialization and immigration affect what kinds of tactics best address specific experiences of sexualization. Since women are differently positioned within local and national power structures based on race, immigration status, and sexual orientation, not all interventions into dominant spatial norms address their varied needs. Accordingly, even when spaces are held by people with shared concerns, not all participants are embraced fully.

The next part analyzes two examples of feminist responses to war: Women in Black's silent vigils and CODEPINK's direct actions. In some ways, these two organizations are polar opposites—one silent, one loud, one contemplative, one disruptive—yet each organization works from the position of outsiders left out of national decision-making processes.

PART II

Gendered Responses to War

Deploying Femininities

Introduction

Women activists, including many feminists, have long focused on peace. Militarism, like other cultural ideologies and practices, is deeply gendered. Despite growing numbers of and greater responsibilities for women in militaries worldwide, soldiers are still generally viewed as male or at least masculine, and women are generally viewed as patriotic, feminine supporters of individual military men and military campaigns. Additionally, women are frequently perceived as symbolizing the nation and the people whom men are protecting through military campaigns. Women have contested both the gendered division of military labor and the assumption that they will support war efforts, nurture injured veterans, and mourn men lost in battle. They've also questioned the misogyny within much mixed-gender antiwar activism. Moreover, as historian Say Burgin argues, "gender becomes reconstituted as much *through* antiwar experiences as it acts as a predictor *for* those experiences."[1]

In exploring these dynamics, this part of the book includes two quite different examples of antiwar protests: CODEPINK, a direct-action organization formed in response to the post-9/11 move toward and eventual declaration of war, and Women in Black, a transnational network of vigils that originated in Israel and now occur in numerous countries, including the United States and U.K. Looked at together, they provide a window into the ways that women in the early twenty-first century build on a rich history of feminist antiwar activism and, in the process, transform public space.

U.S. women have long organized against war as mothers, as feminists, and as part of both national and transnational peace organizations. In the early twentieth century, advocating for peace was closely linked with the expansion of women's sphere of influence to include explicitly political issues.[2] In addition, peace was frequently viewed as a specifically womanly investment, in contrast to a manly obsession with war. A number of national and international organizations were founded in the early years of the twentieth century. The International Alliance of Women, established in 1904 by women predominantly from European countries, began advocating for peace in 1913.[3] In 1915 the Women's International League for Peace and Freedom (WILPF) formed because other international organizations were either supporting or not protesting the emerging war in Europe.[4] Both of these organizations had U.S. chapters from their inaugural years onward. In the United States, the explicitly feminist Women's Peace Party, formed in 1915 in response to Germany's military aggressions and other nations' investment in military response, "emphasized three basic beliefs: that women best understood the supreme value of preserving human life; that women were committed to providing each individual with the best possible quality of life; and that women insisted on resolving conflicts without severing relationships between individuals or nations."[5] Party members believed that women had been socialized to better appreciate peace and that society could benefit from their unique views. In 1921 absolute pacifists and suffragists who had worked with the Women's Peace Party formed the Women's Peace Union.[6] Additionally, the relatively moderate National Committee on the Cause and Cure of War (NCCCW), a coalition of women's organizations, was founded in 1925.[7] Other women's organizations included peace among the issues they addressed. For example, in 1930 91 percent of chapters of the National Council for Jewish Women, which was part of the NCCCW, held regular peace programs.[8] These organizations were comprised primarily, if not exclusively, of women from privileged national, class, and racial backgrounds.

Activists continued linking motherhood and antiwar activism in more recent years. For example, Women's Strike for Peace (WSP) was founded in 1961 with a strike from housework and wage-earning labor to protest the arms race and militarism in all forms. On November 1, 1961, fifty thousand largely white and middle-class women, mostly housewives, demonstrated in sixty communities nationwide, blending the tactic of striking, traditionally associated with factory laborers, with antiwar organizing. According to literary and legal scholar Catherine Stimpson, these women "were angry, passionately and rightly so. They were mothers whose sanctioned task was to nurture children and human life."[9] This motivation for stopping housework and entering public spaces justified political involvement as an extension of their caregiving roles as mothers and wives. Children were threatened, according to WSP, by a nation amassing nuclear weapons and participating in military aggressions abroad. Although they relied on their maternal roles to justify their activism, participants often had pacifist, Quaker, anarchist, and socialist backgrounds.

Despite their reliance on traditional gender norms, WSP was called before the House Un-American Activities Committee, an episode that affected how people responded to their public activities. When thirty-five members tried to place a wreath in front of statues of women's rights leaders in the basement below the U.S. Capitol Rotunda, they were blocked by Capitol police and physically shoved into the statues, despite a previously agreeable relationship with the officers. In the process of being investigated, they "had transformed . . . from respectable peace ladies to dangerous 'Reds.'"[10] Despite losing respectability, they continued their activism into the 1970s, lobbying, marching, and staging sit-ins, as well as distributing literature at shopping centers and churches.[11]

In 1967 Another Mother for Peace (AMP) formed in response to the Vietnam War based on what participants saw as an essential link between motherhood and peace. AMP intentionally distanced itself from feminism, focusing instead on a supposedly natural and therefore apolitical motherly concern for children. In contrast with the comparatively radical WSP, AMP emphasized a moderate position premised on domestic middle-class white ideals.[12] Similar to many forms of "mother-activism," they challenged a more docile version of patriotic motherhood.[13] While WSP worked within gender norms in order to justify seemingly unwomanly behavior such as public protest, AMP left gender norms largely unquestioned. Nonetheless, both groups challenged what geographer Jenna Loyd identifies as "militarized domesticities" that support militarized masculinities.[14]

Women sometimes used antiwar protests to explicitly address gender roles. For example, in January 1968 a group calling themselves the Jeannette Rankin Brigade organized an anti–Vietnam War protest in Washington, D.C. Named after the first U.S. congresswoman, a pacifist, this collective included members of WSP and religious and peace organizations. Five thousand women, most clad in black, participated.[15] Some feminists opposed the motherly rhetoric and images and called for a counterdemonstration. The resulting funeral procession carried a dummy dressed as the corpse of nurturing femininity. "You are joyfully invited to attend the burial of WEEPING WOMANHOOD who passed with a sigh to her Great Reward this year of the lord 1968," the invitation read, "after 3000 years of bolstering the egos of the warmakers and aiding the cause of war."[16] Historian Say Burgin described their intervention:

> Perhaps condescendingly, Burial organisers applauded Brigade participants for refusing to participate in normative pro-war feminine capacities. Such "traditional" functions (the "hankywave" and reception of "regretful telegrams" and "worthless medals of honor") were infused with nationalist aspirations, and the U.S., in turn, was feminised and required protection. . . . Burial participants admonished the Brigade for enacting a similarly "powerless" and "ineffective" feminine role by appealing to Congress to end the war. This group recognised that the cultural ideas that "allowed" U.S. women to protest war rendered their protest ineffective because of the equation of passivity with femininity. Thus, "traditional" femininity infused the Brigade, the organisers of the Burial felt, and rendered it futile. Indeed, it was the very form of femininity enacted by the Brigade that Burial organisers felt ensured the political inefficacy of the action.[17]

This performance-based intervention demonstrated differing ways of relating and responding to gender norms among feminist antiwar activists. Similar tensions about how to best address social problems, including militarism, in a patriarchal society continue to plague current women's and feminist activism.

While women have often opposed war in greater numbers than men, not all women oppose war, and many actively support it. In contrast to philosopher Sara Ruddick's description of women's potential to be mothers leading to a greater investment in caring for and repairing the world, anthropologist Nancy Scheper-Hughes points out that many women, including mothers, not only support but also call for war.[18] In reference to the 1991 Gulf War led by George H. W. Bush, she asked, "Where . . . were the voices of U.S. women clamoring for 'world protection, world repair' during the Gulf War? Instead we heard women and mothers claiming the right to fight on the front lines and the equal opportunity to master the tools of organized violence."[19] In light of women's role in the Abu Ghraib torture scandal and the recent lift of the ban on women in combat, similar questions can be raised about more recent wars.[20] Nonetheless, many women, including participants in the organizations discussed in the next two chapters, still explicitly link feminism and/or womanhood to antiwar activism.

In the upcoming chapters, I address women's participation in mass mobilizations, creative lobbying efforts, and vigils designed to witness ongoing atrocities. Together these chapters explore a range of responses in an array of affective registers, most of which rely on racial and class privilege. The first chapter examines the generally silent vigils of Women in Black. Rather than protesting using loud chants and movement through streets and other spaces, they demonstrate the peace they desire by standing in silent vigil. In the process, they hope to remind civilians of their complicity in ongoing wars. The following chapter examines CODEPINK's direct actions targeting politicians and participation in mass demonstrations. I focus on their creative, attention-grabbing tactics, including their use of the feminizing color pink, creative costumes, and songs. In contrast to Women in Black's contemplative vigils, they try to disrupt the everyday workings of power in the hopes of drawing attention to these practices and halting related military campaigns.

4

Demonstrating Peace

Women in Black's Witness Space

Just before 5:30 p.m. on a sunny Wednesday afternoon in July 2004, five women gathered outside the Main Branch of the New York Public Library where 41st Street meets Fifth Avenue in front of the southernmost lion statue. All wore black, some head to toe, some with bare shoulders and arms. One woman had a pink logo on her short-sleeved T-shirt, another wore an undyed straw hat with a black band. They formed a silent line facing rush-hour pedestrian and automobile traffic, holding a large black banner identifying them as Women in Black Against War. One woman slowly pulled one flyer after another out of a folder to hand to passersby. The first lines of the handout asserted: "Women in Black New York stand in silent vigil to protest war, rape as a tool of war, ethnic cleansing and human rights abuses all over the world. We are silent because mere words cannot express the tragedy that wars and hatred bring. We refuse to add to the cacophony of empty statements that are spoken with the best intentions yet may be erased or go unheard under the sound of a passing ambulance or a bomb exploding nearby." Over the course of an hour a few more women joined the group. At one point the group numbered eight—all over thirty, most over fifty, and all white, except for one black woman who appeared to be in her fifties. Most onlookers were also silent. Some took flyers soundlessly. Others nodded in agreement. Many kept walking, some giving the silent women a quick glimpse, others focused on other concerns. One younger woman en route to somewhere else spontaneously stopped and stood for a few minutes. Passengers on commuter buses observed the vigil from the comfort of their air-conditioned seats. Other commuters queued for buses, staring into the empty parking spots in front of them and stealing occasional glances at the vigil. A few people verbally asserted support or gratefulness for the women keeping vigil. Still fewer grumbled or made disparaging comments. One middle-aged white man in a business suit asked, "Are your thongs black too?" A middle-aged black woman in a vest covered in prowar buttons tried to engage the woman handing out flyers, but then left, aggravated when she was met with silence.

This small group transformed a section of concrete into a site for quiet contemplation in the midst of late afternoon pedestrian traffic. The stillness of their bodies and their silence shifted the tone of the space. Given associations between black clothing and mourning in the United States and other Western countries, the women's attire marked them as separate from the locals in business suits and tourists in summer tank tops and shorts. Together, their silence, immobility, and monotonal black outfits and the seriousness of their demeanor lent a ritualistic tone to their presence. Despite the bustle around them, they stood, rupturing the ordinary chaos around them. This small area became witness space for the duration of their vigil.

The weekly midtown Manhattan Women in Black vigil demonstrates opposition to war by positioning participants as witnesses to violence occurring in the name of their nation's security. In the process, they assume an ethical orientation to military violence that seeks accountability while refusing to engage in acts of violence. Witness space enables people to focus their energy on atrocities near or far. As opposed to protest space that provides opportunities for people to contest unjust practices, witness space allows people to acknowledge and contemplate appalling actions and situations. Witnesses refuse to look away. In situations where the injustice is far away, this beholding is metaphorical. The goal is to demonstrate an ethical relationship between themselves and the people experiencing violence or disenfranchisement. Transforming hectic urban space into witness space requires bodily presence and affective investment.

Public protests bring bodies together to convey a message, demonstrating how events and issues can evoke responses that exceed rational public debate. As such, demonstrations have the potential to evoke the affective aspects of trauma.[1] Women in Black's silence emphasizes the unspeakable nature of military violence and the linguistic limits of verbal testimony. Participants witness violence and request that others do the same, using their bodies rather than verbal rhetoric. By embodying political beliefs and feelings, they invite additional responses from the people observing them while simultaneously evoking other bodies in distant battle zones. This performance, rather than the messages printed on signs or flyers, creates Women in Black's witness space.

These women hope to serve as reminders to others of ongoing wars that can easily be forgotten in the midst of everyday business and busyness. This is their way of demonstrating solidarity with people experiencing military aggressions and occupations. From a wealthy city in a wealthy and militarily aggressive nation, these women stand, silently using their gazes and their bodies to evoke faraway events. By disidentifying with the silence expected of them as women in a male-dominated society, they attempt to transform the passivity expected of them into an active refusal to support or engage in violence. Instead, they demonstrate the peace they hope to see.

This tactic for dissent is fraught with perils and possibilities. Playing with norms risks reinforcing them. Few Women in Black participants risk their lives or their bodily integrity by witnessing.[2] Most participants are privileged within their own societies in terms of race and class even if not gender. These women leverage their privilege by claiming spaces that might not be available to others without their race and class privilege. Combined with the passivity of their vigil, it's easy to read their actions as complacent, for the benefit of participants rather than observers or the people experiencing violence; however, this vigil complicates such concerns without alleviating them. Apparent passivity can communicate in ways that more assertive tactics cannot.

While each Women in Black vigil is grounded in a particular location and bears the marks of that location and the specific participants, each vigil is also linked to others through transnational networks. These networks primarily function virtually through the presence of a consolidating website (www.womeninblack.org); however, there are periodic international conferences, the most recent of which was in 2005 in Jerusalem and provided one of the people I interviewed grounding for her work with Women in Black in Amherst, Massachusetts. For most of the other participants I interviewed, this connection was more peripheral, based on shared feelings about war and a desire to demonstrate solidarity with other women. The connections were nonetheless meaningful, appearing in comments about why they kept vigil and in the leaflets they handed out.

The transnational context was central to their understanding of themselves, their relationships to their governments, and the wars they memorialized. The relationships they highlight are between groups of women, often comprised of individuals who had spent much of their adult lives as antiwar and/or feminist activists and who vigiled week after week despite changing local weather and global patterns of military conflict. Occasionally, they meet women from other locations or vigil in other locations while traveling for business or vacation. Even though some had never met women who vigiled elsewhere, the sense of belonging to something beyond their locality was central to all participants' understanding of why they claimed public spaces week after week. These affective connections link particular people and places across a vast global network of predominantly developed nations responding to conflicts initiated by their nations in regions often understood as less developed. Thus, the connections drawn are transnational but are primarily among women who question their governments' engaging in or sponsoring of military violence rather than the women experiencing that violence.[3]

Women in Black's witnessing ruptures temporal and geographical continuities, haunting urban spaces in wealthy countries by referencing the violence that enables prosperity and demonstrating another mode of engagement. It also reinforces some social continuities, given that participants occupy spaces that reflect racial and class hierarchies they benefit from. The witness space created is, therefore, complicated even while it demonstrates a way of responding to conflict that emphasizes the humanity of all people.

Beginnings

Women in Black began in Jerusalem in 1988 in solidarity with the first Palestinian Intifadah. Soon there were groups throughout Israel.[4] Participants in this first incarnation of the nearly thirty-year-old framework for responding to military violence and occupation held vigil weekly for six years before disbanding temporarily in 1993.[5] Core elements of current international demonstrations began there: wearing all black, standing in the same public place week after week, and demonstrating in women-only groups. Some Israeli groups stood in silence; others were simply quiet, not arguing with passersby or chanting slogans. The message was simple and uniform: "End the Occupation" written in white Hebrew, English, Arabic, or Russian lettering on a black octagonal placard reminiscent of a traffic sign. A smaller group of women began vigiling again in 1994 as soon as it became clear that the election of a more left-leaning government would not translate into the promised withdrawal from the occupied territories.[6]

Not all Women in Black groups focus on the same conflicts. Yet this framework for responding to violence appears compelling for a variety of women in the United States and worldwide. These women (and a few men) who wear black, the color of mourning for many cultures, as a protest strategy are from a variety of regions with a range of experiences of war, occupation, division, and violence. Despite myriad differences, all have histories of male dominance of public spaces; thus, using women's bodies to publicly express political opinions resonates in each location.

Women in Black vigils in the United States draw predominantly white economically privileged women. Many groups focus on the continued Israeli occupation of Palestine. Of these, some, like the now-defunct Atlanta group, are comprised primarily of non-Jewish women. Others, such as another Women in Black group that vigils in Union Square in New York City each week, are comprised primarily of Jewish women. The midtown Manhattan vigil described above is among many that focus on twenty-first-century U.S. aggressions in Iraq and Afghanistan. The London vigil I describe below focuses on a different war each week, including

Israel's occupation of Palestine and the U.S. and U.K. presence in Iraq and Afghanistan. Non-Jewish women generally dominate demonstrations focused on military aggressions outside of Palestine.

It is politically and symbolically important that it is mainly women who witness these atrocities, generally happening simultaneously in other locations. Women's proscribed roles in nationalist warfare have generally been to support the men who make decisions to go to war and men who fight the wars. Women's increasing military service has shifted the gender polarity of this framework somewhat, but military service continues to emphasize the masculinity of soldiers. From the home front, women have been expected to make financial choices that support the war, keep households going, and wait for the return of the men in their families. Once men return, women support men, deal with their rage, relinquish control, and try to create a "normal" life. If men don't return, women mourn and hold things together in men's absence. This dance of strength and weakness is necessary to continue the machinery of warfare.

The militarization of society is ideological and embodied. Petra Kuppers explains that the "politics of somatics" require addressing "specific bodies, not 'the body'; bodies in specific cultural alignments and webs, not 'just' bodies."[7] The bodies on the line in military actions are usually men's. Women's bodies are supposed to provide domestic comfort upon men's return. Too often, this means that women's bodies are on the line in their homes, dealing with the effects of wartime violence on the psyches of the men in their lives. While women are expected to provide sustenance for this gendered aggression, many women have viewed women's traditional role of caregiving as extending to caring for soldiers and civilians by contesting the wars that harm them. For Women in Black participants, this means presenting their womanly bodies as witnesses to ongoing violence.

In what follows, I describe the London vigil I attended in June 2005 before examining what it means to witness violence occurring in other locations, the possibilities and limits of this tactic, and the function of privilege in these vigils. Finally, I wrap up the chapter by returning to questions about the ethics of silent vigils. Throughout, I focus on how groups of women hold space through stillness and quiet rather than movement and sound. The resulting witness space enables public contemplation of violence for those participating and, possibly, those who encounter these vigils.

The Geography of Witnessing

On a Wednesday afternoon in late June 2005, I walked to St. Martin-in-the-Fields church near Trafalgar Square with a member of London's Women in Black I'd just met. Like me, she was white, middle class, and wearing black clothing. I was in my early thirties at the time and at least twenty years younger than this woman, whom I refer to here as Judy. We retrieved signs from a small room in the basement of the church along with another woman, who met us at the church. I had contacted Judy before my arrival in London for a conference, where I was presenting my research about midtown Manhattan Women in Black, and was invited to attend the vigil. The three of us carried signs back to the Edith Cavell memorial in St. Martin's Place and began setting up for the vigil. Two other women joined us. I was assigned a position on one side of the square base of the statue, where I stood with a sign contesting war in Iraq. Over the course of the next hour, two more women arrived to vigil. One stood with me for part of the vigil and with another Londoner for the rest.

Edith Cavell is a fitting muse for Women in Black London. A British nurse who saved lives regardless of nationality during World War I and who was executed by a German firing squad, she represents values held by the vigilers opposing military violence by a variety of governments, including their own. Above a statue of Cavell, the word "Humanity" is carved into the stone. Below her image, a quote from her is etched: "Patriotism is not enough. I must have no hatred or bitterness for anyone." The memorial situates Women in Black's protest in relationship to a pacifist internationalism that rejects isolationist nationalism and war.

The vigil wasn't officially silent, but there was very little talking, and what little was said was spoken quietly among demonstrators. There was no verbal engagement with bystanders. One woman stood to the side and handed out leaflets critiquing militarism. As I stood with these other women, all white, older than me, and, I assumed, more seasoned peace activists, I took in the surroundings and thought about my position in this vigil. The U.K. had troops deployed in Afghanistan and Iraq, although the United States had led the charge in both cases. The two countries are generally viewed as allies, both economically and militarily. Yet I'd also perceived some resentment of the United States in my readings of British antiwar writings posted on the internet. What was my role here? What was I witnessing? What connected my participation to theirs?

Creating witness space requires addressing the geographical process of militarization. Geographer Jenna Loyd explains that "geographic imaginations that distinguish neatly between battle zone and home front—and thereby citizen and soldier, civil society and military—dangerously shape understandings of wars, and hence what it might mean to end and prevent them."[8] War requires seeing soldiers as holding unique positions separate from yet supported by society. Additionally, "we" must be imagined as separate from "them," and "here" must be distinguished from "there." Connections, whether material, emotional, or geographical, must be ignored, denied, or minimized in order to effectively construct enemies worthy of our ire and to justify sending soldiers to engage them. Loyd explains that these "conceptions obscure uneven geographies of war-making . . .

and the historical geographies of social, economic, and political relations that enable militarized conflict in particular places to appear disconnected from 'peace' in other places."[9]

Public protests often seek to reveal the fiction of these divisions by bringing images of war zones or people in those zones to protests, naming the people who have died in battlefields far from the site of the protests, and chanting slogans that highlight a shared humanity, such as "we are all Egyptians" at demonstrations in the United States during the protests in Tahrir Square. People take to the streets hoping to prevent wars and to stop them once they've begun. After wars become commonplace, marches, vigils, and rallies seek to remind people that war doesn't have to be the status quo or that militarization has specific implications for women. In each of these instances, participants emphasize links between the site of the demonstration and the location of the military aggressions.

A central part of Women in Black's impetus is to collapse the distances required to maintain a militarized mindset, to make the "historical geographies of social, economic, and political relations" visible through their vigils. Rather than bringing images of those places or chanting slogans that risk collapsing differences, they position themselves as witnesses, haunting the home front in order to highlight a shared humanity with those in other locations in the uneven geographies of war making. Thus, the witness space they create relies on these topographically distant yet politically close places and emphasizes affective connections among women differently situated in relation to military aggressions. These locations enable the peaceful veneer of "normal life" in wealthy parts of the United States and U.K. This semblance of peace relies on the wars and systems of economic exploitation occurring elsewhere and violence and exploitation occurring in other parts of these wealthy nations. Women in Black's vigils attempt to reveal these connections while simultaneously demonstrating what peace based on shared recognition of humanity can look and feel like.

Witnessing War from the Home Front

In coming together to publicly bear witness, participants become Women in Black, demonstrating critical theorist Donna Haraway's assertion that "actors are the products of relating, not pre-formed before the encounter."[10] Prior to donning black clothing, gathering, organizing themselves into formation, holding signs, and standing in silence, these vigilers are Janice the actress, who waits tables to pay the bills; Hannah the Jewish grandmother, who is freed of her child-rearing duties; Alyssa, who works with young people at a local university in Atlanta; and others with various unrelated lives. Yet on specified afternoons, they become Women in Black through their relations to each other and to the people who view them.

With their various responses, bystanders are part of this process—spitting on the vigiling women, providing supportive comments, giving engaged glances, not turning their heads to look. All are formed through the encounter, participants and observers alike. The witness space is created by vigilers' relations to each other and the focus of their vigil, which can be augmented or shattered by bystander responses. This public interaction among participants and between participants and observers shapes them and the space they use.

Witnessing remembers and documents traumatic events that risk being forgotten and, in the case of ongoing violence, continuing uncontested. Both direct witnesses and the witnesses to their testimony are necessary to effectively respond to horrific situations. Education scholars Roger Simon and Claudia Eppert explain that "the first-order witness initiates a chain of testimony-witnessing held together by the bonds of an ethics forged in a relationship of responsibility and respect."[11] Survivors' testimony can establish an ethical relationship with people who listen to their testimony. Then, these observers can bear witness to the horrors described to them. While second- and thirdhand testimony cannot replicate survivor accounts, without it political responses remain limited.

Vigiling can be a part of a chain of witnessing. Participants witness the trauma of first-order witnesses, and observers witness the vigil, extending the sequence. Women in Black participants acknowledge and remember violence as they stand on sidewalks and street corners. They demonstrate that the violence they remember is consequential and seek to remind passersby that they too should recognize ongoing violence. In this way they engage in a countermemorial practice that contests dominant value systems that actively forget about people suffering in faraway places.[12]

CREATING WITNESS SPACE

In order to set off time and space to bear witness to military violence and occupation, participants need to alter how they interact with each other and nonparticipants in order to signal that something is different, that there is something serious happening that requires different ways of interacting. An affective shift must occur. This is often accomplished by some kind of ritual, the use of props such as clothing and signs, and the strategic use of participants' bodies.

Women in Black vigils use ritualized elements to transform urban spaces into sites for witnessing violence and demonstrating investment in peace. As part of this process they also rework associations between women, passivity, and emotions. Participants wear black to communicate their belonging in the collective and the emotional register of the event. They gather at the same time and in the same place week after week. They stand in a set configuration such as a line facing traffic or a circle surrounding a memorial. They are quiet or silent, not raising their voices to explain their presence or engaging bystanders in discussion or debate.

Silence facilitates witnessing. Judy, from the London vigil, describes the importance of silence to her group's public presence using her experiences with other forms of protest.

> I think most of the slogans that people shout at marches and demonstrations are pretty stupid. I mean, they are so reduced in their thinking by the time they're a slogan that they are 90 percent of the time so simplistic as to be wrong. . . . I like singing on a march. As long as it's started with the band, and as long as there's some good voices around, I think that's fun. . . . But . . . silence is terribly important here, and I like that. I don't need to come shouting slogans. The slogan is on the banner I hold or the ones I've helped prepare, and so that is very clear. We are so clear as long as somebody reads even the fractional amount of English. Probably even if they don't read English at all, they get the message. I think if you said to somebody who spoke not a word of English, couldn't read a word of English, and saw us standing there, then you said, "What the hell are those women doing?" They might get it fractionally wrong, they might say they're in mourning for somebody because they're in black and they're silent, they might say that. But I think most of them get the message.

She breaks down a range of experiential and auditory protest experiences that produce different affects: shouting, singing, and silence. Slogans, she points out, are necessarily simplistic. They're soundbites, quick and pithy, easy to say and easy to report. Nuance is difficult. Singing, in contrast, helps create a joyful gathering. It communicates with both sound and words. Silence, in comparison with these other tactics, conveys gravity through its lack of noise. For her, the silence of Women in Black is meaningful for two reasons: it avoids the oversimplicity of slogans, and it helps create the desired mood for their vigil. It can be marginally misread—someone might think that participants are mourning an individual's death, for example—but the staging communicates in ways that slogans cannot. This ritualized organization of costumed bodies transforms sites into witness spaces that can be read as such by passersby. The affective quality of Women in Black demonstrations communicates messages that political rhetoric cannot.

COMMUNICATING FEELING

Women in Black vigils' ability to communicate feeling is linked to their immobility and silence. Participants work with the cultural relationships between passivity, emotionality, and women. "The fear of passivity is tied to the fear of emotionality, in which weakness is defined in terms of a tendency to be shaped by others," Sara Ahmed explains. "The association between passion and passivity . . . works as a reminder of how 'emotion' has been viewed as 'beneath' the faculties of thought and reason. . . . Emotions are associated with women, who are represented as 'closer' to nature, ruled by appetite, and less able to transcend the body through thought, will, and judgment."[13] Participants take on these associations, but they do so in ways that transform them into authority. Judy explains the productive contradiction here: "Although it looks quite passive, it's actually not. I can't explain the dynamic of it: it is *so* active—even though it is silent and people are not doing anything. It is so active that some men, [and] very occasionally women—enough to make one really surprised—men find the strength and the activeness of our demonstration *completely impossible* to take. And they swear, they shout at us, they cannot bear the strength of a group of women standing there doing nothing and saying nothing and looking strong." Women in Black's apparent passivity is intentional. They choose to stand in silence, not moving, not speaking. This passivity is also active in the sense that it communicates something besides unresponsiveness. This aspect is what Judy describes onlookers, especially men, as objecting to. Participants use this passivity to communicate their feelings and opinions. Their quiet immobility expresses the strength required to stand publicly, making themselves vulnerable to verbal and, potentially, physical abuse in order to communicate their responses to ongoing wars, the connections between "here" and "there," and peacefulness. In the process they transform urban space into witness space.

EMBODYING PEACE

For some of the people I interviewed, witnessing had religious or spiritual overtones. Their claiming of public space, therefore, enabled them to transcend the secular and mundane associations of the vigil locations. For example, Janice, a lifelong Quaker, explained that Women in Black transform witnessing from an intellectual exercise to an embodied action: "[The Quakers'] thing is to bear witness in public. It's a long tradition. [Women in Black] are saying that with our bodies," she proclaimed. She and her fellow vigilers' bodies demanded that people remember the dead and injured bodies of civilians, journalists, activists, and soldiers, thereby evoking absent bodies and faraway places.

Blending politics and spirituality was important for Kathleen, a seventy-year-old white woman from Long Island who also demonstrates with CODEPINK. She described taking part in weekly silent vigils as becoming "a presence," something that was explicitly spiritual and feminist for her. Through the process of standing on a sidewalk at a busy intersection each week, her political values took on physical form. She and her colleagues demanded public acknowledgment of dissenting views. The small group claimed and held the space through their physical and emotional presence. Some of the vigils she attended in Long Island drew from her Wiccan practices by beginning in a circle. Others were dedicated to particular people, providing an emotional and spiritual focus for participants. Merging political and religious practices transformed public, seemingly mundane spaces and created the perfect outlet for her feminist values.

For some, the rituality of Women in Black vigils had less explicitly religious but still spiritual dimensions. Hannah, a white Jewish woman in her seventies who was part of the Manhattan vigil and also had long-standing ties to feminism, explored the meditative dimensions of vigiling when describing her first vigil:

> It was the most powerful experience I've had in a long time. There was something very profound about it. At first I realized I wasn't going to be able to speak, and it's not the usual way we do it at these demonstrations and rallies. So I was quiet, and just being quiet I got so deep into my head and such a calmness came over me. . . . I felt at first very calm and tried to keep my eyes off people just to be there with this message. Then I felt strong, very strong about the group, that such a small group was together in this quiet vigil for some very important message. Then I just found it was so profound. . . . I thought, This is what Gandhi was saying. If you just can be quiet. If you feel strong about your message, you don't have to dialogue all the time. I felt people looked at us, and people took the literature, and some people said "I agree" or gave us a high-five kind of sign. The presence was very, very deep. When I left I felt incredibly moved by what I had just done. I still feel it.

Not being able to speak shifted how she understood public demonstrations. Standing in silence required an inward focus, something like meditation. The calmness altered her experience during and after the vigil; it changed her. Refusing to look away from the continued violence became all the more profound by standing in silence. This private meditation strengthened the message of nonviolence and her commitment to it. The space was held for her by other participants, and, in turn, she held the space for them.

Through silence and stillness, Women in Black seek first to calm themselves and then, hopefully, to calm others who view their demonstration. As Hannah's discussion of her experience makes clear, she calms by standing in silence. By thinking of the teachings of a renowned nonviolence advocate, she transforms her own response to ending war. She carried the calm with her to our interview the next day. Janice described a similar experience. "I get really frustrated and angry. Then if I go to my vigil and I'm silent, I can deal with all that stuff. I'm meditating," she explained. For Janice, yelling feels antithetical to demonstrating for peace. Silence fits the message of peace better: "Silence means to me that we're not arguing with you, these are our feelings. Silence may touch people, whereas if you're arguing with them or yelling or chanting, it cuts [them] off and makes them angry, and then you can't reach them at all." Instead of initiating a conflict about whether or not war is warranted, she communicates her views through silence without resorting to rhetorical violence. For her, this is practicing peace, a process that bridges self-care and engagement with geopolitical processes.

The embodied nature of this demonstration is key to its communication of feeling. Women's bodies, loaded with cultural associations about passivity, nurturing, and sexual availability, silently convey the gravity of ongoing wars. By making themselves vulnerable in a culture invested in women's vulnerability, they demand that people recognize that something significant is happening in other places and that violence elsewhere enables the everyday workings of places like Manhattan and London. These places are intricately connected through flows of money, arms, people, and ideas. London's tourist sites and Manhattan's boutiques rely on money made via military aggressions, past and present. These vigils witness these processes, seeking to reveal the connections that are generally covered over by violent and exploitative geopolitical processes.

This approach to protest also provides a way to address disagreements among people opposing war by demonstrating the peace they seek. For Janice, the silence of the Manhattan vigil allows participants to focus on what they have in common rather than their differences: "The silence is very good because we're not arguing about what we're going to agree on or disagree on, and that's a blessing." Rather than arguing with each other, rather than being rigid in advocating for their own methods, they soften together in their collective, silent vigil. The individualism of Hannah's meditative experience is transformed in Janice's observation. Individual experiences of calmness can change communal spaces. They can prevent people from arguing with each other over ideal tactics and outcomes. Instead, by silently standing together, the group creates a small island of peace in a hectic urban site.

This peace is particularly poignant when there is opposition. When bystanders yell at participants or attempt to disrupt the vigil, this peace can be hard to sustain. During the first Women in Black vigil I attended in San Francisco in 2003, I couldn't maintain silence in the face of an angry spectator. Rather than softening when confronted by her outburst, I responded. I tried to "reason" with her, causing escalation. Another vigiler reminded me that we were supposed to be silent. My calm irredeemably broken, I left, allowing others to hold the space. Women in Black's witness space is held by a reciprocal agreement among participants to silently hold vigil. Maintaining the vigil requires that participants collectively maintain the space for each other. In Hannah's statement above, her calm strength was supported by and supporting of the group. My outburst at the San Francisco vigil ruptured the witness space and threatened to transform the space into a site for debate rather than reflection.

NOT SPEAKING FOR OTHERS

Because participants in the vigils discussed in this chapter are not the people experiencing the violence they witness, it's not clear that the violence is theirs to witness. In philosopher Linda Martín Alcoff's explorations of speaking for others, she explains that both "collective action and coalitions would seem to require the possibility of speaking for."[14] This necessity doesn't occlude ethical concerns. We must still be attentive to what is spoken by whom and the "social space" of any given speech act.[15] Thus, while she refuses strict limits on speaking for others that would foreclose collective action, she insists that one should only represent the views of others based on "a concrete analysis of the particular power relations and discursive effects involved."[16]

The social space of a text or utterance includes not only the speaker and the immediate audience but also the context and the destinations where the text or utterance travels. In a protest, this social space is immediate and, potentially, mediated. It is the moment of the event, the people attending, and the bystanders. In some cases, it is also the people who learn about it through a newspaper, radio, or internet report. Thus, the speech that happens in one of these spaces—for example, CODEPINK's claim that "Women Want a Peace Vice President" (see chapter 5)—can potentially be read by a wide range of people who might feel appropriately or inappropriately spoken for.

Women in Black navigates this differently than most protest groups. They still have signs—"Women in Black Against War," for example—but without the accompanying chants and verbal exchanges with bystanders. Also, the slogan is more precise; this isn't women against war—it's Women in Black against war. This claim signals a collective but doesn't purport to represent all women. Thus, participants are not speaking for others broadly; instead, they speak for a transnational, voluntary collective of which they are part.

These rituals of witnessing follow a script that enacts peacefulness by refusing to yell or engage in verbal conflict and thereby provides embodied testimony about ongoing military violence. By not speaking for others yet still taking collective action, participants avoid many of the pitfalls outlined by Alcoff; however, their inattention to the complexity of the social space they inhabit still raises concerns. In my interview with Janice, a white heterosexual woman in her fifties, she declared the space Manhattan Women in Black use as "our area of Manhattan," circumscribing their social space and relegating other women who might also oppose war as outside the scope of their protest. She drew a spatial boundary that reinforced existing race and class segregation. This was compounded by her description of her group as having a "certain sophistication about politics," a view that erected an ideological barrier. Thus, the social space she set for her vigils relied on geographical and ideological divides. While this view is hers and not that of other women who attend Women in Black vigils, it demonstrates how a potentially liberatory mode of engagement can be limited by a narrow sense of community and a lack of interest in coalition building.

Additionally, it is not participants' children, their loved ones, or citizens of their nation who are suffering under a military occupation. In fact, it is their nation coordinating the killing. Their tax dollars fund the campaigns that deprive others of their lives and their loved ones. They want to demonstrate their solidarity with those who are killed and the people who love them. They claim this violence as theirs to witness and memorialize because they are on what journalist Myrna Kostash refers to as the ideological front lines, even if they are geographically far from the military front lines.[17] Their vigils attempt to link these fronts.

In the process, the women avoid representing other people's feelings and views by not claiming to know how other people feel. Instead, they focus on their own feelings about military violence. This can be read as solipsistic, as astute, or as some combination. Beginning with the self as a way to make social change is a ritualized part of our culture found in self-help manuals and academic discussions of the aesthetics of the self. This individualistic starting point may be *both* selfish and a good foundation for addressing state-sponsored violence. The ethics of such public presence are not simple.

While emotions are often seen as individual responses, under the right circumstances they can become the basis for communal political actions. According to critical theorist Judith Butler, grief displays "the thrall in which our relations with others hold us . . . in ways that challenge the very notion of ourselves as autonomous or in control."[18] Thus, anguish can reveal connections to others even when it arises in response to a specific, individualized event. In the examples discussed here, the violence these women respond to is already communal, shared within and among nations. Through coming together to respond, they transform their individual responses into a collective public vigil that highlights the collective effects of war. By slowing down and contemplating the effects of war, they demonstrate another way of being in relationship with the people the U.S. and U.K. military are engaging. Nonetheless, the geopolitical location of the vigils and the social location of participants affect their efficacy.

Matters of Location

Location matters for these vigils in at least three ways. First, whether or not the vigil occurs in a country with an active military conflict or occupation matters. Second, where the vigil is in a city affects who sees it and how it is viewed. Third, the social location of most participants worked with the spatial location of these vigils to simultaneously challenge and reinforce social norms. The two vigils I discuss in depth in this chapter are quite similar on all three counts. They both occurred in spaces likely to draw tourists and privileged members of the cities where they occur. They also transpired in countries with troops deployed elsewhere, rather than in nations experiencing active military conflict. Most participants were also from privileged racial and class backgrounds.

Vigils actively work with their disparate locations, seeking connection among sites where vigils occur and the places where war rages. Participants use their location in "peaceful" places to remind people of the violence occurring elsewhere and to demonstrate what peace could look like. They see themselves as part of a feminist and pacifist international community rather than simply members of their home nations and communities.

This challenges nationalist beliefs that see people from other parts of the world as separate from members of our own nations. As Judy's comments and the opening description of the Manhattan vigil make clear, this orientation opens them up to verbal abuse by angry bystanders who disagree or question women's public presence; however, this risk is quite minimal compared to what vigilers in Belgrade and Israel have experienced. In describing her experiences with Women in Black in post-9/11 Edmonton, Alberta, Kostash opens with a description of Belgrade Women in Black: "No matter how long the wars raged on and how many Wednesdays the Women in Black stood speechless in witness of the hope for peace, people stared and scowled and spat at them as though the outrage of their dissent from war was freshly registered each week."[19] Similarly, feminist scholars Sara Helman and Tamar Rapoport examine the violent, gendered insults hurled at the Jerusalem group, including "you should all be fucked and killed" and accusations that vigilers were "Arab fuckers."[20] While such provocations are possible anywhere, the likelihood of experiencing violent responses is greater in locations where conflicts are active.

In contrast, Kostash claims that her "experience of strength and visibility 'empowered' no one but [her]self."[21] Like the women from the Manhattan and London vigils quoted here, she benefited from her vigiling experience but left feeling like her peace of mind was the only thing vigiling achieved, and it wasn't sufficient. Her assessment that she had only empowered herself was related to her location outside war zones and sites where military decisions were made: "Since we had never been expected to speak in the first place as Canadians far removed from the front lines, ideological and military—our silence was unremarkable."[22] The contrast she makes between Canada and Belgrade, the military front line, makes clear the difference between her vigil and the long-standing Belgrade vigil. What she leaves unexplored is how vigils at the ideological front lines should be assessed.

Solidarity can take many forms. Pushing those in power to make changes is the one that Women in Black participants in the United States and U.K. take up. Their role is to work at what Kostash describes as the ideological front lines of what the two countries refer to as the "war on terror." Women in Black's target audience is civilians, and their method of persuasion is demonstrating peacefulness. They work at a specific point in the decision-making chain, focusing on people who vote and might write letters or lobby their representatives.

These vigils also influence some of the people who view them. While it's impossible to know how many people continue thinking about war after encountering vigils or how many people decide to do something after interacting with these women, Judy's descriptions of people getting angry about the London vigil show some effects. Their presence gets at least a few people thinking and responding. The woman who stopped and joined the Manhattan vigil was also moved. Likely, others also respond in various ways. Mary Wentworth, a white woman in her seventies who helped found the Amherst, Massachusetts, vigil, which met weekly in front of the local Bank of America near the city's major intersection, explained the changes in people's responses between 2001 and 2005, when I spoke to her:

> At first there was not much of a public display of support for us. Not like today, where you saw people giving us the thumbs up, tooting their horns. It was much more reserved, cautious, and a lot of people disagreed with us. People might come along and very quietly say, "I support what you're doing," but we got many more people coming to us and saying, "You shouldn't be doing this." In fact, there was a vet who dressed in uniform and held a big American flag on a pole who stood not too far from us on a traffic island kind of protesting, contrasting the two approaches.

Mary believed that their vigil, which initially was only three women and later grew to six, "gave a lot of people sustenance to continue in their own line of thinking and maybe to speak up more." This is a microlevel effect, but it extends beyond the individuals bearing witness.

My final concern about location focuses on the socioeconomic location of vigil participants. It's certainly not out of the ordinary that participants in a demonstration would reflect the race and class composition of the space the demonstration is in. Yet, to apply Loyd's insights on a local rather than a global level, "peace" in a wealthy area of town might well be related to war in other areas of the same city.[23] Peace requires not only the personal meditation and calm enabled by these vigils or the suspension of arguments about which version of progressive ideology is represented by an organization but also working across race and class difference. The Women in Black groups discussed here do not take that final step. Consider Janice's response to my question about which women attend the midtown Manhattan vigil.

> It's our area of Manhattan. There is a group on 182nd Street. When I've been organizing with other women who've been murdered in Juárez, Mexico, people have said, "You're going to come uptown, aren't you? Up where we live?" That would be the way. If we went to neighborhoods where more black women lived, that would be different. It's in education level—I didn't mean to say education—no, it's a certain sophistication about politics and reading the *New York Times* every day or something. It's a very specific kind of witnessing. I don't know why there are not a lot of black pacifist women standing with us. But we haven't gone out of our way to open it up. We didn't follow up with outreach to the young black teenagers. We didn't follow up because we don't have enough energy. We don't have enough time. We could have gone up there and said, "Let's have a reception. Let's have a meeting. Let's get together. Let's follow up with emails and phone calls." But we didn't, because we just have time to go there once a week. So the people who feel moved to join us will. We don't have time. It's too bad. We need a couple of interns. We need apprentices. Some Women in Black [groups] have committees they delegate, and we're just not that type of vigil. It might be good if we were, but that's our style. We meet and we do it every Wednesday all year round. That's just our style. I'm sure there's a lot of young and middle-aged black women who are active in their churches and active in their colleges and active in their communities. They don't happen to come to our vigil.

Janice struggles to define and defend her complacency about inclusion. "This is our area of Manhattan," she explains, claiming a small slice of the urban landscape of the central borough of New York City. She does work in other areas, for example, organizing around the murders of women in Ciudad Juárez. Yet for vigiling with Women in Black, she's rooted to the space outside of the public library, and it's hard for her to describe why. "We don't have time," she explains, to do outreach. Yet time isn't the only part of her explanation. "It's a very specific kind of witnessing," she says, and she links it to "sophistication about politics and reading the *New York Times* every day or something." That something could be many things: comfort in their space, class privilege, racial privilege. In all likelihood, it is some combination of these elements.

This complacency about local racial and class dynamics, as well as ignorance about the racial spectrum in New York City ("I'm sure there's a lot of young and middle-aged black women"), seems constitutive of the women's presence. They're also not in contact with women in Iraq or Afghanistan. Their connections to international groups come primarily through their presence on the international website. None of the participants in the London vigil articulated this kind of condescending view of other activists, but the group's composition read similarly, leading me to wonder who else was protesting war elsewhere in the city.

In her exploration of the Jerusalem Women in Black vigil, which she was a part of for many years, feminist scholar Erella Shadmi raised similar questions about the dynamics of privilege and oppression: "The *simultaneous coexistence* of female exclusiveness and Ashkenazi dominance . . . constructed an internal tension between hegemony and marginality, center and periphery, powerfulness and powerlessness, resistance and compliance."[24] As women, participants in the vigils I discuss here are marginal and vulnerable. Thus, this form of resistance works from that position, manipulating cultural expectations of women in order to demonstrate their rejection of war. Yet most of the women who perform these actions also enjoy the power that comes with race and class privilege. The spaces they created for witnessing also reflect this privilege.

Conclusion

I continue to struggle with the question of whether Women in Black's witnessing is complacent or profound. The likely answer is both. Compared to other forms of work to end war, their work is undemanding; it only takes a little time out of one's week. It's also easy to focus on the imperfections of such vigils, such as Janice's dismissal of the work required to build coalitions. That too is a form of violence. Yet despite such limitations and the privilege that enables them, there is something compelling in the process of creating a space on a busy street to enact another way of being in the world. The affective intervention they make in hectic public spaces does important work.

Women in Black occupy public spaces each week to demonstrate a way of responding to violence and relating to each other. They demonstrate that peace is possible if only people would be peaceful. By creating witness spaces each week on busy sidewalks, plazas, and street corners, these small groups of women refuse the usual modes of engaging political and military power. Instead of transforming these spaces into opportunities to voice opinions not represented in public policy or engage in verbal debates, their "neither/nor" politics of witness transform spaces into sites for contemplation, for remembering, for being the peace they want to see in the world. They hold spaces for being with each other and, hopefully, with others in ways that refuse the violence of armed warfare and loud argumentation.

5

Uncivil Disobedience

CODEPINK's Unruly Democratic Practice

On September 2, 2004, a conservatively dressed, forty-year-old white woman stood on her chair while delegates cheered George W. Bush, who accepted their nomination as the Republican presidential candidate. When delegates sat down she remained standing, holding a pink banner reading "Bush Lies, People Die." Within seconds June Brashares, who entered the Republican National Convention (RNC) in New York City by claiming she had lost her delegate pass, was dragged out of the convention hall. A few minutes later another conservatively dressed white woman stood up in the press stands and removed her dress to reveal a pink slip with a handwritten message across the front: "Pink Slip Bush! Women Say Bring the Troops Home Now!" Due to the commotion caused by Brashares, Jodie Evans, the pink-slip-wearing cofounder of CODEPINK: Women for Peace, was able to remain standing for a brief moment before being hauled away. Both were arrested, and Brashares was charged with felony assault. These accusations were later dropped.[1]

For a few brief moments the focus of the convention was on Brashares and Evans rather than on President Bush. His voice faltered, and the crowd's tone shifted. The adjustment was temporary, but it demonstrated how easy it is to interrupt formal political proceedings. Two women's tactical use of a banner and a pink slip drew attention away from Bush's assertion of masculine military bravado.[2] These women transformed the already gendered spectacle of the convention into a site for feminist protest and delivered a message to the man who led the United States into two controversial wars and to the people who supported his continued leadership. Through media coverage they also held the attention of people across the nation.

Brashares and Evans successfully evoked the image of conservative professional women in order to enter the convention. Their white, middle-class, normatively feminine, able bodies allowed viewers to see the image they projected rather than the subversion they intended. A form of drag that relied on proximity to respectable femininity, their performance succeeded until they willingly revealed the ruse. This politicized feminine drag evoked the civility they would later reject as part of their disruptive democratic practice. In describing how they acquired passes, cofounder Medea Benjamin explained, "We have some very nice-looking women in Code Pink that have been hanging out in some nice bars, and these delegates like to impress the women."[3] A blazer, a conservative dress, classy bar attire, and appropriately styled long hair signal class status and, potentially, political persuasion. These women's skin color also referenced belonging in a white-dominated space. That this proper, conservative veneer could be easily shed—by the unfurling of a protest banner or the public removal of a dress—also showed the fragility of appropriate femininity.

These activists' politicized drag performances, like their participation in large-scale protests and sonically disruptive lobbying efforts, which I explore below, are forms of dissident citizenship practice. Political theorist Holloway Sparks defines dissident citizenship as "the practices of marginalized citizens who publicly contest prevailing arrangements of power by means of oppositional democratic practices that augment or replace institutionalized channels of democratic opposition when those channels are inadequate or unavailable."[4] Institutionalized channels for opposition such as "voting, lobbying, [and] petitioning" are most available to people who resemble, somatically and behaviorally, those in power.[5] These forms of opposition generally rely on behavioral norms that emphasize rationality and civility, which have been constructed in ways that privilege interactional norms associated with masculinity, whiteness, and educated middle- and upper-class people. Views of women as inherently less rational and possessing excessive communication styles pose particular challenges for women's use of accepted channels for contesting policies and institutions.

Protesters challenge both current institutions and the ideas and policies produced within them, taking an affective position that places them on the edges of civility norms regardless of protest style. Some manifestations of dissident politics work as closely as possible with expectations of civility in order to increase the likelihood that observers will deem them "good," rational citizens and therefore consider their claims. However, given the role of behavioral norms in upholding social hierarchies, sometimes "incivility is also a rational response to injustice."[6] CODEPINK works from this premise, insisting that current structures and ideologies limit who can effectively express dissent and the ways that dissent can be expressed. Their disruptive interventions into political processes seek greater participatory opportunities for women and other political outsiders while simultaneously highlighting the race- and class-inflected masculine norms of accepted political processes. Their awareness of civility norms and proper feminine comportment helps them access elite events.

The responses protesters elicit in these settings have ideological dimensions, but they operate primarily in an affective register. This dynamic highlights an often-unrecognized aspect of political power. As sociologist Deborah Gould explains, power "operates through ideology and discourse, but it also operates through affect, perhaps more fundamentally so since ideologies and discourses emerge and take hold in part through the circulation of affect."[7] In the example that opens this chapter, the angry responses to CODEPINK's disruption of Bush's speech are not the only affective dimensions operating. Bush's charisma relied on his successful harnessing of the affective dimensions of nationalism and masculine political authority. Affect circulated in the space during his speech and in the rhetorical responses to events, including the September 11, 2001, tragedy that preceded his renomination. That women disrupting his speech, which affirmed his position as figurehead for a conservative social and political agenda, were met with emotion-laden force is not surprising. Brashares and Evans likely knew that their uncivil behavior, which grew out of their own affective responses to political processes and figures, would elicit affective and possibly violent responses.

Not all women could have pulled off this stunt. A combination of creativity, bravery, and successfully leveraged privilege helped them achieve their goal on September 2, 2004, as well as in other actions before and after. As part of a group comprised primarily of white, middle-class, middle-aged, able-bodied women, participants are able to access elite spaces while risking arrest. In exploring dissident citizenship, Sparks argues "for a conception of citizenship that recognizes both dissent and an ethic of political courage as vital elements of democratic participation."[8] CODEPINK's uncivil direct actions require courage and intentionally elicit affective responses. Their participatory democratic process not only questions the exclusion of most women from the formal political process but also challenges norms of civility that both mask and uphold social and political hierarchies. In the process they transform formal political and activist spaces into unruly democratic spaces using uncivil sartorial and sonic enactments.

In each of the examples I discuss in this chapter, CODEPINK protesters transform spaces using a combination of privilege, imagination, and courage, generating a distinct protest style that they have maintained for over a decade. First, I briefly explore CODEPINK's origins and contextualize their use of the color pink. I then discuss how they claim spaces, including convention speeches and segments of large leftist mobilizations, by exploiting cultural fascinations with women's sexuality and descriptions of liberty as a feminine virtue, enactments

I refer to as feminine drag. Subsequently, I explore their creative lobbying of elected officials using songs along with pink clothing. In the process, I highlight how they transform political and activist spaces through uncivil enactments of democracy.

Beginnings

CODEPINK's first action took place on November 17, 2002, when cofounders Medea Benjamin, Starhawk, Jodie Evans, Gael Murphy, and Diane Wilson joined approximately one hundred other women on a march through the streets of Washington, D.C. Following the November demonstration, they set up a four-month vigil in front of the White House, culminating in a large demonstration on International Women's Day in March 2003.[9] As part of the day's events, a forty-foot pink banner shaped like a slip reading "Women Say: Fire Bush" hung from a giant weather balloon.[10]

Evans and Wilson met at a retreat in May 2002 in Ojai, California, organized by UnReasonable Women for the Earth and began talking with others about creating a direct-action group that would attract the women who, according to polls, were strongly opposed to war.[11] The group became CODEPINK, named in reference to the Bush administration's color-coded terror alert system and the hospital alarm of the same name, used when a baby is abducted. The organization's moniker reframed a term from the traditionally private, feminine arena of motherhood as a response to the public, masculine-dominated world of politics by playing on public safety rhetoric. In order to emphasize the dangers of militarism and corporate capitalism, CODEPINK reworks affective and ideological frameworks politicians use to exploit fears of terrorism.

The September prior to the first official CODEPINK action in November 2002 Benjamin and Wilson were arrested for disrupting Defense Secretary Donald Rumsfeld's testimony before the House Armed Services Committee. During this feat they utilized what were to become stock CODEPINK tactics: entering an official, male-dominated establishment where voices of civilians are generally not heard, disrupting official political and/or legal proceedings by vocally expressing opposition to war and government policies, and unfurling a banner that created a good media image.[12] By asking "Why are you obstructing the inspections? Is this really about oil? How many civilians will be killed?" they broke congressional silences about the human and environmental costs of declaring war on Iraq. They also insisted that women's voices be heard in a male-dominated arena of public life, highlighting how official public debate usually relies on gender exclusions central to the bourgeois public sphere from its inception.[13]

Playfully reclaiming pink as a primary aspect of their political performances instantly genders their public presence because of pink's deep association with girls, women, and femininity. Since the 1950s pink has symbolized femininity in the United States.[14] The contemporary, often anxious emphasis on color-coded clothing and toys for children demonstrates the link between gender norms and color; pink and blue serve as symbols for a larger set of values. The association between pink and femininity and, by extension, nurturing, purity, frailness, and frivolousness carries beyond childhood. While blue is culturally available to all adults and most children, pink's association with girlhood renders all male-bodied people who wear it suspect and marks adult women who wear it as "in touch with" their supposedly innate, youthful femininity.

CODEPINK members attempt to simultaneously tap into and diverge from the traditionally gendered use of pink. This disidentification with idealized femininity exploits the power of visual culture and reframes the supposed weakness of pink into something authoritative, militant, and explicitly feminist. Katha Pollitt describes pink as carrying "so many meanings we like: female, gay, antimacho, peaceful, playful and, well, pinko."[15] By using pink to assert authority, CODEPINK asserts femininity and leftist values while rejecting the color's associations with passivity, domesticity, and, in the contemporary moment, corporate-sponsored breast cancer awareness.[16]

The group's methods are necessarily tactical. In his descriptions of the differences between tactics and strategies, philosopher Michel de Certeau emphasizes the role of power. A strategy, he explains, is "the calculus of force-relationships which becomes possible when a subject of will and power (a proprietor, an enterprise, a city, a scientific institution) can be isolated from an environment."[17] In other words, strategy is available to those who can act from a position of power where the environment has little effect on them. In contrast, tactics belong to "the other," to outsiders who must grab opportunities on the fly.[18] Operating tactically has both benefits and drawbacks. Creativity flourishes in this flexible environment; however, outsider groups are at the mercy of strategic shifts by those with official power. For example, in an interview with *Roll Call*, Capitol Hill's news magazine, CODEPINK activists explained that the rules they were expected to follow during their occupations of congressional offices, banner drops, and interruptions of hearings shifted over time. An attorney representing many CODEPINK members, Mark Goldstone, explained that because he had "never seen a long-term systematic campaign of this sort" in more than twenty years of practice, security has been figuring out how to respond, and "the ground rules are shifting and enforcement is shifting."[19] By 2011 the opportunities CODEPINK had found to claim and hold congressional spaces in 2007 were essentially eliminated by the Federal Restricted Buildings and Grounds Improvement Act.[20]

Despite setbacks, CODEPINK members' tactical maneuvers have led them to a number of locations in the United States and abroad. For example, they've sponsored delegations to Iraq, Pakistan, and Palestine, among other locations.

In this chapter, I focus on their U.S. actions. In their domestic demonstrations, participants enact an uncivil democratic process that uses femininity to draw attention to their critiques of militarism and, in the process, demonstrates the masculine dominance of political processes and spaces.

Claiming Space: Feminine Drag

In their early public presence, CODEPINK used various pink accessories, including slips and crowns, to create a parodic feminine politicized presence. In many ways, CODEPINK's enactments of femininity function as forms of drag. According to J. Halberstam, "the drag king performs masculinity (often parodically) and makes the exposure of the theatricality of masculinity into the mainstay of her act."[21] Thus, just as drag queens enact femininities and drag kings perform masculinities in ways that expose the theatricality of gender, CODEPINK protesters recite different versions of culturally recognizable femininity in ways that expose the theatricality not only of their own protest personas but also of gender conventions. CODEPINK's drag brings aspects of staged performances to the streets and formal political environments. As in street theater, the audience is often unwitting. Both the pink slips participants frequently don and their enactments of Lady Liberty use culturally salient symbols tied to femininity to transform spaces and highlight their political commentary. Their intentionally parodic performances reference aspects of hegemonic cultural ways of constraining women—treating them as sexualized objects for men's pleasure or as muses to inspire ethical behavior—in order to undermine those same modes.

A pink slip is a piece of very feminine attire, as well as a slang term that denotes being laid off from employment. Thus, an item from the private, domestic realm is symbolically connected to the public arena of paid labor. According to the second edition of the *Oxford English Dictionary*, the first published incidence of "pink slip" referencing job loss was in 1915 and documented the practice of using a pink slip of paper to indicate the end of employment. Since then it has shown up in activist art, from "Pink Slip Blues," performed by Ida Cox in 1939, to an unemployment line staged during the 2004 RNC protests.[22] In October 1992 the Women's Action Coalition (WAC), a group known for their creative actions in the early 1990s, used pink slips with the slogan "Read Our Slips: No More Bush Quayle" stenciled on the front.[23] At a San Francisco Republican fund-raiser in 1992, two women shed their conservative attire while standing on a table to reveal pink slips, a performance they described as a "layoff notice."[24] While WAC and others employed the pink slip tactic first, slips and representations of them became emblematic of CODEPINK's savvy, uncivil claiming of political and activist spaces in the early twenty-first century.

The pink slips, often emblazoned with the slogan "Pink Slip Bush," that participants wore in many early demonstrations function in multiple registers. Intellectually, pink slips show the sharp yet playful critique central to CODEPINK's activist style by connecting labor insecurity to feminist critiques of war. Affectively, pink slips tap into the contentious realm of women's sexuality and representations of women in public discourse. Aesthetically, pink slips highlight the performance aspects of CODEPINK's activism. Bringing cultural fixations on women's undergarments together with anxieties inherent in a capitalist economic system challenges a male-dominated political and economic system; the eye-catching color facilitates participants' ability to claim spaces for these values.

Feminist groups frequently use lingerie to draw public attention to women's political concerns or to claim a voice of authority for women. For example, in 1968 feminists protesting the Miss America pageant in Atlantic City, New Jersey, threw their bras and girdles into a garbage can along with their makeup and high heels.[25] A group called the Axis of Eve created a line of panties with slogans critiquing George W. Bush (including "Give Bush the Finger," "Expose Bush," and "Lick Bush") as part of protests in 2004, including the RNC demonstrations and the March for Women's Lives.[26] The Raging Grannies also presented a basket of briefs at a hearing on uranium mining as part of their performances of meddlesome grandmotherhood.[27] Like these other groups, CODEPINK exploits the cultural fascination with women's sexuality and sexualized attire in order to draw attention to their political critiques.

Clothing, including lingerie, is an indicator of gender, social class, age, ethnic and racial belonging, and subcultural group membership. A person's choices provide links between individual expression and social meaning. As Carole Turbin explains, "Dress is inherently and simultaneously both public and private because an individual's outwardly presented signs of internal or private meaning are significant only when they are also social, that is comprehensible on some level to observers."[28] People of all genders put effort into how they present themselves; however, in U.S. culture, the time and money many women put into their appearance, including dress, are intricately tied to our understandings of women and "the labour of looking feminine."[29] CODEPINK's pink slips are comprehensible to a society that associates seductiveness and frailness with women and both punishes and rewards women for their enactment of these qualities.

By drawing on these associations using an item of clothing partially stripped of its sex appeal through handwritten political messages, CODEPINK participants demonstrate their understanding of the cultural power of feminine clothing while also working against dominant meanings. Their deployment of sexualized femininity to draw attention to seemingly nongendered issues such as war, corporate greed, and the loss of civil liberties performs three kinds of work: it draws attention; it highlights the gendered aspects of military, political, and corporate culture; and, like their use of the color pink, it marks their critiques as coming largely from women.

Their enactments are intentionally reiterative. The pink slips reference hypersexualized, feminine women, who are the subject of much cultural fascination. Images of women as either virgins or whores are not as common as in the past, and women, especially queer women, have worked to create alternative spaces in order to be sexual on their own terms. Nonetheless, women are still expected to be feminine in ways that hint toward a dormant sexuality only available to the right man. Women are punished for being overly feminine, "too sexual," or sexual in the wrong way. By embodying hypersexualized femininity parodically, CODEPINK participants seek to capitalize on hegemonic femininity's power without surrendering to its limitations.

The politicized feminine drag of pink lingerie was soon augmented by another symbol: the Statue of Liberty's crown. Often cut out of pink paperboard or foam, these handmade accessories signaled CODEPINK's investment in liberatory politics by highlighting the erosion of civil liberties in a wartime political climate. Below I explore CODEPINK's participation in a large national demonstration and their intervention into this leftist space before exploring the relationship between their use of Liberty's crown and other aspects of their emancipatory drag performance.

Emancipatory Drag: Embodying Liberty

On August 29, 2004, CODEPINK protesters led a contingent in the United for Peace and Justice (UFPJ) march, which was the centerpiece of protests against war and social conservatism on the weekend prior to the RNC. National leaders, including Benjamin and Evans, were present. Most of the 250 or so CODEPINK marchers appeared to be white. There were quite a few men present, but only a few wore pink or any other visual indication that they were part of the group. Exceptions included two men who carried a large pink sign that read "Keep Choice Alive" from a reproductive rights march the day before and one who wore a pink sequined shirt and held a sign that asserted "Gay Men Want to Lick Bush Too." The group gathered at a park a few blocks from the main march route, and after a short rally, including dancing by the Pink Bloque, a group of young white anarchist women, music and cheers by the Radical Cheerleaders, and comments from Benjamin focusing on the "positive energy" CODEPINK was generating despite all the "negative energy" created by the Bush administration, marched to join the main procession. Women at the front of the contingent carried a huge pink sign with the slogan "Peace on Earth" handprinted above CODEPINK's website address.

Other participants carried signs shaped like pink doves and slips. Many wore pink lingerie slips with handwritten slogans or dressed like pink Statues of Liberty. Five women carried a huge banner shaped like a pink slip that read "Fire Bush." Others carried a laundry line with pink slips clipped on it. Once the contingent joined the march of approximately five hundred thousand people, they continued chanting, differentiating themselves from other marchers via sound and appearance.

In these circumstances and many others, CODEPINK activists reclaimed the quintessential U.S. image of liberty: the statue of a crown-wearing woman holding a torch to guide people toward enlightenment in one hand and a tablet bearing the date of the Declaration of Independence in the other. Modeled on the Roman goddess Libertas, who represented personal freedom and, like many other personified virtues, was depicted as a woman, the statue that stands above the New York harbor has served as a liberatory image for immigrants and citizens alike. Numerous activists have questioned the degree to which a nation that was built by enslaved people on land taken from Native peoples actually represents freedom, including African Americans who requested in 1886 that her torch not be lit until racism was eradicated and feminists who took over the monument in 1986 during the Reagan administration's campaign to get individual donors to fund the statue's centennial renovation.[30] Extending this criticism, CODEPINK's enactment of Liberty began in response to a caged "free speech" zone at the 2004 Democratic National Convention and became a central part of vigils and marches leading up to the RNC.[31]

This version of feminine drag draws from a rich history of feminist reclaimings of feminized, anthropomorphized virtues. Liberty's womanliness has traditionally highlighted the masculinity of the political sphere rather than provided an avenue for women's participation. As political theorist Sharon Krause explains, "The fact that, being a woman, she is meant mainly to engage *male* desires reflects the extent to which citizenship and political agency have been largely the province of males in the past."[32] Perhaps the most notable historical reclaiming of Liberty was part of the national suffrage procession of 1913. For this performance, activists presented a pageant featuring a silent tableau of women dressed as the virtues. The pageant began with Columbia, the poetic incarnation of the United States, who was then joined by Justice, Charity, Liberty, Peace, and Hope. According to historian Lucy Barber, "With the combination of goddess-like women, dancing young girls, and colorful costumes, the pageant communicated a message of beautiful patriotism that gently rebuked those who would exclude women from political action."[33] In contrast, CODEPINK's version of Liberty was neither gentle nor invested in an aesthetic of idealized beauty. Their unpolished, handmade costumes were frequently worn in direct confrontations with politicians and police, as well as in direct confrontation with an aesthetic defined by the male gaze.

Liberty was a perfect symbol for participants to emulate, given her womanly representation and the post-9/11 era descriptions of national safety and civil liberties as mutually exclusive goals. By emphasizing a collective vision of liberty focused on freedom of speech and assembly, they provided a progressive, feminist revision of a national icon. Putting on the paper and foam crowns along with pink slips transformed them into a democratic ideal; their womanly bodies became otherworldly representatives of an idealized feminine virtue. The handmade pink accoutrements highlighted their self-conscious performance of a feminized ideal in order to enact a more participatory form of democracy. Their actions demanded democracy and demonstrated its absence.

The small core of CODEPINK's national leadership performs most of the group's interventions, yet the contingents in large mobilizations enable greater participation. Additionally, the organization's involvement in these manifestations allows them to demonstrate the importance of gendered analysis within leftist circles. In addition to the UFPJ March during the 2004 RNC, CODEPINK members have participated in other convention protests, anti-NATO demonstrations, and various manifestations of Occupy in New York City, Oakland, San Francisco, and other locations. While questioning hegemonic gender norms is often associated with left-of-center politics, progressive organizations have long been sites of struggle for women and people with nonnormative gender presentations. As political scientists Margaret Farrar and Jamie Warner point out, "Even the voices from the unruly margins of the public sphere [are generally] male voices."[34]

CODEPINK's feminine drag facilitated the protesters' visibility within the UFPJ demonstration and thereby their ability to insert gender into the space they occupied. This visibility requires investment. As Kammie, a thirty-year-old white woman, noted, it is much easier to move in and out of a demonstration when you are not in costume. In contrast, when dressed up with CODEPINK, she says, "I had a very clear sense of being a part of the protest as opposed to an observer. . . . Because you're dressed up you're making more of a commitment." For Kathleen, a seventy-year-old white woman who also demonstrates with Women in Black, the visibility and theatricality of wearing pink created a sense of belonging: "It changes things. It changes your persona. You can put on a pink persona." Wearing pink or dressing up as a Statue of Liberty is part of being a CODEPINK demonstrator, a visibly political and discernibly feminine role. Costuming created a sense of cohesion for observers and participants. It also produced an explicit boundary between the CODEPINK contingent and other marchers, enabling them to draw attention to their gendered critiques.

Because of the not quite respectable femininity of this costuming, this pink persona reflects the relative privilege of most participants. Wearing lingerie in public risks association with excessive, working-class femininities. Proper femininity has long been associated primarily with racially and class-privileged, able-bodied women who were designated female at birth. Women of color, working-class white women, disabled women, and transwomen are often understood to be inadequately or excessively feminine.[35] Proper gender expression is linked to privileged bodies, rendering other ways of expressing femininity suspect.

Appropriate femininities are culturally recognizable without seeming excessive or theatrical, markers of working-class femininity.[36] Ideal femininity should appear "natural," masking the required cultivation and upkeep. This "natural" femininity results from the right amount of attention: feminine attire appropriate for the occasion, flowing hair in understated styles, subtle makeup, and clothing in colors and patterns that don't draw too much attention. In contrast, blouses that are too low cut; skirts that are too short; heels that are too high; hair that is too big, too obviously nonwhite, or too obviously dyed; lipstick that is too loud; eye shadow that is "inappropriate" for daytime; and bright colors and patterns push people to the edges of propriety. The drag is too obvious when the gender expression doesn't fit middle-class norms. Thus, wearing pink slips moved protesters out of middle-class respectability into an arena of corporeal excess in order to draw attention to themselves and, by extension, their message. While this tactic risks undermining their message, it also enables them to reach their primary audience: other people who also question war, corporate greed, and restrictive gender norms.

Despite the perilous terrain protesters navigate, the theatrical context of a protest and the racial privilege of most participants rendered this flirtation with impropriety relatively safe. They could leave this arena of excess once the protest was over. Given this, one could argue that women without their racial and class privilege could not have risked appearing publicly in undergarments, as many black women have in response to SlutWalks.[37] CODEPINK members' use of theatrical attire is marked as performance because of their racial privilege. The dominance of racially privileged women codes their public presence as not only feminine but also white, middle-class, and normative. Kammie portrayed CODEPINK as "fairly homogenous": mostly white middle-class women from the baby boomer generation, with a substantial number of younger white women and a few women from different racial and ethnic backgrounds. After the 2004 RNC the group was never the same, Alice, a forty-two-year-old white woman, claimed; most of the "young gay women" and women of color quit coming. Regardless, depictions of CODEPINK as a "white lady" group bothered her because she believed that CODEPINK's actions successfully challenged gender norms and contributed to important political conversations.

CODEPINK's membership isn't exclusively white or cisgender; nonetheless, because of their leadership and activist style, their public presence reflects the privilege enjoyed by most of their leaders and members.[38] In describing institutional whiteness, Sara Ahmed explains, "Whiteness is what the institution is orientated 'around,' so that even bodies that might not appear white still have to inhabit whiteness, if they are to get 'in.'"[39] A similar process seems to be at work with CODEPINK. The few nonwhite members take on the normative racial affect of the group. In white-dominated societies, white bodies render spaces white through use, and space associated with whiteness becomes comfortable for white bodies.

This deployment of privileged femininity was considered strategic by some participants. Kathleen described CODEPINK's largely white and middle-class composition as unfortunate but beneficial in some circumstances. For example, she depicted Gael Murphy's ability to enter and interrupt Dick Cheney's speech at the 2004 RNC by playing the part of a "Republican lady" as an example of using what she refers to as the "cloak of invisibility" that women have had to wear during "five or six thousand years" of male oppression. The demeanor of a Republican lady and the associated cloak of invisibility are available to women who fit race and/or class standards.

In recent years, conversations about feminism and racial inclusion have focused less on overt exclusions and more on the ways that the topics emphasized and approaches advocated by feminist organizations frequently reflect privileged women's perspectives. Most feminist groups want their work to appeal to a diverse set of women; however, just as male leadership of leftist organizations often leads to campaigns and tactics that inadequately address women's concerns and organizing styles, white women's leadership of feminist organization frequently results in campaigns and tactics that insufficiently address women of color's interests and ways of organizing. While CODEPINK has an expansive understanding of democracy, both the leadership and ways of claiming a public presence favor racially privileged perspectives, which limits the reach and impact of their uncivil dissent.

Transforming Tactics, Shifting Messages

CODEPINK's public presence has transformed considerably in recent years due to shifts in messaging, protest style, and personnel. Their messaging has changed, no longer emphasizing women's views but instead simply articulating their critiques of corporate-influenced government policies. Nonetheless, their use of varying forms of feminine drag continues to explicitly gender their actions. They combine these sartorial claims to space with the sonic disruption of creative chants and songs, sometimes on their own and sometimes with other organizations. Additionally, their high-profile actions are no longer exclusively performed by normatively white women. A few women of color and an openly transgender woman have participated, and one white man became a key part of their more disruptive actions.

One of the few prominent CODEPINK members outside of normative whiteness, Desiree Anita Ali-Fairooz, was the "Pink House Mama" and "den mother" of the headquarters they maintained for a few years in Washington, D.C.[40] Notably, her participation in the organization focused primarily on the domestic space of the Pink House, which CODEPINK maintained for three years, rather than on more public spaces. Regardless, despite her self-described shyness and generally matronly role, she approached Condoleezza Rice with her hands covered in fake blood and accused her of war crimes, heightening the organization's notoriety.[41] Her light skin, demeanor, and attire, which fit within both mainstream U.S. and CODEPINK norms, didn't challenge the normative femininity of the group.[42] She was, in Ahmed's words, able to inhabit a white-dominated organizational space. Her dark hair and olive complexion complicated rather than changed CODEPINK's public presence. Similarly, Midge Potts, an openly transgender naval veteran, participated in many of the group's 2007 events and shifted CODEPINK's public image in Washington, D.C., but left their national image remarkably unchanged.[43] This tall, white, blond woman added another dimension to CODEPINK's deployment of normative femininities rather than radically transforming them.

The biggest change to CODEPINK's public presence came from Tighe Barry's participation. As a white man, his presence didn't alter the racial valences of their actions; however, his participation in smaller, more high-profile events required shifts in their messaging in ways that men's participation in large demonstrations didn't. Since around 2007, with a few exceptions, most notably, Sarah Palin's 2008 RNC speech, their slogans had become less gender specific. "Women Say: Fire Bush" gave way to "Don't Buy Bush's War," and their message for Palin, "Women Need a Peace Vice President," was replaced by gender-neutral slogans, for Mitt Romney's ("People Over Profits") and Donald Trump's ("Build Bridges Not Walls") RNC acceptance speeches. Their foci—militarism and politicians' relationships with corporations—remain the same, as does their deployment of the feminizing color pink, which Barry wears along with the group's women members. This change in messaging hasn't changed the organization's self-description as "a women-initiated grassroots peace and social justice movement" or perceptions that they are a women's organization.

Where they perform their interventions has also changed largely due to a changing political and activist landscape. While they continue to disrupt major speeches, particularly at Republican and Democratic conventions, the number of large demonstrations in the United States has decreased since 2004, and, in response, while they were able to, they maintained a presence in Washington, D.C., with frequent visits to congressional offices. In the following sections, I discuss their presence in Washington, D.C., in 2006 and 2007 as a way to emphasize these changes and explore the creativity of their lobbying efforts. While their feminine drag became less overt, they still marked themselves as feminine through their use of the color pink and in the process highlighted the masculinity of congressional spaces. Their playful reframing of a traditional avenue for dissent, lobbying, into a more unruly and creative method for approaching elected officials enabled them to claim official political spaces.

CODEPINK draws on a long history of women activists' challenges to congressional spatial norms. For example, when members of Women's Strike for Peace (WSP) were called in front of the House Un-American Committee (HUAC) in 1962, one reporter noted that they "had been using the Congress as a babysitter, while their young crawled in the aisles and noisily sucked their bottles during the whole proceedings. With a mixture of awe and wonder [reporter Mary] McGrory described how the ladies themselves, as wayward as their babies, hissed, gasped, clapped entirely at will."[44] Participants cheered each other on, transforming the space with their uncivil behaviors and unruly children.

In the political performances I examine below, CODEPINK, sometimes in collaboration with Reverend Billy and the Church of Stop Shopping, provide twenty-first-century versions of WSP's subversion of HUAC.[45] In both cases, activists went through the motions—testifying when called and visiting congressional offices during appropriate times—but then transformed these formal spaces into arenas for creative dissent. Both groups also capitalized on gender norms and masculinized political spaces.

There is also feminist legacy for CODEPINK's tangles with authorities over the limits of free expression in the Capitol. In the 1980s, a long-standing vigil in support of the ERA resulted in a series of court cases about the use of space around the White House.[46] The implications of this 1983 ruling for subsequent protests are wide-ranging. Some aspects of the regulations, such as the restrictions on the placement of parcels, are understandable as long as they aren't applied in overly stringent ways. Others, such as the restrictions on signs, seem paranoid at best and demonstrate the willingness of the National Park Service, which drafted the regulations, to limit free speech due to far-fetched possibilities. Perhaps the most telling aspect of the law is what the court of appeals described as the "legitimate aesthetic goal" of making the White House a tourist destination rather than a site for free speech. The 2011 Federal Restricted Buildings and Grounds Improvement Act further restricted people's ability to demonstrate in places where elected officials will encounter them.

While there are many more women elected to and hired to work in congressional offices than there were fifty years ago, Congress remains a masculine space. As journalist Margaret Carlson explains, in the Senate "there are still spittoons, more men's than women's rooms, and unequal gym facilities."[47] In an interview, Senate historian Donald Ritchie explained, "There's a veneration of the way the chamber has always operated."[48] New ways of doing things are frowned upon. Maintaining these traditions limits who feels comfortable in the spaces and, by extension, which issues are considered important. CODEPINK's visits to congressional offices attempted to shift this.

Congressional buildings are public in the sense that they are state rather than private property. Representatives are also supposed to be available for people to approach regarding pressing political issues. At the same time, security personnel are ever present due to real and perceived threats. This contradictory set of circumstances—a publicly owned place that is open to the public and overseen by security—creates incongruent norms about who can use the space for what purpose. Prior to 2011 the rules were quite loose, which provided openings that CODEPINK exploited in order to deliver messages to politicians and, through media coverage, the U.S. public. In the process, participants transformed elite political spaces into sites for voicing citizens' views. Below I describe four of the many visits CODEPINK activists paid to congressional members in 2007 in order to explore how they exploited the openings provided for them in these publicly owned spaces governed by loose rules.

It's March 21, 2007, and Medea Benjamin, dressed in pink, including a Statue of Liberty crown and a T-shirt reading "Troops Home Now," held the door to Senator Hillary Clinton's office open for members of CODEPINK, in their usual pink attire, and members of the Church of Stop Shopping, most of whom were wearing pink signs with antiwar slogans over their red robes. Among them was their figurehead, Reverend Billy, a character based on southern white televangelists created by actor Bill Talen.[49] The vocalists who joined Reverend Billy and CODEPINK in congressional offices and the choir members profiled on the Church of Stop Shopping's website are racially diverse, although predominantly white.[50]

In published video footage, the primarily New York–based group quietly filed into the foyer of their senator's office to perform an exorcism. Lining the walls, participants from both organizations begin quietly singing "no more Bushit" and "don't buy Bushit." Soon Reverend Billy broke into testimony, declaring, "Senator Clinton . . . don't spend our tax money that way" while the choir continued to sing. A young black woman staff member headed toward the camera shaking her head, shutting the door to block the camera's view. The door reopened, bringing Reverend Billy and the choir back into view. "Don't buy Bush's war. . . . Vote for peace. . . . We're from New York City and we want peace. . . . Don't spend 100 million dollars for that war," the Reverend demanded as the chorus continued to sing "no more Bushit" interspersed with declarations of "hallelujah."[51]

Later the same day, they visited Senator Barack Obama, who would soon be engaged in a battle with Clinton for the 2008 Democratic presidential nomination. His staff seemed amused. Two men, one black and one white, engaged dissenters in light banter while a black woman tried to talk on the phone. Reverend Billy exclaimed, "Senator Obama, I'm calling out to your soul right now. . . . I believe that you feel peace inside, but you're letting millions of dollars go to this criminal, illegal war. Senator Obama, listen to us. We appeal to the peace you have inside. Senator Obama, peace-allujah. . . . Be that man. Be that leader. You don't need to fight Hillary Clinton on her terms" while the choir sang about the war budget. Police officers stood on the far side of the glass office doors observing and speaking into CB radios. After their song was finished, the group filed out and paused in the hallway, where Benjamin suggested that they visit Senator Russ Feingold.[52]

Upon entering Feingold's office, Reverend Billy proclaimed, "We are all so proud of Senator Feingold and your staff. We're from New York City. We don't have a peace candidate. You're our peace candidate. We're so grateful to you for your courage" while the choir sang, "I just want to thank you, thank you" to two young white women staff members who appeared embarrassed and amused. A white male police officer stepped into the office and declared stiltedly: "You guys have gotten your warning. Disorderly conduct. . . . You do it again, anyone's subject to arrest." Benjamin engaged the officer, highlighting one of the informal rules of the space: "We're invited guests, and we're singing him a thank you." The officer interrupted her, "Here's the deal: at any time today, if you guys disrupt anyone, you have your warning." Benjamin responded: "You come and break into this office where we're invited guests, singing him a thank you." The officer emphasized the impact of their actions beyond the walls of Feingold's office: "Just because you're in this office doesn't mean you aren't interrupting other people's offices." Another activist responded, "The carts that go down the hallway are a lot louder." Benjamin referenced another choir, asking, "Why are we different than the choir downstairs?" The officer responded in a southern drawl, "Ma'am, I'm sorry. I'm in charge of this building, and I'm just breaking the news to you. . . . Continue about your business." As CODEPINK members discussed their next move, the Church of Stop Shopping broke into a choral rendition of the First Amendment: "Congress shall make no law respecting an establishment of religion or prohibiting the free exercise thereof. . . . Free speech, free press, free people." CODEPINK members joined in before leaving the office and, presumably, the premises.[53] End scene.

By performing a political exorcism to rid Clinton of a warmongering demon, they sought to restore a Hillary Clinton who existed before the election, someone who cared about her constituents' wishes. To these New Yorkers, her hawkishness had a particular sting. The destruction of the twin towers of the World Trade Center was used to justify invading Afghanistan and the resulting sacrifice of thousands of lives. Tired of New Yorkers' trauma being used to validate military aggression, the slaughter of civilians, and the sacrifice of U.S. soldiers' lives, these protesters felt that Clinton's support for the war was a particularly grave betrayal. No demon left the office, and it's unlikely that protesters expected one to. Clinton wasn't even on-site to present her body and mind for cleansing. The performance served primarily to remind her and her staff that she had become part of the political machine.

The auditory aspects of the protesters' action rippled beyond Clinton's office, which they held for a short time, prompting the response of the Capitol police officer who found them visiting Obama. The tone and flavor shifted once they arrived in Obama's office, showing the complexity of their repertoire. Capitalizing on Reverend Billy's role as preacher of the Left in a different way, their songs were lighter in tone and more clearly gospel influenced. The reverend evoked Senator Obama's soul not to free it from a demon but to appeal to its better, peaceful nature. Obama was, as of yet, untested. This biblical evocation of his leadership within Washington was realized, sort of, later that year when he successfully secured the nomination as Democratic presidential candidate. As president he did lead the United States out of Iraq, but not to the promised land of peaceful international relations.

The protesters' final stop in Senator Feingold's office was more explicitly political both in their performance of gratefulness and in their engagement with the police. The spectacle the coalitional group of activists created through their choral performances was transformed into a contest over the space. They claimed the space with their grateful song and then engaged in a struggle with Capitol police over control of the space, which they eventually conceded. As geographer Don Mitchell has explained, public space is not a given. It results from struggle and must be maintained through ongoing struggle.[54] The exchange between activists and police revealed an astute understanding of each other's power and the ongoing struggle over interpretations of lobbying.

The curtain opens again in April 2007, a few days after Republican presidential hopeful John McCain joked about bombing Iran during a speech by riffing on the Beach Boys' song "Barbara Ann." A group of seven white-appearing women, including Potts and Benjamin, and one man, Barry, entered McCain's office, singing, "McCain will bomb, bomb, bomb Iran. He'll bomb Iran if he can, he'll bomb Iran, bomb, bomb, bomb Iran. He is an abomination because he wants to bomb the nation of Iran."[55] Barry, wearing a black hat with a pink brim, affixed a small pink sign with black lettering reading "Don't Bomb Iran" on the wall. The group sat down around a table and continued singing. After delivering their message, they walked back out of the office, still singing, while a black woman police officer, gesturing toward the door, demanded, "Stop. Stop. Stop." The sign remained on the wall.

For this visit, CODEPINK appeared solo. Minus the religiopolitical stylings of the Church of Stop Shopping, they focused more directly on political messages. The smaller group was able to claim the space in ways different from those of the coalition. Rather than filling the office with their bodies, they asserted ownership of the space by sitting at the table and redecorating the office. The pinkness of the sign left on the white wall among the drab decorations and furniture drew attention not only to itself but also to the masculinity of the space. They only held the space for a few minutes, but they left physical and sonic traces of their presence.

In her exploration of black and Latino organizing and cultural creation in Los Angeles, Gaye Theresa Johnson emphasizes the importance of sound, especially music, to claiming spatial entitlement. "Sound travels even when people cannot," she explains, and thus can create a distinctive soundscape whose meanings exceed frequency and vibration.[56] The unruly nature of sound works to CODEPINK's benefit, traveling beyond the offices they occupy, infiltrating other offices and corridors. It can also linger long after the performance is over, especially if the song is catchy. One can easily imagine CODEPINK's rendition of "Barbara Ann" floating through congressional staffers' minds long after the pink-clad protesters left the building.

Congressional offices are not intended as musical venues, so they are not "shaped by the practices, aspirations, and indeed power relations of those involved in organising and arranging musical events."[57] Yet power relations still structured the interactions described above. CODEPINK asserted power by pushing the edges of congressional norms and allowing their sonic interventions to travel throughout these unsoundproof spaces. In the end, the threat of physical force by Capitol police in Feingold's office and the specter of that threat in McCain's office ended CODEPINK's physical, affective, and sonic claims to the space.

In each of these examples, CODEPINK exploited flexible norms and rules for lobbying in a publicly owned yet closely surveilled space. They used policies that allow individuals to approach elected officials about key political issues to voice antiwar perspectives poorly represented in Congress, filling the offices with creative lobbyers when they could and demonstrating their absence at the metaphorical decision-making table by sitting at McCain's office table when their numbers were lower. In the process, they held these spaces with their pink-clad bodies and their voices, transforming them into sites that centered women and demonstrated alternatives to militarism.

The presence of women-dominated groups, visually marked by pink clothing and carrying signs, re-created the business-oriented space into an arena for protest. In the process, these groups also questioned the masculine, rule-laden rationality of the space by drawing attention to participants' gender, expressing and eliciting emotional responses, and pushing the boundaries of interactional rules. The sterile, off-white floors and hallways became backdrops. The monotony of staff meetings, phone calls, and memos was broken up by the sonic incivility of chants and songs. As Rae Abileah explained, "We not only brought a flash of hot pink to the sea of drab gray and black Congressional suits, we [also] broke through the inside-the-beltway politics with a refreshing dash of people power."[58] This "people power" provided a foil for a democratic process riddled with corruption and dominated by behavioral norms that privilege wealthy and formally educated white men.

CODEPINK's visits to the offices of members of Congress had become so routine by 2007 that *Roll Call*, Capitol Hill's newspaper, wrote a feature story about the group and their tactics and brushes with Capitol police.[59] In a 2006 interview, Benjamin explained that they had a "cat and mouse game going with the D.C. capitol police."[60] In response, President Bush mentioned them in an address to Congress in early November 2007: "When it comes to funding our troops, some in Washington should spend more time responding to the warnings of terrorists like Osama bin Laden and the requests of our commanders on the ground, and less time responding to the demands of MoveOn.org bloggers and CODEPINK protesters."[61] CODEPINK's outsider tactics (as well as MoveOn's online petitions) had made ripples in the political establishment.

Conclusion: Unruly Behaviors and Spaces

CODEPINK's unruly politics uses spectacle to garner attention and challenge interactional norms that limit women's participation in formal politics. Unruly politics, according to a manifesto cited by Akshay Khanna and colleagues, is

> political action by people who have been denied voice by the rules of the political game, and by the social rules that underpin this game. It draws its power from transgressing these rules—while at the same time upholding others, which may not be legally sanctioned but which have legitimacy, deeply rooted in people's own understandings of what is right and just. This preoccupation with social justice distinguishes these forms of political action from the banditry or gang violence with which threatened autocrats wilfully try to associate them. Far from promoting state disintegration, these forms of unruly political action can lead to fairer, cleaner or simply better government.[62]

This optimistic vision for uncivil dissent highlights the social and political rules that govern public interactions and the reasons for breaking them; it emphasizes that such dissent follows alternative guidelines based in a vision for justice; it also describes outsider political action as able to affect formal politics. Thus, unruly politics is not simply a disorganized action disrupting order for the sake of disruption. It is an ethical vision not only for social change in a broad sense but also for changing political process.

Because CODEPINK approaches the state tactically, the group's interventions do not entirely change the political landscape. Instead, participants cause momentary disruptions. When George W. Bush stumbles during his speech because a banner has been unfurled in the convention hall or tells reporters that they need to ignore CODEPINK and MoveOn.org, CODEPINK's actions jump scale from a moment in a congressional office or hearing to the nightly news. In these cases, their tactics affected the state figurehead's demeanor and speech, demonstrating that those in power are calculating how to respond. Power momentarily acted tactically before stabilizing and resuming strategy.

These momentary shifts do not bring on immediate or transformational change. Nonetheless, they demonstrate how citizens can affect government. Jürgen Habermas describes the public sphere as "a realm of our social life in which something approaching public opinion can be formed. . . . A portion of the public sphere comes into being in every conversation in which private individuals assemble to form a public body. They then behave neither like business or professional people transacting private affairs, nor like members of a constitutional order subject to the legal constraints of a state bureaucracy."[63] Thus, for him, the public sphere is a participatory sphere explicitly outside of the state, and its role is to influence the state by developing and demonstrating public opinion. CODEPINK demonstrates the function of the public sphere while simultaneously expanding "the boundaries of the public sphere" using intentionally uncivil modes of dress and behavior.[64] In challenging other activists to think about gender, CODEPINK protesters also question the masculinity of dissident spaces. CODEPINK's uncivil tactical actions transform domestic spaces into political sites, private convention spaces into spaces for political debate, and public spaces into women-centered demonstrations of unruly dissent.

The next part of the book continues my exploration of citizenship practice. Public demonstration is always about citizenship practice on some level. Understandings of citizenship are also deeply tied to gendered, racialized, and classed conventions of public interactions. Therefore, all of the events explored in this book enact and intervene in norms of citizenship. The demonstrations addressed in the following chapters make this ever-present theme more overt by claiming spaces in Washington, D.C., the site of U.S. political power.

PART III

Engendering Citizenship Practices

Women March on Washington

Introduction

The affective turn in social and cultural theory has shifted myriad scholarly discussions, including conversations about citizenship. While ideals of reason and rationality remain closely associated with the rights and responsibilities of citizenship, and binaries continue to be simplistically drawn between emotion and reason, discussions of affective connections have become part of critical citizenship studies. For example, political theorist Monica Mookherjee emphasizes that "emotional connections and dispositions support citizens' most important reasons for action."[1] U.S. feminist approaches to citizenship have long reflected this. When Women Strike for Peace members were called in for Cold War era congressional hearings, they brought their children and nursed them in the chamber.[2] In the 1990s Lesbian Avengers groups brought their anger regarding homophobia to local legislatures, unfurling signs demanding changes.[3] As I described in chapter 5, CODEPINK's twenty-first-century style of lobbying also worked with and evoked emotional responses. These are only three of many examples of feminist activism merging supposedly private emotions with public citizenship practice.

The next two chapters explore the complex milieu of emotions, affect, and citizenship practice by focusing on the ways that women in the early twenty-first century have used one of the quintessential forms of U.S. citizenship practices, the March on Washington, to advocate for their rights as women at the 2004 March for Women's Lives and as mothers at the 2004 Million Mom March. These two events illustrate how a space chosen for its symbolic link to citizenship practice can be transformed to meet a range of political ends, analysis that could be extended to address the January 21, 2017, Women's March that occurred in the wake of Donald Trump's presidential inauguration. As the seat of domestic political power, Washington, D.C., is where individuals and groups seek representation through their elected officials, lobbyists, letters, phone calls, and public demonstrations.

Demonstrations about numerous issues have transformed this city, and gender has often been a central part of doing so. The first March on Washington occurred in 1894 after an economic depression resulted in widespread unemployment. In response, Jacob Coxey and Carl Browne organized a march of distressed workers under the title of the Commonweal of Christ. The contingent became known as Coxey's Army and by the time they reached Washington, D.C., included approximately one thousand men.[4] Called invaders and tramps, these unemployed men were cast as outsiders to the elite masculine political space of the nation's capital. Yet, over a hundred years later, their "petition in boots" has become a national tradition.[5] Notably, this revered method of enacting citizenship rights has also been associated with masculinity. The Million Man March in 1995 and the Promisekeepers gathering in 1997 solidified this association, which works in tandem with the masculinity of congressional spaces. Masculinity remains part of the everyday workings of government and specific manifestations of citizenship practice, such as protest marches, in the city's public spaces.[6]

Both marches I examine in this section challenged the masculinity of national public spaces; however, the extent of the challenge varied due to the degree to which participants worked within or outside of dominant gender and other norms. In the first example, the focus on reproductive freedom challenged spatial and citizenship norms by linking women's reproductive needs to citizenship practice. In the other, "mothers and others" gathered to advocate for gun control using maternal care as their motivation for organizing. While both events claimed masculinized spaces and challenged the norms of these spaces, motherhood is a more accepted reason for women to claim political authority. Nonetheless, as I discuss in depth in chapter 7, linking motherhood and overt politics remains controversial.

Citizenship Norms and Practices

The term "citizenship" references an array of practices of inclusion and exclusion. At its most legalistic, citizenship refers to which nation-state one belongs to and the rights and privileges resulting from that membership. This aspect of citizenship is undeniably important, as immigrants' and refugees' struggles for humane treatment make clear; however, focusing solely on the formal status granted or denied to individuals misses the subtle and overt ways that many people are deprived of full access to the rights and privileges supposedly granted to citizens. In order to address who is viewed as a legitimate political actor, one needs to examine how different ways of interacting are coded as appropriate or inappropriate to political participation.

Geographer Phil Hubbard describes citizenship as "the political and social recognition that is granted to those whose behaviour accords with the moral values underpinning the construction of the nation-state."[7] Moral values tend to reinforce existing systems of power and privilege, and thus people's relationship to citizenship reflects the status accorded to them based on their proximity to somatic norms. Racial, gender, and sexual others are often treated as what geographer Nirmal Puwar refers to as "space invaders."[8] Outsiders' access to citizenship benefits, claims political theorist Shane Phelan, "depends on the willingness of the majority to acknowledge them as members," which is often only begrudgingly or conditionally granted.[9] If outsiders behave like those in power, then they are more likely to access citizenship rights. This has explicit spatial ramifications. According to Hubbard, "A basic right of citizenship is the right to access and use specific kinds of space within a given territory," generally public and semipublic spaces.[10] Certain people, values, and practices are generally deemed inappropriate in public spaces.

In his explorations of the bourgeois public sphere, philosopher Jürgen Habermas defined an arena of engagement separate from both the private sphere and formal politics.[11] In this sphere—comprised of physical spaces such as coffee shops and salons and discursive spaces such as print media—citizens engaged in culturally important conversations. Central to his understanding of this idealized interactional form was people leaving aspects of themselves such as racial, gender, or other differences in the private realm. Several commentators note the impossibility of this requirement for rational debate.[12] Other scholars have claimed that the unified public sphere he idealized was actually only one of many public spheres, even if it was the most easily recognizable due to the gender, race, and class backgrounds of most participants.[13] Additionally, the idea that some aspects of people's lives can be left in the private realm relies on somatic norms. Whiteness, maleness, and heterosexuality are seen not as differences but rather as defaults. Accordingly, these supposedly neutral spaces actually reflected dominant values and, thus, relied on a series of exclusions.

This "bracketing" of differences not only excluded those too different to be recognized as legitimate participants but also helped maintain an idealized bifurcation of emotions from rationality. In Western thought, reason is connected to public political behavior, while emotions are seen as properly contained in the domestic sphere. Political theorist Iris Marion Young emphasizes that norms of rational debate rely on specific cultural values, making them most available to people with cultural capital: "The norms of deliberation are culturally specific and often operate as forms of power that silence or devalue the speech of some people."[14] This false neutrality has gendered implications. Not only are women and femininity generally linked to the private, domestic, and emotional, while men and masculinity are connected to the public, political, and rational, forms of communication expected of women, which emphasize facilitating conversation rather than asserting positions, are also devalued within the political sphere.

Participants in the March for Women's Lives and Million Mom March claimed a space historically linked to citizenship claims. In her exploration of marches on Washington, historian Lucy Barber discusses the creation of what she calls national public spaces through successive demonstrations in the U.S. capital. "It has become a place," she claims, "where groups of citizens can project their plans and demands on national government, where they can build support for their causes, and where they can act out their own visions of national politics."[15] The particular associations of those spaces amplify quotidian associations between citizenship and public space. As geographer Bruce D'Arcus claims, "Public space, put simply, is a medium of citizenship: a material space and representational forum through which boundaries of citizenship are drawn and redrawn."[16] National public spaces in Washington, D.C., emphasize this connection due to the symbolic weight carried by the act of marching on Washington. Demands to enter and utilize public spaces in the nation's capital are part of a larger process of demonstrating that a group of people belongs to the public in addition to the counterpublics to which that group contributes.[17] For Barber, this carving out of space where people can gather, march through the streets, and make political speeches is one of the primary successes of the now-ritualized demonstrations that began in 1894 and continue to the present day.[18]

While most early national marches were comprised exclusively of men, women are integral to this history. Five thousand women took part in the Woman Suffrage Procession in Washington, D.C., on March 3, 1913. By bringing themselves and their demands to Washington, they not only sought legal changes but also challenged gendered spatial norms. In doing so they sought to present themselves as socially acceptable in other ways. According to Barber, they wanted to show "an alternative to the grubby, disorderly world epitomized by the bowery conditions surrounding Pennsylvania

Avenue."[19] Suffrage women wanted to improve society using the caregiving skills they developed keeping homes and nurturing children, which they demonstrated through lady-like comportment in the streets. Parade organizers grouped marchers into factions to highlight different arguments for suffrage. Male sympathizers brought up the rear, after African American women.[20] Participation by women of color was important to show greater numbers but considered risky by organizers because of continued white political dominance. Dressed in white, most suffragists strove for an image of themselves as pure white women not challenging society's racial hierarchy.[21] Thousands of mostly male spectators rioted, injuring more than three hundred women. Women's complaints about the violence were dismissed. Their public presence was considered a valid excuse for violence.[22]

Despite these challenges and limitations, Barber describes the tradition of marching on Washington as part of a progressive history of opening up spaces to women of all races, men of color, and working-class people of all genders and racial backgrounds. Geographers Don Mitchell and Lynn Staeheli provide a less optimistic analysis of public spaces in the nation's capital. While "Washington is the 'protest capital' of the US," it also "has perhaps the most advanced, and the most institutionalized, system of protest permitting."[23] Restrictions on when and where protests can happen are indicative of social control under the guise of the liberalization of free speech. For Mitchell and Staeheli, this is a dialogic game of give-and-take through which those in power maintain a great deal of control. Limiting location and timing of demonstrations through requiring protest permits also enables control of protest content, since people who disagree can avoid demonstrators. Like Mitchell and Staeheli, I recognize contemporary moves to control dissent as undermining democracy. Nonetheless, I share some of Barber's optimism, especially regarding the effects of women claiming and regendering national spaces.

Gendered, Affective Citizenship

In the following two chapters, I investigate how national public spaces, imbued with cultural understandings of who counts as a citizen and how citizenships rights can be exercised, were transformed into topographic and discursive sites for negotiating movement meanings and boundaries through the explicit blurring of emotional attachments with political reasoning. In both cases, participants held these spaces for each other through their physical and affective presence. In chapter 6 I examine participants' evocations of embodiment and emotions within an explicitly feminist citizenship practice. They transformed national public spaces into venues for advocating for women's self-determination. In chapter 7 I explore how demonstrators emphasized links between maternal care and citizenship practice. Participants held spaces for explicitly affective political advocacy. In both cases, marchers performed citizenship in self-consciously gendered ways.

The March for Women's Lives modeled a feminist, embodied, affective citizenship that demanded reproductive rights through the physical presence of hundreds of thousands of people exercising their rights to speech and assembly. The daylong event with speakers, musicians, and a march emphasized political aspects of reproductive health, bolstered by the presence of current and former elected officials. Some participants articulated a complex understanding of gendered citizenship, utilizing intersectional analysis that included race, class, and disability within the gendered politics of reproduction. By linking gender, race, and class they generated a justice-based discourse that acknowledged the connections and dispositions Mookherjee identifies as integral to understanding citizenship in a multiracial world.

The Million Mom March drew a few thousand people, some of whom performed additional citizenship duties by lobbying Congress the following day. These moms leveraged the accepted, although limited, authority granted to mothers in a patriarchal culture through their organizing platform and choice of Mother's Day as the occasion for public demonstration. By bringing their grief and anger to Washington, they claimed motherhood and care, forms of enacted emotion, as expressions of maternal affective citizenship. Despite working with the traditional and often conservative framework of motherhood, the Million Moms violated social and spatial norms. Performance theorist Diana Taylor explains that "mothers have been idealized as existing somehow beyond or above the political arena."[24] Thus, through entering the political arena as mothers, they simultaneously accepted and challenged gender norms.

By holding these spaces for explicitly gendered enactments of citizenship practice these protesters demonstrated both the gendered nature of their claims and the ways that, through excluding women's perspectives, political spaces are always gendered. Both groups of demonstrators exposed the masculinity of political spaces through their presence and temporarily "feminized" the National Mall, D.C. streets, and congressional hallways by insisting that the seemingly private concerns of reproduction and maternal care belong in national public spaces. In the process they held these spaces for women's concerns, temporarily centering people usually politically marginalized.

6

Embodied Affective Citizenship

Negotiating Complex Terrain in the March for Women's Lives

On April 25, 2004, a white- and women-dominated crowd walked out of the National Mall, stepped onto Constitution Avenue, and eagerly waited to start marching while thousands lined up behind them. As soon as they began moving, a small group of predominantly white and male anti-abortion protesters started yelling "Stop killing your babies, you perverts," "Stop being a lesbian now," "Do you know the meaning of the word 'submit'?," while conservatively dressed women silently held mass-produced signs asserting "Women Need Love Not Abortion" and "I Regret My Abortion." One counterprotester tried to police the masculinity of the men participating with a sign that read "Stop Being Sissies, You Mama's Boys." Another group of men standing a few feet away stuck to overtly religious proclamations on their signs, including "Have You Considered What Jesus Has Done for You" and "You're Sinners." The only vocal woman called the crowd "losers" before demanding "Get a life, be a wife" and "Act like a lady." Homemade signs held by the anti-choice protesters included "Family = One Man, One Woman and Children," "Your Right Is a Wrong, Bitches," "Abortion Is Genocide," and "Good Choice, Mom's Life." Many stood silently waving Bibles in the air. The louder, more contentious group of men held large photographs of bloody, aborted fetuses described by one of my interviewees as "fetus porn."

Meanwhile, the mass of women and their supporters slowly filed past. Some of the marchers exclaimed, "My body, my choice" or "Jesus was a liberal," others increased the volume of their chants of "choice, choice, choice" and "right to life is a lie, you don't care if women die" when they encountered the counterprotesters. A few carried signs claiming that "77% of Anti-abortion Leaders Are Men, 100% of Them Will Never Get Pregnant." Some noted the small numbers of counter-demonstrators by yelling "That's all you've got?" and "Where are the pro-lifers?"

Anger, sarcasm, and defiance animated this struggle over rhetorical and physical space. This heated encounter between marchers and counterdemonstrators was a battle of belief systems. This exchange's location at the site of federal political power contextualized protesters' and counterprotesters' demands within long-standing negotiations about the nature of citizenship, especially women's role in the political process, and the relationship between reproductive rights and citizenship practice. Despite the presence of a few people invested in maintaining men's exclusive claim to the political sphere, marchers held the space for each other and a feminist vision of citizenship practice premised on the centrality of embodied, affective experiences.

This chapter brings together three overlapping concerns—embodiment, affect, and citizenship—by focusing on how this women-dominated group claimed a public space integrally tied to citizenship practice. These concerns are often addressed separately, yet as Sara Ahmed, Teresa Brennan, José Esteban Muñoz, and other affect theorists emphasize, affect is experienced bodily.[1] When we feel, we feel with our bodies. We also feel, emotionally and bodily, the ways that we are granted or denied citizenship. Belonging, which can be conferred by institutions, communities, and individuals we encounter, affects us. It is an emotional and embodied experience, as well as a legal and political process. Similarly, as sociologist Deborah Gould and political scientist Cheryl Hall have each demonstrated, political life is deeply emotional.[2] By marching on Washington, participants brought this complex web of experiences, what I'm calling embodied affective citizenship, to what historian Lucy Barber refers to as a "national public space."[3]

In claiming that this group collectively transformed the space, I'm not asserting that there was unquestioned unity among participants. As geographers Ash Amin and Nigel Thrift explain, our world is "imperfectly unified and never unitary."[4] This imperfect unity was palpable during the demonstration, most notably in different degrees of engagement with the reproductive justice platform advocated by many organizations led by women of color, a perspective influenced by intersectional analysis of reproductive issues. Thus, there were different understandings of embodiment present that relied on greater and lesser consideration of the experiences of women from a variety of racial, class, en/disabled, and sexualized backgrounds. Marchers interacted with others representing different approaches to establishing reproductive freedom, transforming the space into a site for negotiation around the ideal direction for national organizing and, in the process, how citizenship practice would be understood during and after the event.

As I explain in more detail below, the physical terrain of the march route provided opportunities for marchers to encounter counterprotesters, for people advocating a pro-choice agenda to engage with those forwarding a reproductive justice platform, for women of color to encounter the overwhelming whiteness of national organizing, for young women to be with hundreds of thousands of other people invested in reproductive autonomy for the first time, for people in wheelchairs to struggle to navigate the route and other marchers' inattention to their needs, and for local organizers to vent their frustrations about top-down organizing models. The space was claimed by 1.15 million participants in a movement with long-standing divisions and used as a location to continue negotiating what the national platform to achieve reproductive freedom would be.

In the end, many claimed the demonstration as a victory. The national organizations that first proposed the march were pleased with the results. Organizations representing women of color claimed that gathering the largest number of women of color at any national feminist march was also a victory. Individuals left the event invigorated to continue their local organizing. Yet people also left feeling frustrated by broken promises, sidelined by other marchers' ignorance of their concerns, condescended to by national organizers, and exhausted by the process of navigating a route not designed for their bodies. The range of emotions expressed in interviews demonstrated the complexity of the relationship between emotions and organizing for social change and between claiming citizenship and the feelings that accompany the process of demanding reproductive freedom.

In what follows, I provide a brief contextualization of the event, followed by an exploration of how marchers demonstrated the embodied and affective nature of citizenship practice. Throughout I address the negotiations among different constituencies in order to explore the ways that the march became a site of encounter among different visions for feminist affective citizenship.

Context: Negotiations Prior to the Demonstration

The beginning of this chapter explored some of the more obvious tensions at the March for Women's Lives; however, conflicts and negotiations among different segments of participants were also palpable during both the event and the organization of it. These tensions demonstrate some of the cleavages within national organizing around reproductive issues, especially as they relate to race and poverty. Deeper exploration of these divergences also provides an example of how the boundaries and goals of a community are challenged within a public demonstration.

In exploring marches on Washington for LGBT rights, sociologist Amin Ghaziani focuses on the productive aspects of what he calls infighting, which he claims "does more than just give voice to abstract, cultural concerns; it also serves as a guide for future organizing. Through infighting, a cluster of assumptions, agreements, and meanings are developed that structure future conventions of argumentation, disputation, and decision-making."[5] In the organizing that preceded the 2004 March for Women's Lives, different constituencies advocated for their agendas in what I view as a process of negotiation rather than infighting. Focusing on negotiations emphasizes the shifts necessary for groups with different stakes to work together and the incomplete and often tentative unity within the organizing scene. Negotiations about the direction and focus of movement around reproductive issues occurred in numerous forums prior to the march and continued during the demonstration, transforming the physical space of the march into negotiated and negotiating terrain.

Accordingly, the National Mall became a site not only to demand political and cultural rights but also to sort out competing visions for achieving reproductive freedom. The range of perspectives about which issues were most pertinent highlighted differences between segments of the movement, each utilizing distinct ways of describing their foci and, by extension, differing visions for feminist citizenship practice. The term "pro-choice" generally refers to organizing to guarantee women the right to choose abortion. While the term "choice" has more expansive meanings for many people, in response to equations of the term with abortion advocacy, activists working on a wider range of issues began defining their work as reproductive rights, reproductive health, and reproductive freedom to indicate concern about coerced sterilization and birth control, access to health care, and other impacts of racism and poverty on women's reproductive lives.[6]

Focusing on choice, which remains the dominant framing of the movement to ensure that women have access to reproductive services, is insufficient for many organizers working with women of color and impoverished women. For example, Lottie, who worked for the Black Women's Health Imperative, explained why the term "choice" does not adequately address the needs of black women:

> Black women very often don't have the luxury of even deciding whether or not to have a child if they don't have access to the information or access to contraceptives or [are] in relationships where they're not empowered to negotiate contraceptive use. So the issues are much bigger and more complicated, and, again, we're talking about, in many regards, life-and-death issues. Talk about the AIDS rate going through the roof among black women. For black women in their prime childbearing years, ages twenty-five to thirty-four, it's the number one killer. . . . If a woman who goes on welfare has children already, those children are covered, but in certain states, if she has any more children, those children are not covered. So she's penalized and more or less told in a de facto way by these laws and regulations not to have any more children. There are a lot more issues than just the narrow focus on abortion rights and the decision of whether or not to carry a child to term.

Andrea, a Latina in her twenties and a National Latina Institute for Reproductive Health employee, shared many of Lottie's concerns. She explained that almost half of Latinas are uninsured, that those who are insured are not as likely as white women to see doctors, that there are higher rates of HIV and cervical cancer among Latinas, and that abortion, although legal, is inaccessible for many. This occurs in a political climate where Latinas, like African American women, are frequently vilified for having too many children, for not instilling "proper" values in their children, and for being "unfit" mothers.[7] Native American and Asian American advocates voice similar concerns about depictions of women from their communities.[8] In responding to such critiques, most "pro-choice groups now use the language of reproductive rights—though their agenda is still focused on abortion rights," according to Jael Silliman, Marlene Gerber Fried, Loretta Ross, and Elena Gutiérrez. In response, "some women of color organizations are using 'reproductive justice' to recognize that the control, regulation, and stigmatization of female fertility, bodies, and sexuality are connected to the regulations of communities that are themselves based on race, class, gender, sexuality, and nationality."[9] Disability rights advocates have found greater comfort with this model as well, since discussions of choice cover over "the ableist context in which women make decisions about pregnancy, abortion, and reproduction in general."[10] Reproductive justice fuses critiques of structural racism, classism, and ableism with work toward reproductive freedom.

Many women pushing for more inclusive movement were frustrated because their perspectives were not addressed by the march leadership, the media, and other marchers. A comprehensive vision for feminist citizenship was sidelined in favor of a narrower understanding of reproductive rights. Carmen, a queer Latina in her twenties from the National Latina Institute for Reproductive Health, explained: "This was a march that had been corporately messaged, corporately logoed. It was as if a lot of the organizing groups didn't trust the people to be there to put across their own messages. . . . What they did was dominate the messaging and the scene, and they did so through their financial investment, and it was a smart move on their part. Mission successful: choice march. It just wasn't our mission, unfortunately." As Carmen indicated, like many marchers, some speakers, and the counterprotesters, the media generally saw abortion as the focal point despite press releases, letters to editors, and other stories insisting that abortion was only one of many issues at stake. The right-wing press utilized narrow moral arguments, claiming marchers were part of a pro-abortion movement based on "hideousness and evil."[11] Most of the mainstream media also focused on abortion, an issue that, while very real for women who desire or require one, has also become a symbol of either morally bankrupt modernity or a society supportive of women's rights.[12] Even *Democracy Now!*, a news program known for its leftist analysis, described abortion as the "centerpiece of the march."[13] The media focused on the most sensational aspect of reproductive rights. The march leadership's failure to effectively articulate a broader agenda fed into this narrow focus.

As these diverse perspectives indicate, organizing coalition members had multiple agendas that created an array of messages and allowed for a diversity of interpretations of the event's focus; however, power differences between organizations and varying degrees of resonance with dominant media conversations made some frameworks more available for onlookers to take away. The signs carried by marchers demonstrate the way that some messages dominated rhetorically and, by extension, spatially.

Many marchers held signs mass-produced by the four largest members of the organizing coalition: the Feminist Majority, NARAL, the National Organization for Women (NOW), and Planned Parenthood. The Feminist Majority's and NARAL's placards emphasized choice. The Feminist Majority's included "Choice = Freedom" and "Another ____ for Choice," allowing individuals to fill in an identity. Signs declaring "Who Decides?" on one side and "It's Your Choice . . . Not Theirs" on the other were supplied by NARAL. NOW and Planned Parenthood used a broader range of terminology. NOW's signs read "Keep Abortion Legal" and "Young Feminists Mobilizing." Planned Parenthood provided "My Body Is Not Public Property" and "Reproductive Justice for All." These signs were easily available, lying in tall piles along the walkways on either side of the National Mall.

A smaller number of mass-produced placards asserting "Women of Color Taking Steps" were distributed at a table in the vendors area rather than along the walkways with the signs from the four major organizations, making them more difficult to find. This spatial segregation of signs created explicitly for women of color served as a reminder of the limited attention many movement leaders and participants give to women of color's specific needs. Finding these signs required additional effort.

The unquantifiably small number of handmade signs contributed to the overall feeling that this march was what many commentators called a "corporate feminist" event rather than a grassroots effort. Nonetheless, slogans handwritten on poster boards gave voice to the anger and playfulness of some participants and signaled the negotiations between large organizations, smaller groups, and individual marchers. Handmade signs addressed President George W. Bush ("Maybe Barbara Should Have Considered an Abortion," "Only My Bush Belongs in My Panties," and "The Only Bush I Trust Is My Own"), critiques of public policy ("Responsible Sex-Ed Is Better Than Pregnant 13 Year Olds" and "Pro-life Laws Kill Women"), and serious and ironic religious commentary ("Saquen Sus Rosarios de Nuestros Ovarios" and "If Men Got Pregnant Abortion Would Be a Sacrament").

Sensationalist media priorities and racialized power dynamics gave more discursive space to organizations focused primarily on the needs of white and middle-class women, especially those often referred to as "the big four": the Feminist

Majority, NARAL, NOW, and Planned Parenthood. These groups did not initially include other, smaller organizations on the organizing committee. In early 2003 they announced a coalitional national march called the March for Freedom of Choice. That fall the name was officially changed to the March for Women's Lives. NOW and the Feminist Majority initially proposed the latter moniker but after months of debate with NARAL and Planned Parenthood agreed on the March for Freedom of Choice. The marches in 1986, 1989, and 1992, sponsored by NOW rather than a coalition, had been called the March for Women's Lives.

When approached about supporting the march, women of color activists demanded that the organizing coalition better address their needs. In November 2003 SisterSong, a collective of thirty women of color organizations representing five major ethnic groups (African Americans, Arab Americans, Asian Americans, Latinas, and Native Americans), held their first annual conference in Atlanta organized by the National Center for Human Rights Education (NCHRE). After enough participants expressed interest in discussing the upcoming march and Ross was asked to codirect it, organizers added the national manifestation to the program.[14] Representatives from the four national organizations presented arguments regarding why SisterSong organizations should participate. In response, conference participants created a list of demands. According to Rose, an African American woman in her fifties who worked for SisterSong: "We asked for women of color to be included on the steering committee. We asked for the name of the march to be changed from the March for Freedom of Choice back to the March for Women's Lives. . . . We felt that it was much more inclusive, broader, and it talked more about the realities that women face. We asked that money be allocated to enable women of color to participate, because even if we wanted to drop everything we were doing and organize on the march, our organizations would die." The stipulations were accepted. The march's name was changed, and the Black Women's Health Imperative and the National Latina Institute for Reproductive Health became part of the organizing coalition.[15] SisterSong participants claimed space within the march and the movement. These negotiations over the focus of the march and how to address a diversity of needs continued until marchers left the National Mall.

Divisions within reproductive rights, health, and justice organizing based on race and class differences are long-standing. Divergent perspectives about the founder of Planned Parenthood, Margaret Sanger, exemplify the difficult relationship between contemporary activists. Sanger was a pioneer of women's right to self-determination, but she was also an important link between feminism and the eugenics movement. For her, birth control both allowed women to control their fertility and helped prevent the birth of undesirable children.[16] According to Sanger, the results of unchecked fertility would range from widespread physical and mental defects, crime, women being forced to labor outside the home, child labor, and, through the ability of the undesirable to cast votes, a political system marred by scandal.[17] Populations considered unwelcome by Sanger and many other native-born European Americans included recent immigrants, as well as African Americans and Puerto Ricans. The so-called feeble-minded were also among those supposedly putting the nation at risk.

This legacy is central to the race- and class-inflected divisions within cultural movement toward reproductive freedom. Some abortion opponents use Sanger's example as a reason to disparage the entire reproductive rights movement.[18] In contrast, some feminists defend her positions as the result of her time, during which eugenics was considered a legitimate scientific field.[19] Not addressing the unsavory aspects of Sanger's life within reproductive rights organizing may inadvertently support detractors. For example, Gail, a white heterosexual woman in her twenties from Minneapolis, reported seeing an older white male anti-abortion protester at the march tell a group of black women that "Margaret Sanger founded Planned Parenthood because she thought you were an inferior race." While she experienced this comment as harassing rather than educating, a woman of South Asian descent speaking at a postmarch rally in Atlanta described feeling conflicted when a group of black anti-abortion counterprotesters referenced Sanger's legacy. This marcher wasn't sure whether the counterprotesters or the predominantly white marchers better understood her perspective as a young woman of color concerned with reproductive freedom and combating racism. These divergent responses demonstrate why organizers continue to grapple with Sanger's connections to eugenic practices.

SisterSong members' frustration with national organizations also had more recent precedents. In 1986 NOW organized the first March to Save Women's Lives, which drew more than six hundred thousand demonstrators to the capital and an almost equal number to Los Angeles the following weekend.[20] NOW organized two other national marches in 1989 and 1992. Both were critiqued for not effectively addressing women of color's needs. For example, a few days before the 1992 March for Women's Lives, a coalition called the Women of Color Reproductive Rights group criticized NOW for "failing to contact woman-of-color groups in time for them to participate in planning and strategizing for the march; failing to acknowledge the suggestion that a woman-of-color delegation be prominently located in the march line-up; and failing to seek their input about rally speakers."[21] The coalition then asked march participants to wear green armbands as a sign of protest and to march together to demonstrate their presence and concerns.[22] Thus, including organizations that worked with women of color on the steering committee, even if they were brought on late, marked an important shift in the organization of the 2004 march.

Embodied Affective Citizenship

The March for Women's Lives emphasized bodies, particularly women's bodies, which are often the focus of legislation. Within political spaces, women's bodies are marked as bodies in ways that men's, or at least able-bodied white men's, are not. Liberal understandings of citizenship emphasize forms of self-possession and independence generally understood to belong most fully to racially privileged men. Emily Russell explains the centrality of embodiment to citizenship practice in the United States:

> One's ownership of one's body—and one's capacity or ability to labor—stands as a founding concept in the construction of U.S. citizenship. But if citizenship assumes corporeal self-possession for all its subjects, bodies read as normal slip back into a position of invisible neutrality. Consequently, it is those with visible bodily difference whose political participation is read as inescapably embodied. The features that exclude those with anomalous bodies from full access to the national ideal are the same features that make their acts of citizenship legible. "Embodied citizenship," then, stands for the unacknowledged embodiment of all citizens, but more directly calls upon the ideological weight attached to bodily difference as the overdetermining force of political participation for those marked as different.[23]

All citizens (and noncitizens) are embodied, yet those bodies considered normal—white, middle class, male, heterosexual, able-bodied—don't call attention to themselves in political spaces. Accordingly, those outside somatic norms appear uniquely embodied. Russell focuses on disabled bodies, yet her observations also apply to other political outsiders, including the women-dominated group that claimed the National Mall during the March for Women's Lives.

The presence of so many women in an explicitly political space challenged commonly held understandings of who should direct policy. As political theorists Carol Lee Bacchi and Chris Beasley explain, social policy generally assumes that there are bodies that act and bodies that are acted upon, people in control of their bodies and people whose bodies need to be controlled.[24] By and large, women are still figured as people whose bodies are acted upon. Thus, women assembling in Washington, D.C., demonstrated and reaffirmed their political agency. Yet, counterdemonstrators' descriptions of marchers behaving inappropriately demonstrate how a women-dominated march on Washington still challenges political norms.

In order to address the complex relationship between bodies and citizenship, Bacchi and Beasley use the term "social flesh" to "capture a vision of interacting, material, embodied subjects."[25] Like Monica Mookherjee's insistence that affective bonds be understood as central to citizenship practice, Bacchi and Beasley's emphasis on the embodied nature of citizenship pushes back against long-held associations between reason and citizenship and both categories with privileged, able-bodied men.[26] Additionally, their idea of social flesh bears some relationship to anthropologist Elizabeth Povinelli's concept of enfleshment, which emphasizes the somatic aspects of social life, including affective conventions.[27] In a multicultural society, different affective conventions interact, and encounters among different behavioral norms and life experiences are felt somatically. Accordingly, people bring different ways of expressing joy, anger, and disappointment, as well as distinct expectations regarding what makes a successful demonstration, to an event such as the March for Women's Lives.

Participants expressed joy, awe, anxiety, disappointment, and bitterness about the same event. These multivalent responses were not the result of misunderstanding or faulty transmission of a collective feeling but were instead the unsurprising result of different social locations and divergent past experiences. Thus, I focus on the complexity of feelings among a diverse group.

In marching to demand continued and increased access to prenatal care, birth control, abortion, and support to raise their children, march participants embodied their own demands while simultaneously being affected by encounters they had with other marchers and counterprotesters and with ideologies about women, choice, and justice they supported and challenged. This embodiment was twofold: their presence in the National Mall presented bodily representation of their views, and the demands they made emphasized the importance of addressing women's bodies in social policy. The particular experiences of marchers deepened the experience of social enfleshment when women of color were forced to hunt down signs printed especially for them and, as I discuss more below, wheelchair users struggled to navigate the march route.

Affective Engagements

Public demonstrations elicit emotional responses from participants, bystanders, counterprotesters, and people who consume media reports. People demonstrate about issues they feel passionate about. Marches on Washington in particular tap into deep wells of historical demands for inclusion—from African Americans, poor people, women, and LGBT people—or demands to address points of view seen as outside the norm or bringing seemingly private issues into a public forum—worker's rights, women's equality, antiwar perspectives, or, in this case, reproductive freedom. It's perhaps unsurprising, then, that emotional responses figured prominently in my interviews with participants.

Marchers' discussions of being at the march, like many of the chants and slogans used during the event, often emphasized the affective aspects of participation. For many, the experience was overwhelmingly positive. Being among like-minded people was, quite simply, exhilarating. For others, enthusiasm about being among other people devoted to reproductive freedom was tempered by past experiences of racism and ableism, frustration with the organizing process, and irritation with other participants' inattention to their needs.

Holly, a white heterosexual woman in her early thirties from Minneapolis, demonstrates how exciting the march was for some participants: "We got up out of the subway station, and we walked into the crowd, and there were so many people there. It was overwhelming, and I don't know who was speaking, but the woman who was speaking over the intercom, she just impressed us. I looked at my husband, and he looked at me, and we had tears in our eyes. We were so moved." Seeing the vast number of people gathered and hearing views they agreed with expressed over the loudspeakers affected them deeply.

Aimee, a black lesbian in her twenties from Atlanta, had a quite different, although equally strong, reaction.

> When we first got there, I didn't see any other black people. . . . We were in section B12 or B21, it was B something. We get up there, and everybody around us are the colored women. I was like, "Is this the colored section of the march?" At first I started flipping out because people had signs "Women of Color," and then we turned around and there was a group of Asian women, and there was a group of Indian women, and I was really [wondering] if that was where [we were]. I remember walking from the back up to the front and seeing nothing but white women. At first I thought that was weird and that was going to be a problem. But since we were all there for the same thing, that brought things together. Once the march started you end up being pushed back or pushed to the side, so it's like this diffusion thing. Everybody turned into these little particles that float into the air, and then you hit each other, and it was different. It was this bonding. At first I saw this separation, but as the march continued it turned into everybody being there for one thing. When that happened, that was better.

While Holly saw a big group gathered for the same purpose, Aimee saw a huge mass of white women. Thus, her initial experience was alienation. Over time, as she encountered other marchers with goals that approximated hers, that estrangement transformed into bonding over a shared purpose.

Their different responses are instructive: the same gathering may feel very different to people differently situated in relationship to the dominant somatic norm in a space. While both Holly and Aimee were in a crowd dominated by other women, Holly's racial privilege translated into comfort more quickly and definitively. In contrast, Aimee had to be in the crowd for longer and begin marching before she could experience anything similar to Holly's reaction. The physicality of moving together, of becoming part of the body of the march, shifted her experience. Nonetheless, she never experienced the unbridled positivity that Holly did. Instead, after the march began she felt "better."

Emotions experienced during the event sometimes resurfaced during my interviews with participants. Brandy, a white bisexual woman in her thirties from Minneapolis, teared up while discussing the day of the event after helping organize Minnesota's contingent: "This is my work, and it still makes me feel [pauses as tears fill her eyes], I obviously feel really strongly about why we were there and why we were marching—and I felt so proud." Her pride in helping bring people together was amplified by the kindness people showed each other. This same kindness transformed Aimee's experience of alienation into a provisional sense of belonging, demonstrating, again, how different relationships to somatic norms can give similar experiences different valences.

Demonstrations can also serve as sites for affective transformation. Aimee's comments provide a window into this. Her initial response changed once she became part of the body of the demonstration. Additionally, people can learn new things, gain a greater understanding of how activism works, or deepen existing relationships with the people they attend with. Felicia, a white heterosexual professor from St. Paul, Minnesota, who is in her forties, attended with some of her students, who found the march transformative. Their transformation deeply affected Felicia. She described seeing Loretta Ross speak.

> There was a woman of color who stood up, I think it was a black woman, who said, "We changed the name, and because we were there that's why the name was changed." It really resonated with my students. I was really glad. They really liked the emphasis on all different aspects of women's lives. One of them was especially moved by [Ross's] revelation that poor women even now don't have access to what [the student] has access to. That came as a surprise and really got [my student] motivated to make sure that changes. Others of my students were moved by the third world women, by the gag order and how that has changed access to reproductive freedom and really affected women's lives. I mean, women die because of it.

For these students, the diversity of the march was compelling. They learned how restrictions on reproductive freedom affect a range of people, many of whose lives are very different from theirs.

The movement Felicia describes her student experiencing was both intellectual and affective. Through learning new information, these young women experienced a shift in their own self-understanding. That one was "especially moved by her revelation that poor women even now don't have access to what [the student] has access to" accentuates the relationship between self and others, a privileged young woman and her less privileged counterparts. The march was a space of learning, of experiencing the self differently.

Other attendees also emphasized the transformative potential of demonstrations. Carmen, a Latina organizer in her early twenties from New York, describes protests as playful, joyous occasions:

> Protests and marches are sort of the activists' prom. It's a social event. It's something you dress up for. It's something you make a lot of arrangements for. It's something you get excited to go and hang out with your friends at. . . . A lot of times people who do activist work feel like their work isn't as social as they'd like it to be. . . . You see crazy people on stilts and dressed up and wearing funny outfits and doing street theater. There's music and entertainment and flyers. It's just a giant social carnival for activists. Of course, saying that, I also think that people have very strong views that they believe in, and they go to a protest because it's a public place to vote with your feet, to be present, to create a larger mass of people. . . . It's really powerful. I think that a lot of times those that feel disenfranchised really often lack that feeling of being in a giant, powerful mass. They feel disempowered, and I think standing in that group can sometimes be for people one of the only times in their life that they feel like they are the powerful ones. That's thrilling, exhilarating.

As a site for joy, laughter, and connection, these events can serve as rewards for the daily, often isolating work of organizing while simultaneously helping bring people, such as Felicia's students, to a movement, what Carmen describes as a "sociocultural group that does it often."

The affective shift Carmen describes from disempowerment to empowerment resonates with comments made by many participants in the March for Women's Lives and other demonstrations explored in this book. That this particular event occurred in the national public space of the National Mall made this all the more potent. Women and their allies demonstrated the importance of reproductive freedom and negotiated the direction of the national movement. The spatial location also highlighted the centrality of their bodies to experiences of citizenship. Representing a diversity of frameworks for social change, they dominated the space in their imperfect unity, pushing back against threats to existing reproductive health services and advocating for greater access to prenatal care, birth control, abortion, and other aspects of comprehensive reproductive health care.

Affected Bodies

Because of its focus on reproductive issues, the March for Women's Lives was about bodies—the bodies that produce life and the bodies of fetuses and infants. In the fraught political discussion of reproductive issues, these bodies and the rights they do or do not have are frequently pitted against each other. Women seeking birth control or abortions are described either as exercising their choice and their sexuality or as seeking to prevent or end another enfleshed being. Within these debates, mothers are sometimes erased from the conversation: their wombs and, by extension, their bodies become the "fetal environment."[28] When women are seen as containers rather than people, they are stripped of the ability and right to make decisions about their own lives. Within this rhetoric women are not agents able to make the rational decisions necessary to address public, political issues; they are not full citizens. Being described as a "fetal environment" rather than as a person or, to paraphrase the counterprotesters, as unwomanly when refusing to relinquish agency elicits strong responses.

Dominant understandings of politics emphasize rationality, which is generally described as diametrically opposed to emotions. Yet, at base, these modes of engagement are tied. As political scientist Cheryl Hall explains, "Passion depends on a perception of its object as deeply valuable. Such a perception in turn depends on both an *interpretation* of the object's nature and qualities and a *judgment* that these qualities are worthy of one's emotional commitment, particularly in view of competing alternatives. These interpretations and judgments are cognitive components built right in to passion. . . . [P]assion actually requires a mental vision of the good. In this sense, it is inherently rational as well as emotional."[29] Passion, which encompasses many affective states, including joy, love, anger, and frustration, utilizes the interpretative and analytical facilities generally understood as being part of rational decision making. It makes rational sense that experiences bring us joy or make us angry.

Sociologist Deborah Gould pushes this relationship a little further, similarly declaring that "feeling and emotion are fundamental to political life" but refusing to avoid a connection to irrationality and nonrationality: "I see no reason to deny the irrational components of human motivation and action—*all* human beings have the capacity to be irrational if by that term we mean something like engaging in illogical, senseless, and unreasonable behavior that goes against one's interests. But my rendering of affect is agnostic with regards to irrationality. Affect *may* generate irrationality, but it does not necessarily do so. Affect is always *non*-rational, by which I mean *outside of*—but not necessarily *contrary to*—conscious, cognitive sense-making."[30] She carefully parses the difference between irrational behavior and nonrational behavior. Tying affect inextricably to nonrationality, she emphasizes that affect can nevertheless align with conscious, well-reasoned decisions.

In Hall's explanation, a thinking person allows herself to be affected by events and ideas. Rhetoric describing women as simply "fetal environment" should produce a passionate reaction once it is assessed as denying women agency. Similarly, repeated erasure of women of color's concerns within national reproductive rights campaigns understandably results in feelings of alienation, anger, and bitterness. These feelings are based on sound judgments.

Within this framework, positive responses are also based on rational thinking. The presence of thousands of people gathered to support an issue dear to one's heart should make a person happy. Successfully organizing a state contingent or coordinating the largest number of women of color at a national reproductive rights events reasonably produces feelings of pride among the organizers. Such feelings, while sometimes coming upon people in ways that feel uncontrollable or surprising, make rational sense.

Gould introduces a more complex yet perilous approach to emotion, refusing to simplistically link it to rationality, which is afforded higher value within contemporary U.S. society. Instead, she emphasizes that all political life is also affective life. Thus, there is an inherently nonrational aspect to politics that may or may not be reconciled with well-reasoned decision making. Such a focus risks reaffirming existing associations between women, people of color, and other people outside somatic norms with the emotional rather than the rational; however, just as all citizenship is already embodied, so all political thought is already both rational and emotional. Congressional votes and Supreme Court rulings, especially on topics as sensitive as abortion and same-sex marriage, always reference both emotional and rational investments. Public demonstrations, similarly, always focus on topics in which participants have deep investments. The presence of a woman-dominated group highlights the always present embodied, affective dimensions of political practice. These experiences have explicit spatial dynamics, which are highlighted when people who seem "out of place" claim public spaces.

Memories of places are marked in our minds with the emotions we experienced while inhabiting them. Our memories record the topography, as well as how we were affected by our interactions with the space and other people in the space. Disability theorist Eli Clare explores this process:

> For as long as I can remember, I have avoided certain questions. Would I have been a good runner if I didn't have CP? Could I have been a surgeon or pianist, a dancer or gymnast? Tempting questions that have no answers. I refuse to enter the territory marked bitterness. I wondered about a friend who calls herself one of the last of the polio tribe, born just before the polio vaccine's discovery. Does she ever ask what her life might look like had she been born five years later? On a topo map, bitterness would be outlined in red.[31]

His embodiment produces complex emotional responses structured around his supposed lacks in relationship to society's expectations.

Bitterness and other emotions can be mapped onto the terrain of a mountain, to extend the supercrip metaphor Clare is working with, or a march route, as one of the women I interviewed noted. These experiences not only register in the physical bodies of those affected but also are intertwined with the topography of the places where people experience them. When Marie, a queer disabled woman of color organizer from Atlanta in her midtwenties, described her participation in the March for Women's Lives, her affect shifted over the course of our interview from excitement, to frustration, to irony, to bitterness, to resignation, to thoughtful engagement, to hope, to anger, and back through many of these modes. Her discussion of navigating the march route as a polio survivor began tinged with frustration:

> I think that if I was somebody who lived in a wheelchair all of the time, I would probably have had a better wheelchair. I would probably have been able to take the gravel on the Mall better or maybe a stronger, maybe an electric one, because my girlfriend pushed me the whole time. But, as it was, . . . I just had one of the push-from-the-back ones, and it was definitely very hard to get across the grass on the Mall, as well as the gravel, and then we didn't actually march because it was so big. The special seating was up at the front of the stage, but the people we had come with were back down, way far on the Mall, so by the time we found where we needed to go and once they said they were starting, it was just too much ridiculous effort to get through crowds and, people, they don't move for you. It just took twice as long, so we just decided to stay on the Mall and make our way up to the stage on the other side. By the time we made our way up to the other side people were coming back, so it was perfect. Yeah. Well, Washington itself, you know, big cities—it's hard. Practically anywhere is not accessible or as accessible as [it] should be. It's not necessarily the march's fault. It's nobody's fault; it's the culture. So it was accessible, but in the time it takes to get through a crowd of people who are not conscious that people are coming from different levels of height, I guess. Yeah.

Her experiences were marked by the difficulties she experienced navigating the route: being in a poorly organized section that didn't differentiate between people with different kinds of disabilities, sitting separate from her friends, and not really "marching" due to the arduousness of being pushed through the Mall filled with people unwilling to move for her. The National Mall became a topographic map of her joy, hope, frustration, irony, bitterness, and resignation. Like Clare she wonders, What if? What if she'd been a more consistent wheelchair user? What if she'd had an electric chair? Implied in her comments were also the questions, What if march organizers had thought in a deeper way about what it would mean to make the march accessible? What if people actually paid attention to people in wheelchairs? What if Washington, D.C., was accessible? By the end of her comments about access, frustration had shifted to irony tinged with bitterness ("It was perfect. Yeah") and then to resignation ("It's nobody's fault; it's the culture").

Marie's responses register in relation not only to the difficulty of navigating the march route but also to the vexed position of people with disabilities in discussions of reproductive rights. As disability theorist Alison Kafer explains, many discussions of ideal futures, including feminist utopias, explicitly exclude disabled bodies.[32] Additionally, anti-abortion activists often frame their campaigns as supporting disabled children.[33] Thus, disabled people and people supporting abortion rights are often depicted as diametrically opposed. This understandably produces complex, passionate responses. In response, some disabled people have forged a reproductive justice platform that affirms disabled lives and reproductive freedom simultaneously. In a statement responding to the use of reproductive technologies to select against disability, Kafer and several cowriters refused "to accept the bifurcation of women's rights from disability rights, or the belief that protecting reproductive rights requires accepting ableist assumptions about the supposed tragedy of disability." Instead, they asserted that "reproductive rights includes attention to disability rights, and that disability rights requires attention to human rights, including reproductive rights."[34] Marie's commitment to a reproductive justice platform for the national movement thus includes such a vision alongside her investment in a reproductive freedom platform that address women of color's struggles. Unfortunately, a march on Washington, despite its important symbolic weight, wasn't accessible for her or other wheelchair users.

Marie wasn't the only participant concerned about the limited inclusion of people with disabilities. Maggie, a nineteen-year-old queer-identified white undergraduate student from Atlanta, attended as part of Choice USA's "youth all access contingent." The organization, which focuses on empowering upcoming leaders in the reproductive freedom movement, pledged full access for all youth interested in attending. This tall order was, unsurprisingly, unmet. She explained:

> We heard a lot of rhetoric about youth empowerment and how youth should be there and youth are great and all this. Then there was a lot of ageism and ableism when we were sleeping on the floors, which is something that I can handle but recognize that other youth can't handle that for whatever reasons. Also with Choice USA we ended up sleeping in a church basement, [and] I've slept in a church basement before and I'll probably do it again, but the location of a church is really loaded and problematic for a lot of people, [and] there weren't other options.

Ableism was intermixed with ageist expectations that youth didn't need many of the things older people needed while traveling, including beds. Youthful bodies were viewed as resilient and willing to sleep on whatever floors could be found. This had both emotional and somatic affects. For people not raised in Christian households or who'd experienced alienation from Christian communities, sleeping in church basements wasn't a viable option, even though these were the only spaces Choice USA found once organizers discovered that promised hostel beds were full. While these issues did not intentionally target any particular group, as

Maggie points out, the results of these decisions were felt unevenly, depending on participants' histories and embodiment.

Before wrapping up my analysis, I explore negotiations among different constituencies regarding the direction of the contemporary movement. The change in the event name from the March for Freedom of Choice to the March for Women's Lives provides a jumping-off point for this larger discussion because race, class, and tensions between local and national organizations were so central to dialogues preceding and succeeding the shift. Questions about whose interests the national movement emphasizes remain salient. Women of color's social enfleshment was at the center of these conversations.

Navigating National Politics

As discussed above, negotiations about movement priorities began well before demonstrators arrived in Washington, D.C. A central part of SisterSong's demands of the original organizing coalition was a change in the demonstration's name back to the name used for the prior three feminist marches on Washington. For initiators, this change signaled recognition of the broader affective context and health concerns of women without class and racial privilege. Responses to the name change varied widely. Due to the relatively late change, some people didn't know the name had changed and continued to refer to it as the March for Freedom of Choice or the March for Choice. Others thought the change was shortsighted or an example of "too little, too late." Still others believed it demonstrated the national movement's willingness to listen to women of color and organizations that work predominantly with women of color. Many thought it did little if anything to change the event itself; however, some believed that as part of the changes that brought organizing focusing on women of color's needs to the organizing table, it affected, even moved, national organizing priorities.

In this section I consider the range of responses to this change and how they tap into concerns about the top-down mode of organizing the march and the rhetorical domination of narrow messaging focusing on choice rather than justice or freedom. This diversity of perspectives demonstrates, again, how the National Mall was transformed into a site for negotiating the direction and meaning of the national movement toward reproductive freedom.

Some people believed the name change depoliticized the march. Brandy didn't mince words. "First, let me say I think it's crap," she asserted. The Minnesota organizing coalition she was part of "felt a little bit deserted or a little bit like people had to step back because choice is too polarizing of a word." Yumi, the coordinator of New York Radical Women and a queer-identified Asian American woman in her forties, had a similar reaction. For her, the new name "watered down the issue of abortion." For both women, a move that was intended to broaden the issues included within the movement seemed like an attempt to take away the radical edge. Additionally, Yumi "thought it was a little patronizing to women of color . . . to say that women of color wouldn't be as supportive of the word 'choice.'" Regardless of the name change's origin in demands by organizations led by women of color, how the decision to change the name was described within reproductive rights circles simplistically communicated the message that women of color were uncomfortable with the term "choice" and presumably with discussions of abortion. Therefore, the attempt to make the event more inclusive backfired in some ways, leading to some women of color feeling misrepresented or blamed for a shift in perspective that was often described by many as depoliticizing the movement rather than broadening it.

Vicky, a white queer-identified organizer from Atlanta in her early thirties and executive director of Georgians for Choice, understood the impetus for the change but wasn't sure it achieved the intended focus on less privileged women:

> Whether or not [the name change] worked, I think it's kind of ridiculous, frankly, because they spent two months revising the name, revising the logo, revising the colors, all that to try and make it more inclusive. And I felt like they would have been so much more productive if they took that chunk of change, however much it was, reprinting posters and redoing the website and all the stuff they had to redo and . . . had deconstructing institutionalized racism workshops in every single state with the organizers. How much further ahead would we be?

For her, changing the name of the march did very little to address the bigger issues. As Trina, a white heterosexual woman in her late twenties who worked for the New York City NARAL affiliate, explained, it was "a committee of people sitting down and deciding to change the letterhead" or, in Vicky's words, the logos and the colors. In other words, it was a symbolic gesture that did little to change the actual organizing. Nonetheless, this symbolism was important to those who requested it. For them, it demonstrated a willingness on the part of powerful organizations to listen to women of color.[35]

The change also introduced an additional issue. Due to the focus on a binary understanding of gender (women versus men), the change in the march moniker may have been exclusive in ways that the name "March for Freedom of Choice" wasn't. Kat, a white queer-identified woman in her late twenties, thought that the name "may have turned some people away within the transgender community." The only transgender person I interviewed, Jamie, was glad he attended both for himself and to support his woman-identified partner. He felt comfortable but wondered if people whose gender presentations were more ambiguous would have felt excluded.

Changing the name didn't transform the event into a grassroots demonstration. It remained a top-down event organized primarily by large organizations whose agendas were less progressive than some of their smaller counterparts. The organizing process reinforced divisions rather than erasing them. As Vicky explained, this was demoralizing for organizers working at the state or community level: "We were told the march was happening, and here's the fliers, and here's the logos, and send all your people to the national website, and you'll never get their names. We were never connected to the people who signed up at the national website." This centralized mode of organizing kept the information and, thereby, the power in the hands of the organizing coalition. Small, local organizations were seen as supporters rather than partners of the national organization.

The national focus of the March for Women's Lives was strategic and in some ways fitting; it demonstrated that reproductive autonomy mattered for women across the nation. Yet, how the same issues transpire at different geographical scales—local, national, international—is intertwined. The particular concerns of women in rural Georgia, Atlanta, rural Minnesota, and Minneapolis, to name only a few examples, are all unique, even though they fit under the umbrella of reproductive justice and freedom. Thus, when local organizing platforms are dictated from the top rather than coordinated into a multivalent whole, the national takes precedence over the local in ways that obscure the complexities of women's experiences.

This tension between the local and the national was not unique to the 2004 March for Women's Lives. For example, in Ghaziani's exploration of national LGBT rights organizing, he examines how some national march organizing committees worked closely with local communities to shape the national platform while others did not. The 2000 march was particularly fraught. Many local organizers believed that devoting the energetic and financial resources to a fourth March on Washington, called the Millennium March on Washington (MMOW) for Gay, Lesbian, Bisexual, and Transgender Equality, was a mistake. The Boycott MMOW Coalition came together, claiming that the decision to have a march came not from local communities, as it had to some degree in the past, but from national organizers with little understanding of the experiences of people across the nation.[36] Coalition members believed that organizing autonomy was at stake in the decision whether or not to travel to Washington.

As SisterSong's discussion of whether or not to endorse and attend the event reveals, the reproductive justice community raised similar concerns. Local organizations did not decide to hold a national march. Instead, the four national organizations created an event and wanted local organizations to attend. Like the members of Boycott MMOW Coalition, SisterSong members recognized that the demonstration would happen with or without them. Rather than boycotting or just going on with the usual business of doing their work, they decided to negotiate with the leaders of the larger organizations. Their demands were met, to some surprise.[37]

These divergent responses by local organizers demonstrate some of the possibilities available to groups without the amount of institutional power that Planned Parenthood, NARAL, NOW, and the Feminist Majority have. To use philosopher Michel de Certeau's language, local organizers have to work tactically, since the agenda was set by organizations with more power.[38] Among possible tactics are boycott, negotiation, capitulation, and simply proceeding as if the event wasn't happening. In choosing negotiation, the organizations comprising SisterSong risked co-optation. However, speaking with media outlets and researchers enabled them to tell their side of the story, making the negotiation process transparent. While the national organizations retained much of their power and continue to dominate national organizing, their tactical decisions paid off. They set a precedent of having organizations representing women of color on the organizing committee, women of color had a strong presence at the demonstration, and numerous discussions of the event, including this one, reflect their perspectives.

The overall success of this decision didn't make the process easy. One organizing effort designed to engage a racially diverse set of youth demonstrates some of the logistical difficulties. Gwen was an Atlanta-based march organizer for Choice USA, a national organization based in Washington, D.C., focused on empowering youth. As part of a plan to have a "youth all access contingent," Choice USA enlisted local organizers such as Gwen. Like Vicky, Gwen was frustrated by the power dynamics between the big organizations and other groups:

> I feel like it was important to have youth leadership, and I feel that the initial objective of the youth all access contingent was very important. However, because of organizational politics and because of financial politics that exist, which are real within nonprofit organizations as well, I feel that there is a dichotomy between wanting to really promote youth leadership and really give youth the space to mobilize themselves to D.C. to participate, to stand up, to take a leadership role, and for organizations to access some power, because it's political power, and you're dealing with some organizations who were organizing the march who have well over a million-dollar budget and have PACs and [501](c)(3)s and (c)(4)s.

The funding structure that funnels money into established nonprofits also helps keep those organizations in power. It is inherently competitive rather than collaborative.[39] Some argue that this also minimizes the radical potential of organizations, since funders' priorities affect the work done by organizations.[40] Gwen, Vicky, and others felt demoralized by this process.

Among the issues participants working with grassroots organizations had to navigate was the rhetorical dominance of large organizations. Andrea, a Latina in her twenties who worked for the National Latina Institute for Reproductive Health, lauded the organizers for broadening the message. Yet because most people were used to a few ways of framing the issue, a more complex understanding was hard to convey. "I feel like the organizers did great work in terms of making that [broader] message and putting it out there, [but] I think there was something lost in the transmission. Most people didn't come away with that," she explained. "We don't even know the right chants" that could convey a broader understanding of what reproductive freedom means, she asserted.

Whatever the intent of organizers, and there was a diversity of intentions among organizers from national and local organizations alike, the standard messages that people had been using for years benefited bigger organizations that have been central in defining the movement rhetoric. Marie described "the ridiculous amount of time they spent focusing on abortion when the march was . . . about so much more than that" as "sad." Additionally, the large number of signs from the four major organizations transformed photos of the event into "one big huge advertisement" for NOW, Planned Parenthood, NARAL, and the Feminist Majority. Their logos, combined with their slogans and chants, claimed the rhetorical and topographical space of the demonstration. This messaging not only focused attention on larger organizations to the detriment of local groups and grassroots organizing but also demonstrated a limited analysis of what it takes to create and sustain a movement that addresses the needs of a wide range of women. Carmen described this as evidence that the large national organizations did not have "a real understanding of what it takes to earn diversity." Viewing diversity as needing to be earned rather than simply achieved emphasizes the importance of building trust. Trust doesn't emerge overnight; it requires taking time to learn about other people's concerns. Legacies of cultural and subcultural racism and classism mean that privileged organizers need to do the hard work of learning about other women's needs. A central piece of this is, as political theorist Iris Marion Young explained, listening. In explaining her concept of asymmetrical reciprocity, she explains: "Moral respect between people entails reciprocity between them, in the sense that each acknowledges and takes account of the other. But their relation is asymmetrical in terms of the history each has and the social position they occupy."[41] Earning diversity thus goes beyond the outreach many described as lacking. It requires really listening to people's experiences and needs and responding to them. The positive response to SisterSong's demands was a step toward a deeper acknowledgment of asymmetry and earning the trust of a broader group of women.

While the demonstration was successful in many ways, top-down organizing and the related rhetorical domination by large organizations tempered this success for many people working with small organizations, especially women of color organizers. As Eli Clare emphasizes, bitterness signals resentment about seemingly unchanging or unchangeable circumstances. The bitterness that wove in and out of interviews with women of color organizers responded to ableism, ageism, transphobia, and racism but also to national organizing priorities within the reproductive rights community.

Conclusion

By way of conclusion, I return to my interview with Marie, who explained her approach to activism in the following way: "My response to the march is my response to activism in general, which is that there is no such thing as perfect activism, and that's the beauty of activism. It's never going to be perfect. None of us are ever going to volunteer enough or quit our jobs and live completely out of the system enough to be satisfied with ourselves necessarily, but that's the point. If it was perfect, then there'd be nothing more to push toward. But at the same time you do have to hold yourself accountable." Marie emphasizes that the march, for her, was an example of the imperfection constituent to organizing. While some of her experiences were clearly frustrating—even demoralizing—this framework contextualizes them in terms of movement toward an end that is always elusive: "If it was perfect, then there'd be nothing more to push toward." Her body, with its Asian features, unique gait, and limited mobility, was vital to how she experienced these frustrations and her vision of activism as a process of moving toward rather than arriving. Her affective experiences of joy, frustration, and bitterness were central too. This movement toward an ideal acknowledges embodied and affective experiences within its striving toward an inclusive and expansive vision of citizenship.

This approach also views the negotiations among different constituencies that occurred during and prior to the demonstration as part of the process. While often taxing, pushing for greater inclusion and working to decentralize power are also processes—goals to be worked toward, even if change is slow and gains seem provisional and compromised. The struggle for rhetorical and physical space within the reproductive rights movement is, accordingly, productive.

To be a citizen in the process of becoming keeps the complexity and fluidity of social change at the root of what it means to participate in society. By rejecting rigidity, what it means to be a member of society opens up, allowing reproduction, in all its meanings, to be part of what it means to participate in society and rethinking what social contribution means. Unlike the phallic citizen critiqued by Shane Phelan, this citizen is unfazed by imperfection and adapts to circumstances while working toward change.[42] Like Chicana theorist Chela Sandoval's differential consciousness, which responds to challenges by choosing among various strategies, Marie's vision for change can provide a guide for those working for a more inclusive world and organizing communities that address diversity experiences and share power.[43]

This approach fits this type of demonstration particularly well. The march wasn't focused on a specific policy or event. Instead, organizers and participants sought a cultural intervention in the formal political culture in the nation's capital and in U.S. culture more broadly. Change takes time, and precisely what is needed at a specific moment shifts based on often uncontrollable social tides. The process of pushing toward change, of moving ourselves in the process of trying to move society in a progressive direction, is how transformation happens.

7

Participatory Maternal Citizenship

The Million Mom March and Challenges to Gender and Spatial Norms

On May 9, 2004, between two and three thousand people gathered on the west lawn of the U.S. Capitol. It was Mother's Day, just as it had been four years earlier at the first Million Mom March, which drew 750,000 people. These activists, many of whom had experienced gun violence in their personal lives, commemorated this day, originally conceived as a call for women to unite against war, by making a public political statement supporting gun control. Some traveled from as far away as California, Texas, or Florida to demonstrate support for the soon-to-expire assault weapons ban.[1] Others lived in the Washington, D.C. metropolitan area. These "mothers and others" from diverse locations and backgrounds came together for the afternoon to demonstrate their shared concern for children.[2]

I exited the Metro just after 8:00 a.m. at the Smithsonian stop and walked through much of the National Mall to reach the Capitol lawn. May 3–9 was Public Service Recognition Week, and a series of displays entitled *Celebrate Our Heroes* lined the promenade.[3] The first exhibit I passed contained trucks, tanks, and men in fatigues striding proudly around a miniature compound celebrating the U.S. Army. This presentation was followed by displays for the police, the air force, and the navy, allowing bystanders to view Humvees, helicopters, high-tech robots, and a variety of weapons.

As I walked past, an amplified call to prayer emanated from beyond these living dioramas, creating a counterpoint to the celebration of state-sponsored force. The space, in geographer Nirmal Puwar's words, "was produced anew" through the introduction of a form of religious devotion frequently treated as antithetical to the U.S. nation-state.[4] Brother Parvez Khan, an imam of South Asian descent, finished his devotions as I found a place on the lawn in the already hot sun. Soon the Sacred Dancers Guild, a multiracial troupe, filled the expanse in front of the stage with bright scarves and sweeping movements. Songs and readings from Hindu, Muslim, Jewish, and Christian scriptures finished the service. Then politicians and other speakers began taking the stage in turn to express their grief over lives lost to civilian gunfire and their support for continued gun control. The multiracial, women-dominated crowd claimed this national public space, generally devoted to celebrations of political power, military might, and economic achievements, in order to grieve, pray, and demand policy changes.

The 2004 Million Mom March brought together families who had lost children, other gun control advocates, and law enforcement figures to petition Congress to renew the 1994 Federal Assault Weapons Act, which banned semiautomatic weapons.[5] Their "petition in boots" emphasized connections between "mothers and others" and the children they care for. Organizers from around the country and local families were joined by political dignitaries, including Representatives Barbara Boxer, Jim Moran, Carolyn McCarthy, and Chris Van Hollen, as well as Washington, D.C.'s delegate Eleanor Holmes Norton and other celebrities who collectively underscored the importance of parenting, especially mothering. For example, hip-hop artist Ludacris's mother emphasized the importance of holding children accountable for their behavior and caring for all children in our neighborhoods, including those not related by blood. Other speakers, especially women, frequently evoked the image of a village raising a child. This idealized community collectively imagined by participants was explicitly gendered: in it mothers, grandmothers, and aunties look after children. Women's presence in the lives of children was key to both the present they critiqued and the future they sought. This gendered framing of care served multiple functions. It honored the emotional and physical work of mothering, highlighted the often-gendered labor of caring for children and mourning their deaths, and reinforced these connections. Fathers and other male caregivers were rarely mentioned, despite their substantial representation at the rally.

After listening to speakers and musicians for three hours, roughly half of the assembled crowd marched through the dense, humid heat past counterdemonstrators organized by the Second Amendment Sisters to the Washington Monument.[6] While the rally was the site of most of the day's emotional work, for some, the primary political labor was done the following day when small groups approached congressional representatives and their aides to elicit support for renewing the national ban on assault weapons. This multisited approach was quite different from the other demonstrations discussed in this book and demonstrated a nuanced understanding of the political process and, thereby, the labor of citizenship practice. At each of these sites, the groups enacted a participatory maternal citizenship that brought elements of women's traditional roles as mothers and caregivers into the public political arena.

Million Mom March participants fused maternal care with citizenship practice through gathering, often in familial groupings, on the White House lawn to demonstrate their affective investment in limiting civilian access to firearms. The lobbying that occurred the following day added an additional dimension to their public enactment of maternal care as they engaged in formal aspects of citizenship practice. This mother activism, to use geographer Melissa Wright's term, requires work. Wright explains that narrating "one's pain, loss, and anger is a labor-intensive endeavor that requires mental and sometimes physical strength, preparation, and the willingness to perform publicly."[7] As mothers and others took the stage to tell their stories or crafted signs with images of loved ones, they performed the labor of maternal citizenship. Women's bodies, especially in large groups, are often equated with private spaces. In particular, bodies explicitly marked as maternal are generally viewed as domestic rather than political bodies, despite a long history of fusing motherhood and public political work. Their presence in the public political sphere blurred commonly accepted divisions.

Motherhood has provided one of the most consistent platforms for women's activism both nationally and globally. Temperance and suffrage organizers often justified their organizing in terms of their motherly roles. Temperance organizers, in particular, framed their entrance into the public arena as necessary in order to protect their homes from the problems associated with men's drinking. Suffrage generated a greater challenge to the status quo, yet activists still described their work as a way to "mother" the nation. More recent activism, particularly antiwar organizing, has frequently relied on women's relationships to soldiers as mothers, grandmothers, wives, girlfriends, in particular. Such organizing challenges the status quo by disrupting assumed divisions between the public and the private. Nevertheless, motherhood remains a relatively safe platform for activism, and maternal activists frequently distance themselves from women who enter the public arena for other reasons.

The Million Mom March extends this tradition of mother organizing. The march's articulation of maternal care as citizenship practice challenges political norms that relegate emotions to the private sphere while leveraging the power granted to mothers in a patriarchal society. This power is circumscribed because it doesn't explicitly challenge gender roles or heteropatriarchal assumptions about the proper ordering of society, yet it enables women who organize as mothers to do their work without some of the challenges faced by women who more directly question the social order. Using this platform, the Million Moms contest gendered spatial norms by explicitly blending supposedly private concerns with their public political presence.

This chapter explores the participatory maternal citizenship practices of Million Mom March participants. I begin by providing some background information about the organization, then explore the maternal framework participants use for their public presence. Next, I discuss two other sites of the Million Moms' citizenship practices: congressional offices and a local press conference in Minneapolis. Finally, I wrap up by contrasting their public presence with the short-lived Mothers in White to elucidate the race and class dynamics of the Million Mom March.

Beginnings

Donna Dees-Thomases, a publicist for *Late Night with David Letterman*, formed the Million Mom March in 1999 following a shooting in Granada Hills, California.[8] The organizational website describes this event as a random act of violence; however, other sources describe the attack on a Jewish daycare center in more detail.[9] The white male suspect associated with the Christian Identity movement, a white supremacist organization, sprayed seventy bullets from an AR-17 Bushmaster rifle, injuring five people, including three children.[10] Using a march to mobilize other mothers was suggested by Dees-Thomases's sister-in-law, who was one of Hillary Clinton's advisors.[11] The first national demonstration was a tremendous success, drawing approximately 750,000 "mothers and others" to demand gun laws that would hopefully prevent children's deaths. Like Dees-Thomases, most Million Mom March members' political activity extends from their outrage regarding children's deaths as a result of civilian against civilian gun violence. Their entry into the public political realm reflects concerns that supposedly safe and often suburban spaces no longer seemed to be the havens people assume they are. Since 2004 the organization has merged with their longtime ally, the Brady Campaign to Prevent Gun Violence.[12]

While participants at the 2004 march were predominantly white women, the demonstration was more racially diverse than most of the demonstrations discussed in this book, and a large percentage of participants were men: the assembly was approximately 70 percent white and 65 percent women. After European Americans, African Americans were the best represented; however, Latino/as and Asian Americans were also present in substantial numbers. The racial diversity of the march and rally didn't extend to either the lobbying efforts the following day or, as I discuss below, local organizing efforts. Participants not explicitly tied to local chapters of the Million Moms were overwhelmingly black and Latino/a and often attended in familial groups. Their signs and T-shirts frequently identified specific children killed by gun violence. In contrast, none of the organizers I spoke to had lost a child, rendering their participation more political than personal. Most organizers attended with fellow activists and gathered in groups based on city or state of residence rather than in familial groupings. Most were also white.

Maternal Activism

While the framework for the public memorial, rally, and march was mothering, the focus was on the heterosexual and patriarchal family relations within which a sanctioned variety of motherhood supposedly flourishes. Selfless care for others is central to this vision of womanhood. Participants were not arguing for their own rights as mothers but instead for the safety of children. The organizers and participants I interviewed held a range of perspectives about this political orientation. On one end of the spectrum, one organizer saw the group's maternal framework as tactical. Heather, a white heterosexual Million Mom in her forties from St. Paul, Minnesota, explained:

> It's using a traditional power base, traditional for women. We're not speaking out as strident, angry feminists. It's not feminists marching; it's moms. It's a much softer edge in the same way that using pink softens what we're trying to do, intentionally or not. . . . If I was trying to approach my neighbor and say "Hey, do you want to go to an antigun rally? Want to be an antigun activist?" it would put them off. But if I said, "Do you want to come to this rally? There are going to be a lot of other moms there, and we're really concerned with this gun thing," it's a less loaded way to bring people in.

Throughout our interview, Heather described motherhood as a relationship not necessarily based in blood relation, gestation, or giving birth. Her sense that other participants found the maternal frame comfortable was borne out in my other interviews. This less threatening posture is tactical within a male-dominated political climate, but also reflected many participants' experiences.

For example, Jessica, who is in her fifties, African American, and heterosexual and who lives in Minneapolis, believed that motherhood provides a powerful biological bond between mother and child. She insisted that not every woman is meant to be a mother and that a person can nurture people who are not biological children, but she simultaneously claimed that something special occurs between mothers and the people they carry and birth. This connection between motherhood and gun control was more immediate for her than for the other people I interviewed. The march occurred on the second anniversary of her son being shot by other young men. While sitting with him in the emergency room, she promised to give back in some way if he lived. He did live, and she joined the local Million Mom March chapter. Her maternal citizenship practice stemmed from a devastating personal experience and the resulting commitment to social change.

She was not the only participant navigating multiple discourses of motherhood. Hava, a white heterosexual Jewish woman from Atlanta in her forties, struggled to articulate what being a Million Mom means: "I think 'mom' is a metaphor. We know that dads can be moms too in the sense that there are now two-male-parent families." Despite this openness to men mothering, she also discussed an emotional and biological connection akin to that described by Jessica. "When we talk about moms, we talk about maternal instincts," she mused. "When you've carried a child inside you for nine months . . . there's a primal instinct about doing everything you can when you're physically responsible for carrying a child." The phrase "mothers and others," which sought to broaden the organization's constituency, made intellectual sense to her; however, an essentialist understanding of mothering resonated emotionally.

This approach is efficacious in the current political climate. Paula, a white heterosexual woman in her forties from Minneapolis, also connected with the emphasis on mothering, although her explanation focused more on the political expediency of organizing as mothers. She claimed: "It's mothers, the heart of the family, that are doing this. . . . [I]t's not just a group of rabble rousers or disenfranchised people, it's mothers." Paula made a less critical articulation of the distinction between volunteering and activism than Heather. She also positively appraised this stance that required participants to distance themselves from women who organize as women or feminists. If they organized as women rather than as mothers, Paula worried that people might say, "They're a bunch of bitches, a bunch of dykes—you know, all the bad connotations." Describing themselves as mothers not only gives these women legitimacy, it also distances them from less respectable women.

For Corinne, a white heterosexual wife and mother in her fifties from Minneapolis, the contrast between mothers and other protesters was also poignant. "It was not your typical group of protesters," she emphasized. "This was moms. This was families going for Mother's Day. It was picnickers. These were not weird-looking people." As both Paula and Corinne made clear, the Million Moms are not angry feminists, bitches, or dykes. They are mothers willing to do whatever they need to do to protect their children, including stepping out into the streets and entering the halls of Congress.

Part and parcel of this focus on respectability is drawing attention to the differences between the moms and other political players, including supposedly "angry feminists" and male politicians. "Look, we're women, and we're going to use our power base," Heather asserted curtly to an imaginary male authority figure. "We're not going to try to be like you." They wear T-shirts with pink lettering rather than power suits to indicate belonging and to signal where their power lies. Hava connected this to experiences caring for children: "You do whatever you have to do to make your child safe. . . . I don't think the Tom DeLays and the Dick Cheneys and the Larry Craigs of the world get that. . . . That's the power they can't harness." This ferocious care is resilient. "Mothers don't give up," Corinne insisted.

"We are mothers and others, but it's the mom thing that gives us our gumption." Their relationship to their children and their empathy for other mothers provide powerful motivation and a platform to work from.

Making their relationships and their empathy the basis for the moms' political presence also bridges the supposed divide between civic engagement and care work. The labor of caring is generally part of the unpaid and frequently unacknowledged labor assigned to women and girls. Care is usually viewed as a private familial affair. Sociologists Pamela Herd and Madonna Harrington Meyer theorize that this assumption not only relies on an unstable and incomplete divide between public and private but also misses the ways that care functions as a form of civic engagement. Care, they explain, is a form of participatory citizenship, even when it occurs within the confines of a private home.[13] By stepping over the threshold dividing the private realm of care from the public arena of civic engagement, the Million Moms emphasize the politics already embedded in the labor of mothering. They also resist the commodification of intimacy that is so prevalent in neoliberal society.[14]

In their focus on care, the Million Moms present a participatory maternal citizenship in order to claim political authority and the right to enter public political spaces. In exploring mothers organizing in response to the deaths of their daughters in Ciudad Juárez, Melissa Wright describes a similar politics of mother-activism: "The mother-activist in this context represents the woman who, motivated by her private experience as a mother, trespasses into the public sphere, not as a public woman but as a private one whose presence on the street indicates that something is terribly wrong in northern Mexico."[15] Some participants, such as Heather, see this as a necessary tactic. Others are drawn to this organization precisely because it provides a way to enter the political sphere without risking the misogynist ridicule that they then replicate in their worried references to dykes, angry feminists, and "weird-looking people."

This concern with public derision for violating gendered spatial norms is further complicated by the slippage between the social and the biological nature of motherhood. Participants' discussions of the simultaneously essential and social nature of motherhood encapsulate the gendered tension within the organization's rhetorical justification for their political presence. As Paula and Corinne make clear, the tightrope they walk between claiming that care is inherent in motherhood and that all people can mother is tied to concerns about social acceptability. Entering the public domain as mothers allows them to remain within a socially sanctioned role for women. It is a way to mark their difference from predominantly male politicians while also reducing the risk of being dismissed. In the process, they replicate and reinforce assessments of other women as deviant.

Victims of Gun Violence: Present Absences

Victims of violence were present at the march in many ways. Some survivors shared their stories from the stage. Others were present through their representation by family members. These signs with photographs and biographical details turned the Million Mom March into both an archive and a memorial.[16] People who lost their lives to civilian gun violence were present absences, providing an emotional anchor for the event. Political actions by their loved ones sought to make these losses meaningful and to keep their memories alive. The addition of photographs of lost loved ones brought the fact of their absence into the national public space occupied by the rally, connecting personal loss to the political goal of limiting civilian access to assault weapons. In the process, the space became a site for witness and reflection.

Family members of those who lost their lives to gun violence shared their tales verbally from the stage and pictorially on signs. In particular, many participants of color held handmade signs with images of lost loved ones. For example, a young black girl held a sign that read "This is a picture of my uncle Derrick R. White. I never had a chance to meet him because he was gunned down before I was born" next to a photo of a young black man. Such personal, emotive expressions helped generate the link between maternal care and citizenship. Marchers evoked deceased family members to demonstrate their grief and, they hoped, to persuade politicians to renew the assault weapons ban. A middle-aged black woman held a sign reading "Grew up together, played together, graduated together, died together. Skeets and Tee, September 4, 1990." Another held two placards. One included photos of a black boy with the words "James E. Tucker III" and "March 31, 1984–Jan 4, 2003." The other included what appeared to be a high school dance photo depicting the same person some years later wearing a tuxedo. Numerous participants wore T-shirts with photos of lost loved ones. A shirt worn by a young black man read "In Memory of Antonio E. Marquez" on the back, using his body to give his loved one presence. These images lent a somber tone to the events through their continual reminder of the personal losses that brought many participants to the White House lawn.

Like other practices of cultural memory, using these photos in protests links, in performance theorist Diana Taylor's words, the "deeply private with the social."[17] Images of deceased loved ones exceed the expected rationality of public political engagements and our capacity to control our memories and feeling. Thus, these images demonstrate the haunting sociologist Avery Gordon identifies as constitutive of our social order while also seeking to restore the humanity of people usually reduced to statistics.[18] They reveal that the supposed divide between the public political world and the private emotional realm has never held. The political sphere has always been haunted by the ghosts of stolen land, enslavement, rape, denial of language and culture, and violence subtle and overt, quotidian and dramatic, private and public. These specters inspire national politics, along with more rational and optimistic promises of life, liberty, and the pursuit of happiness.

In bringing these images to the White House lawn, Million Mom March participants highlighted the underside of the political process and claimed maternal care as the solution. These ghosts, generally unacknowledged by policy makers, along with the still-alive but apparently at-risk children participants also marched for, provided justification for their presence. By transforming a political space into a site to gather in familial and other affective groupings to remember lost loved ones, they linked citizenship practice with maternal care.

While some white marchers also held handwritten or personal computer-produced signs, most relied more on slogans than on testimony, reflecting the motivational differences between the predominantly white organizers and the multiracial participants. Messages from white women focused on motherhood ("Mother Knows Best," "President Bush, for Our Kids' Sake, Keep Your Promise, Texas Moms Insist!," and "Children Are More Valuable Than Guns") and overtly political positions ("Renew the Ban, Stop Gun Violence" and "The NRA's 9/11: 3,000 Kids Killed by Guns Every Year"). A few white women carried signs that included photos of loved ones killed by civilian gunfire. White men weighed in with signs asserting "Real Men Don't Need Guns to Make a Bulge" and "I'm a Million Dad Marcher." One older white man wore a T-shirt reading "We're Looking for a Few Good Moms," demonstrating a social understanding of maternal care.

Some marchers of color also deployed abstract political slogans rather than emotionally evocative personal revelations. For example, black women held signs declaring "A Safety Lock May Save Your Life," "Our Kids Are Dying for a Chance," and "A TEC-9 Killed My Son." The marcher carrying this last placard was part of a contingent from the Philadelphia-based Mothers in Charge, a predominantly black antiviolence organization that emphasizes maternal responses to gun violence.[19] Some blended these two modes. For example, one woman held a sign reading "Halt the Assault" above a photo of a young Latina with the dates 1982–1999 and her daughter's name, Jasmine Gaxiola.

This combination of the private and emotional with the political came together in the rhetoric and embodied enactment of maternal care as citizenship practice. These people gathered because of their concern for children in a society that allows civilians access to assault weapons. The logical outgrowth of this care for these "mothers and others" is the indirect lobbying of public protest and the direct lobbying of talking to senators and representatives in their offices.

Despite working closely with authorities and explicitly working within gender norms, participants' emphasis on gun control agitated gun supporters. At the national march, the moms were met by a small counterdemonstration of white women sponsored by the Second Amendment Sisters.[20] These women also view gun rights as a deeply gendered issue; however, for them, guns provide self-defense in a violent world. Signs exclaimed: "It's a Woman's Right to Choose a Gun to Defend Her Own Body," "Rapists Love Women Who Hate Guns," and "Nobody Ever Raped a .38." Other placards held by the fifty or so women and children highlighted motherhood ("The Million Moms Don't Speak for This Mom") and crime and safety ("Crooks Don't Register Their Guns" and "Gun Safety Is What Gun Owners Are All About"). These gun-toting women contested the moms' claim to gendered authority and attempted to retake the space they'd claimed for a different, yet equally gendered, message about guns.

Concerns about safety that motivate arguments for and against gun control are especially salient for women. Independent researcher Deborah Homsher argues that the perceived threat for women arguing for and against gun control is always male. For people against gun control, the adversary is a criminal stranger, while for gun control advocates, this antagonist is likely to be a man with whom a woman shares her home.[21] Views of law enforcement and the government also divide proponents of these two positions. Gun advocates often see law enforcement either as unable to react in time or as overtly hostile, while gun control proponents generally work with law enforcement. In general, neither side discusses police brutality or the racial demographics of who is most likely to be killed by civilian gunfire.[22] Accordingly, the Million Moms' positioning of themselves as the motherly arm of a movement for gun control places them at odds not only with the NRA and its allies, such as the Second Amendment Sisters, but also with groups more critical of institutional violence.[23]

Lobbying Congress

On the Monday following the rally and march, approximately one hundred people gathered to coordinate lobbying groups based on state of residency. I noticed only a couple of nonwhite faces in the entire assembly, and no children were present, indicating a gathering that was very different from the one held the day before. In U.S. congressional spaces, like the British parliamentarian spaces studied by Puwar, the white male body continues to be the somatic norm. For example, in the 110th Congress, representatives of color comprised 6 percent of the Senate and 16 percent of the House of Representatives, a total of 14 percent of the seats.[24] Of the seventy-five elected officials of color, only twenty-one were women.[25] In the 112th Congress, women held 17 percent of the seats in both the Senate and the

House.[26] Congress remains a white- and male-dominated space that negatively affects the political power available to other people. Outsiders need to utilize other avenues to advocate for themselves, including public protest and direct lobbying.

Different behavioral norms govern congressional spaces and the outdoor spaces of the National Mall and the White House lawn. These spaces are still public in some ways, since they are government rather than private property, yet congressional offices and hallway spaces are nonetheless closely surveilled and reflect social hierarchies in many ways. While activists stage sit-ins and perform many creative protests in congressional offices and hallways, such demonstrations are less tolerated than in outdoor spaces. The farther demonstrators are from politicians, the greater freedom they have.

Ever cognizant of social norms, the Million Moms who visited representatives presented themselves as ordinary people moved by tragedy to lobby to keep assault weapons out of the hands of civilians. Participants wore everyday clothing—jeans, khakis, polo shirts, and T-shirts, including many with the pink Million Mom March logo. Unlike participants in CODEPINK's creative actions, discussed in chapter 6, the Million Moms demonstrated that they knew their place and respected behavioral norms. These visitors didn't seek to displace the authority of elected officials but instead beseeched them to listen to their personal stories and their well-reasoned conclusions that guns belong in the hands of the military, the police, and hunters and that assault weapons had no place in homes.

As a California resident, I accompanied some moms to lobby Republican Doug Ose, who represented the Third District, including his hometown of Sacramento. Our group included three other women and one man. All of us were white. Two of Ose's aides, a white man and a woman of color, discussed guns with us and listened to the stories of the parents who had lost children. At one point the male staffer, who dominated the conversation, asked why the Million Moms called themselves moms when men participated. The male "mom" in the room replied that all people can mother, highlighting a metaphorical understanding of motherhood. We left without the support we sought.

The presence of a woman-dominated group of lobbyists, many wearing pink, subtly shifted the tone and focus of congressional hallways for the few hours we were there. As I discussed in chapter 6, the masculine norm of congressional spaces is established in a number of ways. The bodies who inhabit the space—primarily men—are a key component, yet comportment is also important. Sartorial norms favor subdued colors—tan, navy, gray, and black—and masculine versions of formality—suits, ties, modest jewelry and adornment. Behavioral norms favor rational debate over other modes of engagement, including emotional expressions. Thus, the Million Moms' rejection of sartorial norms presented a perceptible yet respectable challenge to spatial norms. By expanding the color spectrum and bringing large numbers of women into a masculine space, they demonstrated both their own embodiment and, by contrast, the norms that rendered their presence anomalous.

The Minneapolis Press Conference

On September 8, 2004, the Minneapolis chapter of the Million Mom March sponsored a press conference with local police to argue for the reapproval of the assault weapons ban. Heather was joined by an organizer from Citizens for a Safer Minnesota, another white middle-class woman; ten police chiefs, including one woman; two white women attorneys; and an African American city councilman, the only nonwhite person present.[27] This conference focused almost entirely on the dangers faced by police officers and the threat to both local and national security presented by assault weapons. Children were still of concern, but motherhood was not mentioned. This press conference, then, demonstrated another facet of the Million Moms' public presence: as facilitators for respectable masculine authority. Maternal care receded to the background when representatives of the masculine state were working toward greater safety for children. When the state performed a protective parental role, maternal public presence was no longer necessary.

In this situation, the Million Moms and their maternal rhetoric served as a backdrop for a more masculine, traditionally political discussion of gun politics. Accordingly, the downtown Minneapolis room the press conference occurred in was also masculinized. Dark blue, khaki, and black clothing dominated, blending in with the dark walls and standard-issue brown folding tables.

Below I consider, in turn, quotes from three of the police chiefs. The rhetoric is distinctly different from the Million Mom March's focus on children's safety. One chief began with homeland security, casting his net widely: "If people believe in homeland security, which I know we all do, we need to say that the people on the front lines of that security need to be protected. [Letting the assault weapons ban expire] is an assault on an entire community, including the people who are supposed to protect us, the police officers. In the name of them and in the name of communities who have struggled and succeeded but continue to face challenges, we call on Congress to do the basic commonsense step of extending the assault weapon ban." For him, this is a war, with "front lines of . . . security." His concern is with uneven weaponry if people on the other side, criminals, have assault weapons. While there are greater numbers of women in the military and among the police today than a few decades ago, this framing of gun control as a war taps into deeply masculinized rhetoric while simultaneously beseeching Congress to support another facet of the state, local police forces.

This next quote lacks the military metaphor, yet it is still focused on two sides, the police and criminals. Like his colleague, this police chief emphasized protection rather than care, a distinctly masculine stance. He explained, "That's what criminals are looking for. This gives them an advantage. [In a recent incident] we were outgunned easily. We had five to six officers responding, but that one weapon makes a big difference. It's a threat to law enforcement officers, that's why I am here, but it is also a threat to the innocent civilians out there." In his mind, criminals seek tactical advantage through the use of assault weapons. The weapons issued to the police lack the power of these criminal weapons, leading the police to be "outgunned." The focus was again on representatives of the state, even though this police chief also referenced "innocent civilians" seemingly standing on the sidelines of this war.

The third chief also focused on law enforcement officers even while addressing civilians, including children. His comments move outside of the militarized framing of his colleagues while still focusing on the risks to police officers: "These weapons pose a great, great hazard to law enforcement officers. They pose a great, great hazard to everyday citizens walking down the street, and like Don Samuels, who has two small children, I have three small children. These weapons pose nothing but a great, great danger to everybody out on the street. If this assault weapon ban is allowed to lapse, we are all in trouble." While his comments are less militarized, the hierarchical ordering of concern—law enforcement officers, everyday citizens, and small children—gives precedence to representatives of the state. Nonetheless, by explicitly referencing children, even under a rubric of protection rather than care, his comments move his perspective closer to the maternal rhetoric of the Million Moms.

Safety for these three men, all occupying the official masculinized role of police chief, is first and foremost about the police themselves. All three reference public safety, but the security of representatives of the state is of greater concern. The relationships addressed are antagonistic—criminals versus the police, or criminals versus the public. The public is figured as separate from the police and the criminals. There also is no socioeconomic, political, or racial context here, only stark binaries.

The female police chief's comments present a middle ground between her male colleagues and the Million Moms. She focused on public safety rather than the safety of the police or of children: "I cannot believe that we have to be here to keep the assault weapons ban alive, to keep people alive. Who needs an assault weapon? Terrorists and the most serious of criminals. Who else? This just makes no sense, and it is time for public safety to take over and special interest politics to take the backseat." While she doesn't take up the maternal rhetoric of the Million Moms, she focuses more on care, in this case for the public, than her male counterparts. The militarized logic is gone, and the contrasts, while still present, are less stark.

Not everyone toed this line. Samuels, the only African American speaker, provided the most complex understanding of what leads people to take up guns. In discussing violence in his neighborhood, he referred to young people "seeking extreme ways to protect themselves from perceived dangers." This analysis of the sociopolitical context did not excuse those who, in his words, "hold our communities hostage," yet it still demonstrated an understanding that these people are not simply criminals, they are young people making a life for themselves within their social and political context. He shifted the conversation away from simplistic binaries.

Despite Samuels bridging the divides evoked by his colleagues, there was little reference to individual lives or personal connections during the press conference. There were no names of victims and no photos documenting their lives. Instead, the focus was a seemingly rational approach to policy and the importance of protecting those who represent institutional power. Maternal citizenship had no place; therefore, Heather introduced the speakers and let them make their pleas. In this space, normative masculine approaches to political practice dominated.

The Million Moms' Local Presence

This press conference demonstrates not only the ways that maternal activism takes a backseat to masculine public rhetoric but also the complexity of the Million Moms' local presence. As the participation of the families who lost loved ones shows, the national march and rally were compelling for people from many racial backgrounds; however, the racial and presumably class differences between those who organized the event and many of the participants tell another story about organizing against gun violence.

Some communities of color critique the overwhelmingly white Million Mom chapters for not working to end gun violence until it entered suburban schools. For example, Hava reports responses from black communities in Atlanta: "Where have you been? Our kids have been getting killed for years, and now your kids are getting killed, and now you care." Hava admits that she did not start actively working on these issues until after the shootings at Columbine High School in Colorado in 1999 and that the critiques of her and other middle-class white women are absolutely on target. Nevertheless, she is invested in overcoming this division, especially since she believes that arguments against the assault weapons ban are deeply racialized: "Basically, what the NRA is saying is that it's okay for these gangs to be killing each other. It's like survival of the fittest, and this is a way to weed the population out." Despite the slow response to the deaths of children from poor, darker-skinned communities, she insisted that the Million Moms have the interests of all children in mind.

Heather similarly admitted that the Million Moms framework has limitations despite wanting to be inclusive. She explained, "We are a primarily white organization, which is so sad. Obviously, gun violence affects everybody, but disproportionately people of color." She knew that people of color in Minneapolis and St. Paul didn't trust her organization. While attempting outreach she discovered that some believed that the Million Mom March capitalized on the success of the Million Man March, which felt disrespectful to them. Heather also described the moms' close ties to law enforcement as limiting her involvement with organizing against police brutality and probably negatively influencing the organization's reputation among communities of color. The organization's version of maternal citizenship practice cannot accommodate critiques of the police.

The organization's relationship with law enforcement puts members of color in an uncomfortable position. Jessica described the relief and joy other members of the Twin Cities chapter expressed regarding her participation because she could navigate African American communities and spaces in ways that white women could not. She was in a difficult position: she identified with the Million Moms' mission to protect children from other children but knew that the police are not an innocuous presence for all youth and that young men of color are particularly at risk from police brutality. "It's hard to say that 'we want to make sure that the police are protected from the bad guys' when you know that the police are sometimes the 'bad guys,'" she explained.

The organization's focus on some forms of gun violence over others may not be the only issue for people of color. Cross-race and cross-class work requires more work on internal organizational dynamics than working with people with similar experiences. Topics of greatest interest differ, and distinct cultural norms can lead to misunderstandings and mistrust. For example, Corinne described working with a diverse coalition of people in response to the Reagan administration's conservative policies. "It bombed," she declared. Part of her reason for working with the Million Moms is that it is a middle-class organization. "Middle-class people have organizational skills," she declared. "We know how to do that stuff, and working with people who don't is very difficult. We have to be giving them rides, and . . . this time I didn't want that." While this is only one person's perspective, such condescending attitudes create unwelcoming spaces. Combined with differing relationships with the police, a lack of interest in working across class lines, which are often also race lines, may make local chapters of the group unwelcoming for many people of color. Some, like Jessica, who is middle class, may find the trade-off worthwhile. Yet others, such as those Hava and Heather referenced, may find other groups that are less focused on respectability and more welcoming.

Conclusion

This chapter emphasized the fusing of maternal care and citizenship practice at the Million Mom March in May 2004 and the ways that this framework did and did not extend to the organization's local community work. These "mothers and others" built on a long legacy of mother activism in order to create a national presence that emphasized children—the children who have died and those who remain vulnerable to gun violence in their homes, in the streets, and in schools. They sought authority through their social and, often, biological role as mothers and caregivers to children. By extending the nurturing women are expected to perform in private homes to the political realm, they demonstrated a participatory maternal citizenship.

The sites they chose for their activism—the lawn of the U.S. Capitol, congressional hallways and offices, press conferences dominated by law enforcement—reaffirmed the connection between their work and citizenship practice. By transforming the national public spaces in Washington, D.C., into maternal spaces, they connected their care for children to national political discourses; however, by yielding the pulpit to law enforcement during the Minneapolis press conference, they reaffirmed the secondary role of maternal care in relationship to masculine protective discourses. This move was likely tactical, increasing the likelihood that they could achieve their political goals, yet it still minimized their challenge to gender norms. As participants made clear, their public identity as maternal volunteers rather than activists, feminists, dykes, or "weird-looking people" was central to how they envisioned and enacted their public persona.

The Million Moms' participatory maternal citizenship contested, ultimately unsuccessfully, what is often referred to as the gun lobby—the NRA and weapons manufacturers—while simultaneously reaffirming a traditional and circumscribed role for women. In comparison with other assertions of explicitly feminist modes of public presence, the Million Moms can seem tame and even reactionary; however, as the substantial counterprotest demonstrates, women putting the safety of children before gun rights are seen as radical by some people.

To put their activism in context, a more recent incident and maternal organization formed in response provides a helpful contrast. On October 22, 2013, Andy Lopez was fatally shot by Erick Gelhaus, a sheriff's deputy, in Santa Rosa, California. Lopez, who was thirteen, had been carrying a toy gun shaped like an AK-47, one of the guns that became legal when the 1994 assault weapons ban expired. Gelhaus shot Lopez seven times while another deputy was speaking to the teenager, who was then handcuffed before being pronounced dead. Gelhaus had a history of using excessive force, yet he was still returned to duty after shooting Lopez and was ultimately cleared of the charges.[28] This shooting ignited the community, prompting a lawsuit by Lopez's parents and widespread outrage about police violence against young men of color.

In response, a group calling itself Mothers in White emerged. Wearing white T-shirts with "RIP Andy" handwritten across the front, this Latina-dominated group formed to support Lopez's mother.[29] A poster called for all "Women—MOTHERS—Grandmothers and Community Members" to join them at the board of supervisors meeting to comment on the case. Like the Million Moms, the Mothers in White practiced participatory maternal citizenship. They occupied public spaces, marched to address the safety of their children, and lobbied politicians. Unlike the Million Moms, they explicitly contest the masculine authority of law enforcement and emerge from less privileged communities.

One could imagine Gelhaus as one of the officers the sheriffs at the Minneapolis press conference spoke about: fearing for his own safety at the sight of a gun and seeing the world as militarized, pitting the police against criminals. The supposed criminal turned out to be a civilian not old enough to obtain a driver's license. This case, therefore, also reveals the problems with such a narrow, binary view of society that transforms a brown-skinned junior high schooler into a criminal before finding out if the gun in his hands is real or one of the toys sold in stores nationwide. Gun rights advocates interested in making assault weapons and replicas of them available to civilians not only enabled Adam Lanza to kill children at Sandy Hook elementary school but also set up a situation where Andy Lopez's death may seem justified.[30] Making these guns available enabled both of these tragic incidents; however, seeing law enforcement as uniformly benevolent protectors can only address the children who died at Sandy Hook; it cannot address Lopez's death.

The Mothers in White are only one example of the ways that maternal activism can address socioeconomic inequalities. The framework of protecting children can address gang violence, as Ruth Wilson Gilmore explains; environmental pollution in impoverished neighborhoods, as Mary Pardo addresses; and the disappearance of young women factory workers, as Melissa Wright demonstrates.[31] Doing so requires contesting state agencies designed to uphold social hierarchies and sometimes challenging the police themselves. Such work risks the loss of respectability some Million Mom March participants seek. Yet only by doing so can maternal citizenship practice advocate for all children to be safe from gun violence.

Conclusion

Holding Space: The Affective Functions of Public Demonstration

In June 2015 I returned to the New York Dyke March for the first time since 2004. It was also the first Dyke March in the city since the Supreme Court ruled that same-sex marriage was legal in all fifty states. It was a rainy celebration complete with brightly colored umbrellas, a few topless women, and an energetic drum contingent leading the march. Marshals in their twenties wearing purple shirts declaring "This Is a Fucking Protest" and some hecklers quoting biblical passages filled out the scene. The mood was jubilantly defiant, as it had been over a decade earlier. The crowd was mostly youthful and white dominated, even while racially and generationally diverse. A few participants appeared to be transgender, many butch, many femme, and many not easy to categorize with simple gender labels. The Church Ladies for Choice sang "God Is a Lesbian" from the sidelines, and a group of queer men, some of whom appeared to have been designated female at birth, cheered us on. Members of one march contingent wore T-shirts with the slogan "Abortion on Demand without Apology." A black woman in her late thirties or early forties moved through the crowd exclaiming, "Who let the dykes out? You let the dykes out." Dyke pride mingled with feminism cheered on by drag queens, fags, and transmen, while conservative values vied for attention from the sidelines.

Dyke Marches brought me to this research because of the sheer exhilaration I felt during the first few marches in which I participated and the comfort I felt in public spaces claimed and held by queer women. It was in these spaces that I felt seen and embraced as a queer femme. As such, Dyke Marches taught me the power of transforming public space. I still feel joy and belonging when I take part in feminist and dyke-centered protests. While I also experience affective and ideological connection at other kinds of protests, entering the streets with other people denigrated by heteropatriarchal values and practices feels like coming home. Part of what I love about Dyke Marches is the co-existence of different forms of feminist and queer values.

Like all public protests, Dyke Marches can be sites of boundary setting or negotiation regarding the direction of local and national organizing; however, they can also provide a reprieve from ongoing intracommunity debates. The 2015 New York Dyke March definitely served this third purpose. (Since I didn't interview participants, I am not sure whether or not the march served the first two purposes.) The often-vitriolic debates about whether transwomen should be part of women's spaces, whether or not queer and feminist values are compatible, and whether the overt sexuality of some forms of feminist public presence detracts from other feminist struggles were all left aside during the march. For approximately an hour, we marched in solidarity with each other, reveling in our queerness and womanhood, despite rain and calls from the sidelines to repent. Women wearing T-shirts with links to a feminist website condemning pornography marched alongside topless dykes; dykes with a wide variety of gender presentations strode alongside each other; chants ranged from the playful to the serious, addressing homophobia, sexism, and the power of collectivity.

Protests are always utopic; they reach toward an imagined future. In this potential future, whatever issue brings people together will have been addressed, and new interactional norms will have been established. New patterns for interactions might include a shift in power relationships between the cultural outsiders protesting and those watching from the sidelines, or a reaffirmation of the power of the cultural insiders demonstrating their power by parading through the streets. Thus, a white supremacist march is just as utopic as gay pride or a rally to end police brutality against people of color. The imagined future is vastly different, but the impulse is the same. When people outside of social norms claim and hold public spaces, this process is also, in some sense, queer. Queer performance theorist José Esteban Muñoz described queerness as "that thing that lets us feel that this world is not enough, that indeed something is missing. . . . Queerness is essentially about the rejection of a here and now and an insistence on potentiality or concrete possibility for another world."[1] Public demonstrations by cultural outsiders share this sense that the world as it exists now is not enough. They can also provide examples of other ways of being together in public. The 2015 New York Dyke March demonstrated a sense of potentiality in the joyous embrace of identities and behaviors frequently deemed deviant despite inclement weather and counterprotesters. Just as women advocating for unfettered access to abortion marched alongside topless women and were cheered on by drag queens and queer men, in a utopic future, gender and sexual outsiders will come together in the face of conservatives advocating for restrictive gender and sexual values.

Each of the protests examined in this book evinces some aspect of this potentiality, this "feel[ing] beyond the quagmire of the present" while holding public spaces for each other.[2] They all also demonstrate at least one of the three affective purposes of protest I identified above: boundary setting, negotiation of movement direction, and enabling copresence across divides.

Boundary Setting

Public protests are frequently sites of boundary setting, what feminist philosopher Jo Trigilio describes as a "complicated and messy politics of inclusion."[3] This process is related to what sociologists describe as establishing a collective identity, or a sense of political and emotional connection to others with a shared orientation toward an issue of personal or political import.[4] Identifying who "we" are also requires defining who is not part of "us," which is where it gets messy. In feminist organizing, boundary negotiations often focus on gender inclusions and exclusions. Key questions include whether men should be part of events, how womanhood is defined and by whom, and whether members of the group of people an event honors should be the only participants.

Boundary setting affects not only who is invited to participate in a demonstration but also how issues are approached. For example, long-standing questions about the inclusion of men at Take Back the Night events reveal the ways that concerns about inclusion (and exclusion) of specific groups of people are linked to discussions about how to best address sexual violence. At the 2004 Minneapolis event I discussed in chapter 1, some participants' investment in creating testimonial opportunities for women survivors of sexual violence who didn't want to speak about their experiences in front of men were pitted against tactical concerns about the most effective means to end sexual violence. Many participants argued that men must be actively involved in ending violence that is disproportionately perpetrated by men. How to best create a space dedicated to ending sexual violence was never resolved, leaving most people feeling unsatisfied.

For some protest participants, concerns about men's participation were linked to another key aspect of boundary setting at feminist events: whether birth designation or current identity defines gender. Many Take Back the Night participants were familiar with the most well-known example of lesbian feminist boundary setting, the Michigan Womyn's Music Festival (MichFest), and some feared that excluding men would mean defining people's genders for them, which they didn't want to do. Trigilio contrasts MichFest's policy of only admitting "womyn-born-womyn" with the Boston Dyke March's all-gender-inclusive policy.[5] Similar to Sistahs Steppin' in Pride, which I discussed in chapter 2, the Boston Dyke March welcomes all who want to celebrate dykes. Sistahs Steppin' in Pride gathered people who wanted to celebrate queer women's lives and who understood the centrality of women of color to Oakland's queer community. Participants, therefore, included a few men, a good number of white women, and transgender people of many races, along with numerous children who attended with their parents. Urban space was transformed to honor queer women by a march and ritual led by black and Native women and an afternoon-long celebration attended by a women- and black-dominated crowd.

As these examples demonstrate, some organizers make boundaries porous by identifying an event's focus in a way that includes a wider range of people. Similarly, despite their organization name evoking motherhood, the Million Mom March's organizational literature described participants as "mothers and others" as a way to simultaneously center the experience of mothering and acknowledge a broader constituency. Thus, the "us" was mothers and other people invested in children in a similar way. As I explore in chapter 7, they collectively claimed the National Mall in honor of children killed by civilian gun violence as part of advocating for stricter gun control laws.

Organizational names frequently signal boundaries, although the rigidity of these confines vary. In the examples above, mothers, dykes, and sistahs were the focus of the marches rather than the only people invited. In contrast, Women in Black groups explicitly define vigil participants as women (see chapter 4). This collective identity was more important for some participants than for others. Many of those who enjoyed protesting in an all-women group had histories of feminist organizing extending back to the 1960s or 1970s and viewed women as more peaceful than men (and most had not considered nonbinary gender identifications). The group boundary relied on assumptions about differences between men and women's behavior due to nature, nurture, or some combination. The witness space they created during vigils explicitly exploited the silence women are supposed to maintain in discussions of military aggressions.

How organizational names signify can change over time. For example, CODEPINK (examined in chapter 5) shifted its self-definition over time in order to include some men. The original full organizational title, CODEPINK: Women for Peace, is rarely used anymore, and the website describes the group as "a women-led grassroots organization working to end U.S. wars and militarism, support peace and human rights initiatives, and redirect our tax dollars into healthcare, education, green jobs and other life-affirming programs."[6] Women are identified as the leaders rather than the sole constituents, enabling the organization to maintain a feminist orientation while welcoming participants of all genders. Regardless of participants' genders, the spaces they transform through their creative lobbying and protesting are still feminized by their liberal use of pink T-shirts, accessories, and signs.

As these examples demonstrate, boundaries communicate to participants and observers how participants understand themselves in relationship to nonparticipants. Establishing boundaries is part of a larger set of negotiations about how groups inhabit public spaces and engage ongoing counterpublic conversations. As such, this process is connected to another key affective dynamic in public demonstrations: negotiating movement agenda.

Movement Negotiation

Demonstrations provide sites for negotiating the direction of local or national organizing. Not all participants share movement priorities, including issue prioritization, event and group boundaries, messaging, and preferred methods for addressing issues. Views about who "we" are, as well as what "our" goals are, range widely. Some of these political differences relate to people's social locations in terms of race, class, gender, sexual orientation, disability, and other factors. Generational and ideological perspectives also affect people's investments in movement tactic and messaging.

Perhaps the clearest example of negotiating movement priorities in this book occurred at the March for Women's Lives (chapter 6). This national demonstration provided opportunities for local and identity-specific organizations to push large national organizations to better address women of color's needs and the unique challenges organizers face in different geographical locations. In the decade since the march, discussions of reproductive justice have become more common. This framework, developed by organizations led by women of color, was a key aspect of the messaging these organizations brought to the march. While large national organizations still dominate the national conversation about reproductive freedom, the work done by a variety of organizations before, during, and after the march, especially those associated with SisterSong, a reproductive justice collective that focuses on women of color, shifted national conversations.

A similar set of negotiations happened at other demonstrations on smaller scales. For example, concerns about men's inclusion at the Minneapolis Take Back the Night event reflected different ways of addressing sexual violence. These divergent perspectives interacted in complex ways with two other dynamics that emerged among participants: generational differences and divisions between college and university students and other community members. Negotiations occurred not only between people familiar with an earlier model of feminist organizing to address sexual violence and students working from a multi-issue platform that included addressing sexual violence, but also among people with different relationships to college-based organizing. These divisions reflected conversations that began well before the march. Therefore, the negotiations at the 2004 Minneapolis Take Back the Night march demonstrate how public demonstrations provide physical and affective space to address difficult divisions within politicized communities.

The relationship between on-the-ground organizing for a particular event and broader subcultural conversations was also apparent at the Toronto SlutWalk (chapter 3). After over a year's worth of online debates about whether trying to reclaim the term "slut" was a desirable or an effective tactic, the 2012 Toronto SlutWalk brought together a variety of Toronto organizations and community representatives to contest sexual violence and victim blaming. This effort to demonstrate solidarity with organizations and communities not represented at the inaugural SlutWalk the year before acknowledged diverse perspectives without resolving concerns about organizational tactics and priorities.

Perspectives don't need to be resolved to effectively claim space to demonstrate investment in an issue. The negotiations described above ideally occur in spaces that enable encounter rather than expect singular focus. At their best, protests allow people with different experiences and views to share space while collectively addressing an issue or event.

Copresence

Protests can provide rare opportunities for public copresence among people with diverse experiences and perspectives who are nonetheless committed to addressing a particular issue. Being with each other in public is valuable for those of us who live and work in institutions and communities where we remain outsiders. So is realizing that people who share some aspect of our identities or political investments are very different from us in other ways. Working with others across difference to hold space for each other and for whatever concern brought us together can be powerful. These small glimpses into other ways of being together provide inspiration to continue working toward social change.

Most public demonstrations have explicit or implicit rules that can facilitate effective copresence. People may disagree about the best methods to address a particular problem, but they can still march or stand together to draw attention to it. As Women in Black vigils demonstrate, silence can be a tool to minimize debate about the finer points of how social problems should be addressed or resolved (see chapter 4). Combined with the minimalist choreography of standing together, this style of demonstration provides a channel for the range of emotions people experience about war and military occupations. The collective movement of most of the events explored in this book also provides an outlet for the frustration, pride, joy, and grief that bring people to the streets. Marching together along a designated route similarly provides a loose framework that channels participants' energy.

By focusing on whatever brings people together, differences can be put aside. At the events where copresence was the most difficult, Take Back the Night and the March for Women's Lives, some participants found key moments of collective purpose in moving through the streets together. For example, Aimee, a black woman in her twenties who attended the March for Women's Lives, explained: "I remember walking from the back up to the front and seeing nothing but white women. At first I thought . . . that was going to be a problem. . . . At first I saw this separation, but as the march continued it turned into everybody being there for one thing." The alienation she felt upon encountering the huge white-dominated assembly was mitigated once participants began moving together through the nation's capital. Participants in the New York Dyke March, Minneapolis Take Back the Night March, and CODEPINK actions described similar experiences. Once they began moving with others, feelings of alienation subsided.

The embodied aspects of collectively claiming a space are intricately tied to the affective dimensions of holding space. Holding space both requires and allows people to be together in service of a collective goal despite differences in experience and political persuasion. This aspect of the work toward change can be hard to discuss in academic settings that privilege the mind over the body and reason over emotion. Explorations of the bodymind in disability studies provide an alternative method for thinking about how change happens.[7] Our minds and our analysis of social issues are necessary, but our bodies and emotions are also central to the process. Change requires physical and affective presence. Not addressing who feels comfortable in the alternative spaces we create or who can physically participate in the demonstrations we plan limits who moves with us toward an imagined future.

Conclusion

The hecklers at the 2015 New York Dyke March recognized the challenge to so-called traditional values presented by a combination of dyke pride, abortion rights, and queer allies supporting marching dykes. Women's reproductive autonomy, celebration of lesbian lives, and gender nonconformity all defy conservative Christian beliefs. The cheering queer supporters did too while also demonstrating the importance of supporting each other across differences in the face of outside pressure. This public, queer, feminist copresence can be a model for how to use public demonstrations to build and support coalitions rather than police group boundaries. Differences weren't covered up, but they also didn't undermine the collective movement through the streets.

At the end of the 2015 New York Dyke March, drummers formed a circle in Washington Square Park, claiming it for dyke pride just as they had in 2004. Participants dispersed a bit more quickly in 2015 due to the rain; nevertheless, as I walked through Greenwich Village with my friends to find a place to eat, we spotted other participants among the people moving through the rain toward subway stations, shops, and homes. Our dispersion throughout Lower Manhattan maintained our claim on the space for a bit longer as we gradually became part of the mass of humanity moving through the city. The feminist copresence of the march yielded to urban copresence. Dykes sat on the subway next to grandmothers, sipped coffee next to gay men, shared meals next to heterosexual couples, all while carrying the experience of claiming and holding public spaces with us.

I hope *Marching Dykes, Liberated Sluts, and Concerned Mothers* leaves readers with a similar feeling. The analysis I provide of these women-led and women-dominated demonstrations will hopefully help readers think about the protests they return to year after year, those they feel nostalgic for, and those that left them feeling alienated. Ideally, this book will also inspire readers to think about the importance of claiming public spaces and holding them for each other as we create a future that embraces us all, a task that seems particularly urgent after Donald Trump's election as president in 2016. As we push back against bans on Muslim immigration, privatization of education, the dismantling of health-care systems, and state-supported religious objection to LGBT and reproductive freedom, let's hold space for each other and a radically inclusive vision for the future.

Notes

Preface

1. Currans, Schuller, and Willoughby-Herard, "Negotiating Treacherous Terrain."
2. Starr, Fernandez, and Scholl, *Shutting Down the Streets*, 25–26.
3. Bourne, "Commanding and Controlling," 38.
4. Mitchell, *The Right to the City*, 5; Butler, "Bodies in Alliance."
5. Mitchell and Staeheli, "Permitting Protest."
6. Sturken, "Masculinity," 444.
7. Bickford, "Activism and Service-Learning."
8. Baumgardner and Richards, *Grassroots*, xix.
9. Zucker and Bay-Cheng, "Minding the Gap."
10. Ahmed, "Killing Joy."
11. Katzenstein, "Feminism within American Institutions," 30–31; Mansbridge, *Why We Lost the ERA*.
12. Faludi, *Backlash*.
13. Katzenstein, "Feminism within American Institutions," 27.
14. Thompson, "Multiracial Feminism."
15. Hemmings, *Why Stories Matter*, 132–35.
16. Russo, "The Feminist Majority Foundation's Campaign," 558.
17. Haaken, "Cultural Amnesia," 456.
18. Muñoz, *Cruising Utopia*, 3.

Introduction

1. Ryan, *Women in Public*; Elshtain, *Public Man, Private Woman*; Staeheli, "Publicity, Privacy"; Landes, *Feminism*.
2. Certeau, *The Practice of Everyday Life*, xix.
3. Bornstein, *Gender Outlaw*.

4. Browne, "Drag Queens and Drab Dykes," 117.

5. Neely and Samura, "Social Geographies of Race," 1934; Manalansan, "Race, Violence."

6. Munt, "The Lesbian Flâneur," 124.

7. Manalansan, "Race, Violence," 23.

8. Dowling and Pratt, "Home Truths."

9. Warrington, "'I Must Get Out.'"

10. Re uses the gender-neutral pronouns hir and ze as alternatives to the explicitly gendered pronouns she and her or he and him. I don't explore SlutWalk Detroit in any depth in this book. I analyze it along with another Detroit public event in an essay entitled "Encountering Detroit: The Post-industrial City as Stage," which is under review.

11. Ahmed, *The Cultural Politics*, 8.

12. Foucault, *Power/Knowledge*, 142.

13. Ibid.

14. Lefebvre, *The Production of Space*, 13.

15. Ibid., 42.

16. Warner, *Publics and Counterpublics*, 114.

17. Ibid., 89.

18. Durkheim, *The Elementary Forms*, 469.

19. Gould, *Moving Politics*, 3. AIDS Coalition to Unleash Power (ACT-UP) began in 1987 as a direct-action organization addressing government inaction about the growing AIDS crisis. It continues as a multi-issue direct-action organization today.

20. Ibid., 24.

21. Amin and Thrift, *Arts of the Political*, xiii.

22. Sandoval, *Methodology of the Oppressed*, 58.

23. Crenshaw, "Mapping the Margins"; Berger and Guidroz, *The Intersectional Approach*.

24. Glenn, "From Servitude to Service Work"; Boris, "On the Importance of Naming."

25. Kuppers, introduction.

26. Cheng, "'Diversity' on Main Street?"

27. Rothenberg, "'And She Told Two Friends'"; Manalansan, "Race, Violence"; Hanhardt, *Safe Space*.

28. Kafer, *Feminist, Queer, Crip*; Schalk, "Metaphorically Speaking."

29. Halberstam, *Female Masculinity*, 13; Gopinath, *Impossible Desires*, 22.

Chapter 1. Safe Space?

1. Ludlow, "From Safe Space"; Hunter, "Cultivating the Art"; Stengel, "The Complex Case."

2. Ludlow, "From Safe Space," 40.

3. Matthews, *Confronting Rape*, 9–10.

4. Ibid., 11–12.

5. Ibid.; Fried, "'It's Hard to Change'"; Maier, "Are Rape Crisis Centers"; Bumiller, *In an Abusive State*.

6. Bevacqua, *Rape on the Public Agenda*, 71.

7. Women Against Violence in Pornography and the Media, "Press Release."
8. Lederer, *Take Back the Night*, 5.
9. "Sexual Assault Awareness Month."
10. Enke, *Finding the Movement*.
11. MacKinnon and Dworkin, *In Harm's Way*.
12. Greenberg, "Still Hidden in the Closet."
13. Hanhardt, *Safe Space*, 30.
14. Delany, *Times Square Red*, 122.
15. Bumiller, *In an Abusive State*, 13.
16. Cvetkovich, *An Archive of Feelings*, 3.
17. Kuppers, "'your Darkness Also.'"
18. Davis, "The Color of Violence."
19. Iveson, *Publics and the City*, 202.
20. Browne, "Beyond Rural Idylls."
21. Ahmed, "The Nonperformativity of Antiracism."
22. Bhavnani and Coulson, "Transforming Socialist-Feminism," 90.
23. Bumiller, *In an Abusive State*, 10.
24. INCITE! Women of Color Against Violence, *The Color of Violence*.
25. Delany, *Times Square Red*, 125–42.
26. Valentine, "Living with Difference."
27. Leitner, "Spaces of Encounters."

Chapter 2. Enacting Spiritual Connection and Performing Deviance

1. Spirit Drumz, "Welcome to Spirit Drumz."
2. Ramos, "Mojuba."
3. Jacobs, Thomas, and Lang, *Two-Spirit People*.
4. Jameson, "The Cultural Logic"; Cvetkovich, *An Archive of Feelings*, 9.
5. Ghaziani, *The Dividends of Dissent*, 29.
6. Ibid., 27; Weiss, "Gay Shame and BDSM Pride"; Browne, "A Party with Politics?"
7. Lesbian Avengers, "Communiqué No. 3."
8. Collins, *Black Feminist Thought*; Cohen, "Deviance as Resistance"; Miller-Young, "Hip-Hop Honeys."
9. D'Emilio, *Sexual Politics*; Duggan, "Making It Perfectly Queer"; Vaid, *Virtual Equality*, 202–9.
10. Vaid, *Virtual Equality*, xiv–xv; "Dyke March Los Angeles."
11. Lesbian Avengers, "Lesbian Avengers March"; Roth, interview; "Dyke March Los Angeles."
12. Lesbian Avengers, "Communiqué No. 3."
13. Boutiller, "The Dyke March," 10.
14. Ibid.; Lesbian Avengers, "Lesbian Avengers March"; Ghaziani and Fine, "Infighting and Ideology," 52.
15. Brown-Saracino and Ghaziani, "The Constraints of Culture."

16. Lee, Murphy, and Ucelli, "Whose Kids? Our Kids!"
17. CITYAXE, "To the Lesbian Avengers."
18. Califia, "San Francisco"; Boyd, "Lesbian Space, Lesbian Territory."
19. Rothenberg, "'And She Told Two Friends'"; Zamora, "Oakland, Gays"; Buchanan, "Marketplace."
20. Intertribal Friendship House, *Urban Voices*; Ong, *Buddha Is Hiding*; Rhomberg, *No There There.*
21. Chauncey, *Gay New York*; Armstrong, *Forging Gay Identities*; Boyd, "Lesbian Space, Lesbian Territory"; Ordona, *Coming Out Together.*
22. Duberman, *Stonewall*; Hanhardt, *Safe Space*; Manalansan, "Race, Violence"; Valentine, *Imagining Transgender.*
23. Manalansan, "Race, Violence"; Hanhardt, "Butterflies, Whistles, and Fists."
24. Podmore, "Lesbians in the Crowd," 335.
25. Halberstam, *In a Queer Time and Place*, 5.
26. Cohen-Cruz, "At Cross Purposes."
27. Because pronouns are gendered, some people who don't identify with traditional gender designations do not use he, she, her, or him.
28. Police officers were at the march serving more as a friendly audience than an oppositional force. A rumor circulated among the marchers that someone—possibly a dyke-identified officer—fills out a permit each year to prevent conflict between marchers and police, who would otherwise need to disperse an unpermitted gathering of this size.
29. Blum, "Introduction: The Liberation of Intimacy," 848.
30. Shimizu, *The Hypersexuality of Race*, 57.
31. Ibid., 54.
32. Weiss, "Gay Shame and BDSM Pride."
33. Fukumura and Matsuoka, "Redefining Security," 258.
34. Duggan, "The New Homonormativity."
35. Hanhardt, "Butterflies, Whistles, and Fists."
36. Das Gupta, *Unruly Immigrants*, 15–16.
37. Springer, *Living for the Revolution*; Gore, Theoharis, and Woodard, *Want to Start a Revolution?*; INCITE! Women of Color Against Violence, *The Revolution.*
38. Lorde, *A Burst of Light*, 131.
39. Eller, *Living in the Lap*, 199; Teish, *Jambalaya.*
40. Smith, "Native American Feminism"; Tuck and Yang, "Decolonization."
41. Buchanan, "Marketplace."
42. Zamora, "Oakland, Gays."
43. Swan, "Sistahs Steppin' Out."
44. Ibid.
45. Browne, "Beyond Rural Idylls."
46. Bellah, "The Ritual Roots," 32.
47. Ladd and Spilka, "Inward, Outward, Upward Prayer," 233–34.
48. Mitchem, "Sankofa," 177.
49. Hull, *Soul Talk*, 81, 23.

50. Allen, *Sacred Hoop*.
51. Lorde, "Uses of the Erotic," 56.
52. Fernandes, *Transforming Feminist Practice*, 118.
53. Taylor, *The Archive and the Repertoire*, 19.
54. Das Gupta, *Unruly Immigrants*, 166.
55. Fernandes, *Transforming Feminist Practice*, 13.
56. "San Francisco Trans March"; "Home Page of Disability Pride Parade"; Independent Living Resource Center of San Francisco, "5th Annual Disability Pride Parade."

Chapter 3. SlutWalks

1. Sedgwick, *Touching Feeling*, 128; Doetsch-Kidder, "Loving Criticism."
2. Contreras, "Cop's Rape Comment."
3. Brown and Pickerill, "Space for Emotion," 28.
4. Ringrose and Renold, "Slut-Shaming," 334.
5. Vance, *Pleasure and Danger*; Duggan and Hunter, *Sex Wars*.
6. Borah and Nandi, "Reclaiming," 418.
7. Barnett, "Being a Slut."
8. Murphy, "We're Sluts, Not Feminists."
9. Barnett, "Being a Slut"; Easton and Hardy, *The Ethical Slut*.
10. Kapur, "Pink Chaddis," 15.
11. Muñoz, *Disidentifications*, 10.
12. Butler, *Excitable Speech*, 40.
13. BBC, "SlutWalks."
14. Dines and Murphy, "SlutWalk Is Not Sexual Liberation."
15. Traister, "Ladies, We Have a Problem."
16. Hemmings, *Why Stories Matter*.
17. Miriam, "Branding Feminism." An edited version of this post appeared as "Feminism, Neoliberalism, and SlutWalk."
18. Pollitt, "Talk the Talk."
19. Archer, "Q&A with Alice Walker."
20. Greer, "These 'Slut Walk' Women."
21. Walia, "Slutwalk."
22. Crunktastic, "SlutWalks v. Ho Strolls."
23. Lomax, "SlutWalk."
24. Miller-Young, "Hip-Hop Honeys."
25. Shimizu, *The Hypersexuality of Race*, 3.
26. Some of these exchanges are reproduced in Peterson, "Slutwalk."
27. Crunktastic, "I Saw the Sign."
28. Plaid, "Does SlutWalk Speak."
29. Birdsong et al., "SlutWalk from the Margins."
30. Hobson, "Should Black Women Oppose."
31. White, *Dark Continent of Our Bodies*, 14.
32. Cohen, "Deviance as Resistance," 31.

33. Tahir, "Toronto March."

34. Blogando, "SlutWalk."

35. Habermas, *The Structural Transformation*; Warner, *Publics and Counterpublics.*

36. Lugones and Spelman, "Have We Got a Theory for You!"

37. Moraga and Anzaldúa, *This Bridge Called My Back*; Vance, *Pleasure and Danger*; Anzaldúa, *Making Face, Making Soul*; Alexander and Mohanty, *Feminist Genealogies*; INCITE! Women of Color Against Violence, *The Color of Violence*; Sangtin Writers and Richa Nagar, *Playing with Fire*; Ochoa and Ige, *Shout Out*; INCITE! Women of Color Against Violence, *The Revolution Will Not Be Funded.*

38. Young, "Asymmetrical Reciprocity"; Hemmings, *Why Stories Matter.*

39. Reagon, "Coalition Politics"; Silliman et al., *Undivided Rights*; Martinez, "Unite and Rebel!"

40. "Black Women's Blueprint."

41. Black Women's Blueprint, "An Open Letter."

42. Clay, "Endorsing a Critique of Slutwalk."

43. Black Women's Blueprint, "An Open Letter."

44. SlutWalk Toronto, "Initial Response."

45. SlutWalk Toronto, "From the Ground Up."

46. SlutWalk Toronto, "Racism and Anti-racism."

47. SlutWalk Toronto, "WHO."

48. Kapur, "Pink Chaddis," 18.

Part II. Gendered Responses to War

1. Burgin, "Understanding Antiwar Activism," 29.

2. Schott, "The Woman's Peace Party," 19.

3. Rupp, *Worlds of Women*, 23.

4. Ibid., 26.

5. Schott, "The Woman's Peace Party," 19.

6. Zeiger, "Finding a Cure," 70.

7. Ibid.

8. Klapper, "'Those by Whose Side,'" 644.

9. Stimpson, foreword, ix–x.

10. Swerdlow, *Women Strike for Peace*, 109.

11. Ibid., 129.

12. Ibid.; Loyd, "'War Is Not Healthy,'" 410; Loyd, "'Peace Is Our Only Shelter.'"

13. Wright, "Femicide"; Loyd, "'War Is Not Healthy,'" 415.

14. Loyd, "'Peace Is Our Only Shelter,'" 847.

15. Swerdlow, *Women Strike for Peace*, 138; Burgin, "Understanding Antiwar Activism," 21.

16. Radical Women's Group, "Burial of Weeping Womanhood"; Jeffreys-Jones, *Peace Now!*, 161.

17. Burgin, "Understanding Antiwar Activism," 23.

18. Ruddick, *Maternal Thinking.*

19. Scheper-Hughes, "Maternal Thinking," 353.

20. Ehrenreich, "The End of Naive Feminism"; Bumiller and Shanker, "Pentagon Set to Lift Ban."

Chapter 4. Demonstrating Peace

1. Cvetkovich, *An Archive of Feelings*, 7.
2. In Belgrade in the late 1990s, vigiling became dangerous. For more information, see Knezevic, "Marked with Red Ink."
3. There are exceptions to this, including the group that worked in Belgrade prior to, during, and after the civil war in the 1990s and groups in Israel.
4. Berkowitz, "Can We Stand with You?," 94.
5. Helman and Rapoport, "Women in Black," 683.
6. Emmett, *Our Sisters' Promised Land*, 205.
7. Kuppers, introduction, 12.
8. Loyd, "'Peace Is Our Only Shelter,'" 845.
9. Ibid., 845–46.
10. Haraway, *When Species Meet*, 16.
11. Simon and Eppert, "Remembering Obligation," 51.
12. Bold, Knowles, and Leach, "Feminist Memorializing."
13. Ahmed, *The Cultural Politics*, 2–3.
14. Alcoff, "The Problem," 11.
15. Ibid., 12.
16. Ibid., 24.
17. Kostash, "Visible Silence," 593.
18. Butler, *Precarious Life*, 23.
19. Kostash, "Visible Silence," 591.
20. Helman and Rapoport, "Women in Black," 690.
21. Kostash, "Visible Silence," 593.
22. Ibid.
23. Loyd, "'Peace Is Our Only Shelter,'" 485.
24. Shadmi, "Between Resistance and Compliance," 30.

Chapter 5. Uncivil Disobedience

1. Marinucci, "S.F. Woman Hauled Away"; Jacobs, "Banner-Bearing Protester"; Moynihan, "Ejected at '04 Convention."
2. After accepting the nomination, Bush declared: "In the heart of this great city, we saw tragedy arrive on a quiet morning. We saw the bravery of rescuers grow with danger. We learned of passengers on a doomed plane who died with a courage that frightened their killers. We have seen a shaken economy rise to its feet. And we have seen Americans in uniform storming mountain strongholds and charging through sandstorms and liberating millions with acts of valor that would make the men of Normandy proud" ("President Bush's Acceptance Speech").
3. Santora, "With Spare Passes."
4. Sparks, "Dissident Citizenship," 75.

5. Ibid.

6. Farrar and Warner, "Rah-Rah-Radical," 292.

7. Gould, *Moving Politics*, 27.

8. Sparks, "Dissident Citizenship," 76.

9. CODEPINK, "About Us."

10. Murphy, Benjamin, and Cunningham, "Women Use Weather Balloon."

11. Utne, "Think Pink"; Benjamin, "When Will US Women Demand Peace?"; Wheeler, "Women Send Pink Slips."

12. CNN, "Protesters to Rumsfeld."

13. Fraser, "Rethinking the Public Sphere."

14. Elliott, "Pink!," 525.

15. Pollitt, "Instead of a Riot."

16. Elliott, "Pink!"

17. Certeau, *The Practice of Everyday Life*, xix.

18. Ibid.

19. Palmer and Brotherton, "CODEPINK."

20. Congress of the United States of America, *Federal Restricted Buildings and Grounds Improvement Act of 2011*.

21. Halberstam, *Female Masculinity*, 232.

22. "Ida Cox, Blues Woman"; Hauser, "Demonstrators Toe the Line."

23. Essoglou, "Louder than Words," 349.

24. Berkinow, "The New Activists."

25. Ferree and Hess, *Controversy and Coalition*, 49.

26. Ratner, "Axis of Eve."

27. Roy, *The Raging Grannies*, 5–7.

28. Turbin, "Refashioning the Concept," 44.

29. Skeggs, "The Toilet Paper," 297.

30. "Postponing Bartholdi's Statue"; "WOMEN! Take Liberty in '86."

31. Nanes, "'The Constitutional Infringement Zone.'"

32. Krause, "Lady Liberty's Allure," 2.

33. Barber, *Marching on Washington*, 57–58.

34. Farrar and Warner, "Rah-Rah-Radical," 285.

35. Frankenberg, *White Women, Race Matters*; Skeggs, "The Toilet Paper"; Collins, *Black Sexual Politics*; Kafer, "Gender and Disability"; Serano, "Reclaiming Femininity."

36. Skeggs, "The Toilet Paper," 298.

37. Black Women's Blueprint, "An Open Letter"; Crunktastic, "SlutWalks v. Ho Strolls."

38. Cisgender refers to people who are not transgender. The use of this term is intended to mark all people as having a qualified gender; that is, rather than there being transgender women and women, there are transgender women and cisgender women. Many radical feminists, especially those who don't recognize transgender people's identities, resist the term. More interestingly, some transgender people find the ways the term has become institutionalized problematic (see Enke, "The Education of Little Cis").

39. Ahmed, "A Phenomenology of Whiteness," 157–58.

40. Abileah, "Packing Up the Pink House"; MacDonald, "Rose-Colored Clashes."

41. Abileah, "Packing Up the Pink House"; MacDonald, "Rose-Colored Clashes"; Goodman, "CODEPINK Activist Barred."

42. Abileah, "Packing Up the Pink House"; MacDonald, "Rose-Colored Clashes."

43. Alexander, "Transgender Navy Vet"; Rothstein, "Meet Midge."

44. Swerdlow, "Ladies' Day at the Capitol," 507.

45. "Home."

46. *White House Vigil for ERA v. Clark*, 1983.

47. Carlson, "Let's Not Celebrate."

48. "Spittoons and Quills."

49. Perucci, "Guilty as Sin"; McClish, "Activism Based in Embarrassment."

50. "About the Stop Shopping Choir."

51. *Reverend Billy and CODEPINK in Hillary Clinton's Office.*

52. *Reverend Billy and CODEPINK Visit Obama's Office.*

53. *Reverend Billy and CODEPINK Thank Russ Feingold.*

54. Mitchell, *The Right to the City*, 5.

55. Gonyea, "Jesting, McCain Sings"; *John McCain's "Bomb Bomb Iran" Parodied by CODEPINK.*

56. Johnson, *Spaces of Conflict*, 1.

57. Wood, Duffy, and Smith, "The Art of Doing," 871.

58. Abileah, "Packing Up the Pink House."

59. Ibid.; Palmer and Brotherton, "CODEPINK."

60. "CodePink Sends a Message."

61. Goodman, "CODEPINK Activist Barred."

62. Khanna et al., "The Changing Faces," 14.

63. Habermas, "The Public Sphere," 49.

64. Farrar and Warner, "Rah-Rah-Radical," 298.

Part III. Engendering Citizenship Practices

1. Mookherjee, "Affective Citizenship," 36–37.

2. Swerdlow, "Ladies' Day at the Capitol."

3. Arrillaga, "Lesbian Avengers."

4. Barber, *Marching on Washington*, 33.

5. Ibid., 17.

6. Ibid., 227.

7. Hubbard, "Sex Zones," 53.

8. Puwar, *Space Invaders.*

9. Phelan, *Sexual Strangers*, 139.

10. Hubbard, "Sex Zones," 54.

11. Habermas, *The Structural Transformation.*

12. Fraser, "Rethinking the Public Sphere"; Young, "Communication and the Other"; Squires, "Rethinking the Black Public Sphere."

13. Eley, "Nations, Publics, and Political Cultures"; Ryan, *Women in Public*; Squires, "Rethinking the Black Public Sphere"; Gilman-Opalsky, *Unbounded Publics.*

14. Young, "Communication and the Other," 63.

15. Barber, *Marching on Washington*, 3.
16. D'Arcus, *Boundaries of Dissent*, 20.
17. Warner, *Publics and Counterpublics*, 55, 65.
18. Barber, *Marching on Washington*, 2–3.
19. Ibid., 56.
20. Harvey, "Marching for the Vote," 32.
21. Finnegan, *Selling Suffrage*, 90–92.
22. Ibid., 52–53.
23. Mitchell and Staeheli, "Permitting Protest," 797.
24. Taylor, *Disappearing Acts*, 185.

Chapter 6. Embodied Affective Citizenship

1. Ahmed, *The Cultural Politics*; Brennan, *The Transmission of Affect*; Muñoz, "Feeling Brown."
2. Gould, *Moving Politics*; Hall, "Recognizing the Passion."
3. Barber, *Marching on Washington*, 3.
4. Amin and Thrift, *Arts of the Political*, xiii.
5. Ghaziani, *The Dividends of Dissent*, 6.
6. Silliman et al., *Undivided Rights*, 4.
7. Chang, *Disposable Domestics*, 34.
8. Smith, *Conquest*; Asian Communities for Reproductive Justice, "A New Vision."
9. Silliman et al., *Undivided Rights*, 4.
10. Kafer, *Feminist, Queer, Crip*, 162.
11. Erin Montgomery, "'Abort Bush': The Activists at the March for Women's Lives Take Partisan Shots—and Extol the Joys of Abortion," *Daily Standard*, April 27, 2004, http://www.theweeklystandard.com/Content/Public/Articles/000/000/004/020fkuic.asp; Michael Whitcraft, "The 'March for Women's Lives' Unmasked: A Shocking View of the Pro-Abortion Movement," American Society for the Defense of Tradition, Family and Property, 2004, http://www.tfp.org/TFPForum/TFPCommentary/pro_death_march.htm.
12. Cameron W. Barr and Elizabeth Williamson, "Women's Rally Draws Vast Crowd," *Washington Post*, April 26, 2004, final edition, sec. A; Robin Toner, "Abortion Rights Marchers Vow to Fight Another Bush Term," *New York Times*, April 2004, national edition, sec. A; Gail Gibson, "Thousands Rally for Abortion Rights," *Sun* (Baltimore, Md.), April 26, 2004, final edition, sec. A; Charles Hurt, "Pro-choice Rally Swarms Mall," *Washington Times*, April 26, 2004, sec. A.
13. "March for Women's Lives: Over a Million Descend on DC in One of the Largest Protests in US History," *Democracy Now!*, April 26, 2004, http://www.democracynow.org/article.pl?sid=04/04/26/1346234.
14. Lynn Roberts, "March to Save Women's Lives," *Collective Voices: Conference News, Experiences, Reflections, Highlights*, November 14, 2003, http://www.sistersong.net/Collective Voices_Friday.pdf.
15. The ACLU and NAACP joined the coalition later.

16. Gordon, *Woman's Body, Woman's Right*, 258–59, 281–88.
17. Roberts, *Killing the Black Body*, 72–76.
18. Nelson, *Women of Color*, 85–112.
19. Reed, *Margaret Sanger*, 148.
20. Silliman et al., *Undivided Rights*, 31.
21. Martinez, "Caramba," 1.
22. Ibid., 4.
23. Russell, *Reading Embodied Citizenship*, 4.
24. Bacchi and Beasley, "Citizen Bodies," 325.
25. Ibid., 330.
26. Mookherjee, "Affective Citizenship," 37.
27. Povinelli, *The Empire of Love*, 45.
28. Ruhl, "Disarticulating Liberal Subjectivities," 40.
29. Hall, "Recognizing the Passion," 87.
30. Gould, *Moving Politics*, 3, 24.
31. Clare, *Exile and Pride*, 5.
32. Kafer, *Feminist, Queer, Crip*, 73.
33. Ibid., 163.
34. Kafer includes a statement she coauthored with Julia Epstein, Laura Hershey, Sujatha Jesudason, Dorothy Roberts, and Silvia Yee as an appendix to *Feminist, Queer, Crip*, 177.
35. Ross, "The Color of Choice."
36. Ghaziani, *The Dividends of Dissent*, 279–80.
37. McGee, *Loretta Ross*.
38. Certeau, *The Practice of Everyday Life*, xix.
39. Smith, "Introduction: The Revolution Will Not Be Funded," 10.
40. Ibid., 7; Sangtin Writers and Nagar, *Playing with Fire*, 141.
41. Young, "Asymmetrical Reciprocity," 41.
42. Phelan, *Sexual Strangers*, 157.
43. Sandoval, *Methodology of the Oppressed*, 43.

Chapter 7. Participatory Maternal Citizenship

1. In 1873 Julia Ward Howe sponsored the first Mother's Peace Day, which through time has become an annual day celebrating mothers focused more on gift giving and elaborate meals than larger considerations of war, peace, and femininity. For more information, see Swerdlow, *Women Strike for Peace*, 28.
2. Mothers ROC used the phrase "mothers and others" before the Million Moms. See Gilmore, "You Have Dislodged a Boulder."
3. Gilmore, "Washington Mall Hosts."
4. Puwar, *Space Invaders*, 3.
5. The act was part of the Violent Crime Control and Law Enforcement Act and banned nineteen types of weapons. For more information, see Carter, *Gun Control Movement*, 83–85.

6. "Second Amendment Sisters."
7. Wright, "Femicide, Mother-Activism," 416.
8. Million Mom March, "About the Million Mom March"; Bruner, "Mothers Mobilize."
9. Million Mom March, "How We Started"; Bruner, "Mothers Mobilize."
10. Walt, "L.A. Killers' 'Wake Up Call.'"
11. "Marching Moms."
12. "Million Mom March / Brady Campaign."
13. Herd and Meyer, "Care Work," 667.
14. Boris and Parreñas, introduction, 1.
15. Wright, "Femicide, Mother-Activism," 406.
16. Taylor, *The Archive and the Repertoire.*
17. Ibid., 82.
18. Gordon, *Ghostly Matters.*
19. Mothers in Charge, "Home."
20. Kristinn, "Second Amendment Sisters."
21. Homsher, *Women & Guns*, 100.
22. Gabbidon and Greene, *Race and Crime*, 14–28, 45–50.
23. The Second Amendment Sisters are an internet-based group created in 1999 in response to the first Million Mom March. See Kelly, *Blown Away*, 20.
24. The Gender and Multi-Cultural Leadership Project, "United States."
25. The Gender and Multi-Cultural Leadership Project, "Elected Officials."
26. Center for American Women and Politics, "Facts on Women."
27. The Minnesota Million Mom March has since merged with Citizens for a Safer Minnesota to form Protect Minnesota. See "Protect Minnesota."
28. Lee, "New Accusations"; Payne, "Police Say"; "US Judge Restarts."
29. Bliss, "Mothers in White"; "Mothers in White—Madres en Blanco."
30. Barron, "Gunman Kills 20 Schoolchildren."
31. Gilmore, "You Have Dislodged a Boulder"; Pardo, *Mexican American Women Activists*; Wright, "Femicide, Mother-Activism."

Conclusion

1. Muñoz, *Cruising Utopia*, 1.
2. Ibid.
3. Trigilio, "Complicated and Messy Politics."
4. Flesher Fominaya, "Collective Identity."
5. Trigilio, "Complicated and Messy Politics," 236.
6. CODEPINK, "CODEPINK."
7. Price, "The Bodymind Problem."

Works Cited

Abileah, Rae. "Packing Up the Pink House." *PINK Tank: The Political Is Personal*, February 1, 2010. http://codepink4peace.org/blog/2010/02/packing-up-the-pink-house/.

"About the Stop Shopping Choir." *Reverend Billy & the Stop Shopping Choir*. Accessed December 23, 2015. http://www.revbilly.com/about_the_stop_shopping_choir.

Ahmed, Sara. "Collective Feelings: Or, the Impressions Left by Others." *Theory Culture Society* 21, no. 2 (2004): 25–42.

———. *The Cultural Politics of Emotion*. New York: Routledge, 2004.

———. "Killing Joy: Feminism and the History of Happiness." *Signs: Journal of Women in Culture and Society* 35, no. 3 (2010): 571–94. doi:10.1086/648513.

———. "The Nonperformativity of Antiracism." *Meridians: Feminism, Race, Transnationalism* 7, no. 1 (2006): 104–26.

———. "A Phenomenology of Whiteness." *Feminist Theory* 8, no. 2 (2007): 149–68. doi:10.1177/1464700107078139.

Alcoff, Linda Martín. "The Problem of Speaking for Others." *Cultural Critique*, no. 20 (1991): 5–32. doi:10.2307/1354221.

Alexander, David. "Transgender Navy Vet Protests War in US Congress." *Reuters*, April 7, 2007. http://www.bdnews24.com/details.php?id=58158&cid=19.

Alexander, M. Jacqui, and Chandra Talpade Mohanty, eds. *Feminist Genealogies, Colonial Legacies, Democratic Futures*. New York: Routledge, 1996.

Allen, Paula Gunn. *Sacred Hoop: Recovering the Feminine in American Indian Traditions*. 1st American ed. Boston: Beacon Press, 1986.

Amin, Ash, and Nigel Thrift. *Arts of the Political: New Openings for the Left*. Durham, N.C.: Duke University Press, 2013.

Anzaldúa, Gloria, ed. *Making Face, Making Soul / Haciendo Caras: Creative and Critical Perspectives by Feminists of Color*. San Francisco: Aunt Lute Books, 1995.

Archer, Michael. "Q&A with Alice Walker." *Guernica / A Magazine of Art & Politics*, June 15, 2011. http://www.guernicamag.com/daily/michael_archer_qa_with_alice_w/.

Armstrong, Elizabeth. *Forging Gay Identities: Organizing Sexuality in San Francisco, 1950–1994*. Chicago: University of Chicago Press, 2002.

Arrillaga, Pauline. "Lesbian Avengers Disrupt Texas Legislature." *Bay Area Reporter*, June 10, 1993. Folder "Lesbian Avengers, San Francisco." Lesbian Herstory Archives, Brooklyn, N.Y.

Asian Communities for Reproductive Justice. "A New Vision for Advancing Our Movement for Reproductive Health, Reproductive Rights and Reproductive Justice." 2005. http://reproductivejustice.org/assets/docs/ACRJ-A-New-Vision.pdf.

Bacchi, Carol Lee, and Chris Beasley. "Citizen Bodies: Is Embodied Citizenship a Contradiction in Terms?" *Critical Social Policy* 22, no. 2 (2002): 324–52. doi:10.1177/02610183020220020801.

Barber, Lucy G. *Marching on Washington: The Forging of an American Political Tradition*. Berkeley: University of California Press, 2004.

Barnett, Sonja JF. "Being a Slut and Getting Pissed Off." *SlutWalk Toronto*, May 3, 2011. http://www.slutwalktoronto.com/being-a-slut-and-getting-pissed-off.

Barron, James. "Gunman Kills 20 Schoolchildren in Connecticut." *New York Times*, December 14, 2012, sec. N.Y./Region. http://www.nytimes.com/2012/12/15/nyregion/shooting-reported-at-connecticut-elementary-school.html.

Baumgardner, Jennifer, and Amy Richards. *Grassroots: A Field Guide for Feminist Activism*. 1st ed. New York: Farrar, Straus and Giroux, 2005.

BBC. "SlutWalks—Do You Agree with the Toronto Policeman?" *BBC World Service—World Have Your Say*, May 10, 2011. http://www.bbc.co.uk/programmes/p00ggb5t.

Bellah, Robert. "The Ritual Roots of Society and Culture." In *The Handbook of the Sociology of Religion*, edited by Michelle Dillon, 31–44. New York: Cambridge University Press, 2003.

Benjamin, Medea. "When Will US Women Demand Peace?" *Nation*, January 24, 2006. http://www.thenation.com/article/when-will-us-women-demand-peace.

Berger, Michele Tracy, and Kathleen Guidroz. *The Intersectional Approach: Transforming the Academy through Race, Class, and Gender*. Chapel Hill: University of North Carolina Press, 2010.

Berkinow, Louise. "The New Activists: Fearless, Funny, Fighting Mad." *Cosmopolitan*, March 1993. Folder "Lesbian Avengers, NY (1)." Lesbian Herstory Archives, Brooklyn, N.Y.

Berkowitz, Sandra. "Can We Stand with You? Lessons from Women in Black for Global Feminist Activism." *Women and Language* 26, no. 1 (Spring 2003): 94–99.

Bevacqua, Maria. *Rape on the Public Agenda: Feminism and the Politics of Sexual Assault*. Boston: Northeastern University Press, 2000.

Bhavnani, Kum-Kum, and Margaret Coulson. "Transforming Socialist-Feminism: The Challenge of Racism." *Feminist Review*, no. 80 (2005): 87–97.

Bickford, D. M. "Activism and Service-Learning: Reframing Volunteerism as Acts of Dissent." *Pedagogy: Critical Approaches to Teaching Literature, Language, Composition, and Culture* 2, no. 2 (April 2002): 229–52.

Bilić, Bojan. "Not in Our Name: Collective Identity of the Serbian Women in Black." *Nationalities Papers* 40, no. 4 (2012): 607–23. doi:10.1080/00905992.2012.692510.

Birdsong, Destiny, Donika Ross, Nafissa Thompson-Spires, and Nikki Spigner. "SlutWalk from the Margins." *Feminist Wire*, October 31, 2011. http://thefeministwire.com/2011/10/slutwalk-from-the-margins/.

Black Women's Blueprint. "An Open Letter from Black Women to the SlutWalk." *Black Women's Blueprint*, September 23, 2011. http://www.blackwomensblueprint.org/2011/09/23/an-open-letter-from-black-women-to-the-slutwalk/.

"Black Women's Blueprint." *Black Women's Blueprint*, 2012. http://www.blackwomensblueprint.org/.

Bliss, Shepherd. "Mothers in White Demand Justice for Slain Teen Andy Lopez." *Occupy.com*, January 7, 2014. http://www.occupy.com/article/mothers-white-demand-justice-slain-teen-andy-lopez.

Blogando, Aura. "SlutWalk: A Stroll through White Supremacy." *To the Curb*, May 13, 2011. http://tothecurb.wordpress.com/.

Blum, Virginia L. "Introduction: The Liberation of Intimacy: Consumer-Object Relations and (Hetero)Patriarchy." *Antipode* 34, no. 5 (2002): 845–63.

Bold, Christine, Ric Knowles, and Belinda Leach. "Feminist Memorializing and Cultural Countermemory: The Case of Marianne's Park." *Signs: Journal of Women in Culture and Society* 28, no. 1 (2002): 125–48.

Borah, Rituparna, and Subhalakshmi Nandi. "Reclaiming the Feminist Politics of 'SlutWalk.'" *International Feminist Journal of Politics* 14, no. 3 (2012): 415–21.

Boris, Eileen. "On the Importance of Naming: Gender, Race, and the Writing of Policy History." *Journal of Policy History* 17, no. 1 (2005): 72–92.

Boris, Eileen, and Rhacel Salazar Parreñas. Introduction to *Intimate Labors: Cultures, Technologies, and the Politics of Care*, edited by Rhacel Salazar Parreñas and Eileen Boris, 1–12. Palo Alto, Calif.: Stanford University Press, 2010.

Bornstein, Kate. *Gender Outlaw: On Men, Women and the Rest of Us*. New York: Vintage, 1995.

Bourne, Kylie. "Commanding and Controlling Protest Crowds." *Critical Horizons* 12, no. 2 (2011): 189–210.

Boutiller, Nancy. "The Dyke March: Celebration, Not Separation." *Bay Area Reporter*, June 17, 1993, 10.

Boyd, Nan Alamilla. "Lesbian Space, Lesbian Territory: San Francisco's North Beach District, 1933–1954." In *Wide-Open Town: A History of Queer San Francisco to 1965*, 68–101. Berkeley: University of California Press, 2003.

Brennan, Teresa. *The Transmission of Affect*. Ithaca, N.Y.: Cornell University Press, 2004.

Brown, Gavin, and Jenny Pickerill. "Space for Emotion in the Spaces of Activism." *Emotion, Space and Society* 2, no. 1 (July 2009): 24–35. doi:10.1016/j.emospa.2009.03.004.

Browne, Kath. "Beyond Rural Idylls: Imperfect Lesbian Utopias at Michigan Womyn's Music Festival." *Journal of Rural Studies* 27, no. 1 (2011): 13–23.

———. "Drag Queens and Drab Dykes: Deploying and Deploring Femininities." In *Geographies of Sexualities: Theory, Practices and Politics*, edited by Kath Browne, Jason Lim, and Gavin Brown, 113–24. London: Ashgate, 2007.

———. "A Party with Politics? (Re)making LGBTQ Pride Spaces in Dublin and Brighton." *Social & Cultural Geography* 8, no. 1 (2007): 63–87.

Brown-Saracino, Japonica, and Amin Ghaziani. "The Constraints of Culture: Evidence from the Chicago Dyke March." *Cultural Sociology* 3, no. 1 (2009): 51–75.

Bruner, Borgna. "Mothers Mobilize." May 9, 2000. http://www.infoplease.com/spot/millionmom1.html.

Buchanan, Wyatt. "Marketplace Finds Lesbians an Attractive, but Elusive, Niche." *San Francisco Chronicle*, September 2, 2006. www.sfgate.com/cgi- bin/article.cgi?f=/c/a/2006/09/07/BAG7FL0HUI1.DTL.

Bumiller, Elisabeth, and Thom Shanker. "Pentagon Set to Lift Ban on Women in Combat Roles." *New York Times*, January 23, 2013, sec. U.S. http://www.nytimes.com/2013/01/24/us/pentagon-says-it-is-lifting-ban-on-women-in-combat.html.

Bumiller, Kristin. *In an Abusive State: How Neoliberalism Appropriated the Feminist Movement against Sexual Violence*. Durham, N.C.: Duke University Press, 2008.

Burgin, Say. "Understanding Antiwar Activism as a Gendering Activity: A Look at the U.S.'s Anti–Vietnam War Movement." *Journal of International Women's Studies* 13, no. 6 (2012): 18–31.

Bush, George W. "President Bush's Acceptance Speech to the Republican National Convention." *Washington Post*, September 2, 2004. http://www.washingtonpost.com/wp-dyn/articles/A57466-2004Sep2.html.

Butler, Judith. "Bodies in Alliance and the Politics of the Street." *Transversal*, September 2011. http://eipcp.net/transversal/1011/butler/en.

———. *Excitable Speech: A Politics of the Performative*. New York: Routledge, 1997.

———. *Precarious Life: The Powers of Mourning and Violence*. New York: Verso, 2004.

Califia, Pat. "San Francisco: Revisiting 'The City of Desire.'" In *Queers in Space: Communities, Public Spaces, Sites of Resistance*, edited by Gordon Brent Ingram, Anne-Marie Bouthillette, and Yolanda Retter, 177–96. Seattle: Bay Press, 1997.

Carlson, Margaret. "Let's Not Celebrate More Women in the Senate." *Bloomberg*, November 8, 2012. http://www.bloomberg.com/news/2012-11-09/let-s-not-celebrate-more-women-in-the-senate.html.

Carter, Gregg Lee. *Gun Control Movement*. New York: Macmillan, 1997.

Center for American Women and Politics. "Facts on Women in Congress in 2011." *Center for American Women in Politics*, 2012. http://www.cawp.rutgers.edu/fast_facts/levels_of_office/Congress-CurrentFacts.php.

Certeau, Michel de. *The Practice of Everyday Life*. Berkeley: University of California Press, 1988.

Chang, Grace. *Disposable Domestics: Immigrant Women Workers in the Global Economy*. Cambridge, Mass.: South End Press, 2000.

Chauncey, George. *Gay New York: Gender, Urban Culture and the Making of the Gay Male World, 1890–1940*. New York: Basic Books, 1995.

Cheng, Wendy. "'Diversity' on Main Street? Branding Race and Place in the New 'Majority-Minority' Suburbs." *Identities: Global Studies in Culture and Power* 17, no. 5 (2010): 458–86.

CITYAXE. "To the Lesbian Avengers." May 2, 1995. Lesbian Avengers, New York, January 1996-, Special Collection #99-6-997. Lesbian Herstory Archives, Brooklyn, N.Y.

Clare, Eli. *Exile and Pride*. Boston: South End Press, 1999.

Clay, Andreana. "Endorsing a Critique of Slutwalk." *QueerBlackFeminist*, October 5, 2011. http://queerblackfeminist.blogspot.com/2011/10/endorsing-critique-of-slutwalk.html.

CNN. "Protesters to Rumsfeld: 'Inspections, Not War.'" *CNN.com*, September 18, 2002. http://articles.cnn.com/2002-09-18/politics/rumsfeld.protesters_1_weapons-inspections-capitol-police-rumsfeld?_s=PM:ALLPOLITICS.

CODEPINK. "About Us." *CODEPINK: Women for Peace*. Accessed December 13, 2012. http://www.codepink4peace.org/article.php?list=type&type=3.

———. "CODEPINK." *CODEPINK*, 2015. http://www.codepink.org/.

"CodePink Sends a Message to Capitol Hill." *Washington Post*, March 28, 2006. http://www.washingtonpost.com/wp-dyn/content/video/2007/03/28/VI2007032801891.html.

Cohen, Cathy J. "Deviance as Resistance: A New Research Agenda for the Study of Black Politics." *Du Bois Review* 1, no. 1 (2004): 27–45.

Cohen-Cruz, Jan. "At Cross Purposes: The Church Ladies for Choice." In *Radical Street Performance: An International Anthology*, edited by Jan Cohen-Cruz, 90–99. New York: Routledge, 1998.

Collins, Patricia Hill. *Black Feminist Thought: Knowledge, Consciousness, and the Politics of Empowerment*. New York: Routledge, 1997.

———. *Black Sexual Politics: African Americans, Gender, and the New Racism*. New York: Routledge, 2004.

Congress of the United States of America. *Federal Restricted Buildings and Grounds Improvement Act of 2011*, 2012. http://www.gpo.gov/fdsys/pkg/BILLS-112hr347enr/pdf/BILLS-112hr347enr.pdf.

Contreras, Russell. "Cop's Rape Comment Sparks Wave of 'SlutWalks.'" *Msnbc.com*, May 4, 2011. http://www.msnbc.msn.com/id/42927752/ns/us_news-life/t/cops-rape-comment-sparks-wave-slutwalks/.

Crenshaw, Kimberlé. "Mapping the Margins: Intersectionality, Identity Politics, and Violence against Women of Color." *Stanford Law Review* 43 (1991): 1241–99.

Crunktastic. "I Saw the Sign but Did We Really Need a Sign? SlutWalk and Racism." *Crunk Feminist Collective*, October 6, 2011. http://crunkfeministcollective.wordpress.com/2011/10/06/i-saw-the-sign-but-did-we-really-need-a-sign-slutwalk-and-racism/.

———. "SlutWalks v. Ho Strolls." *Crunk Feminist Collective*, May 23, 2011. http://crunkfeministcollective.wordpress.com/2011/05/23/slutwalks-v-ho-strolls/.

Currans, Elizabeth, Mark Schuller, and Tiffany Willoughby-Herard. "Negotiating Treacherous Terrain: Disciplinary Power, Security Cultures, and Affective Ties in a Local Anti-War Movement." *Social Justice* 38, no. 3 (2012): 60–85.

Cvetkovich, Ann. *An Archive of Feelings: Trauma, Sexuality, and Lesbian Public Cultures*. Durham, N.C.: Duke University Press, 2003.

D'Arcus, Bruce. *Boundaries of Dissent: Protest and State Power in the Media Age*. New York: Routledge, 2005.

Das Gupta, Monisha. *Unruly Immigrants: Rights, Activism, and Transnational South Asian Politics in the United States*. Durham, N.C.: Duke University Press, 2006.

Davis, Angela. "The Color of Violence against Women." *COLORLINES*, October 10, 2000. http://colorlines.com/archives/2000/10/the_color_of_violence_against_women.html.

Delany, Samuel R. *Times Square Red, Times Square Blue*. New York: New York University Press, 1999.

D'Emilio, John. *Sexual Politics, Sexual Communities: The Making of a Homosexual Minority in the United States, 1940–1970*. Chicago: University of Chicago Press, 1998.

Dines, Gail, and Wendy Murphy. "SlutWalk Is Not Sexual Liberation: Women Need to Take to the Streets to Condemn Violence, but Not for the Right to Be Called 'Slut.'" *Guardian*, May 8, 2011. http://www.guardian.co.uk/commentisfree/2011/may/08/slutwalk-not-sexual-liberation.

Doetsch-Kidder, Sharon. "Loving Criticism: A Spiritual Philosophy of Social Change." *Feminist Studies* 38, no. 2 (2012): 444–73.

Dowling, Robyn, and Geraldine Pratt. "Home Truths: Recent Feminist Constructions." *Urban Geography* 14, no. 5 (1993): 464–75. doi:10.2747/0272-3638.14.5.464.

Duberman, Martin. *Stonewall*. New York: Plume, 1994.

Duggan, Lisa. "Making It Perfectly Queer." In *Sex Wars: Sexual Dissent and Political Culture*, by Lisa Duggan and Nan Hunter, 155–72. New York: Routledge, 1995.

———. "The New Homonormativity: The Sexual Politics of Neoliberalism." In *Materializing Democracy: Toward a Revitalized Cultural Politics*, edited by Russ Castronovo and Dana Nelson, 175–94. Durham, N.C.: Duke University Press, 2002.

Duggan, Lisa, and Nan Hunter. *Sex Wars: Sexual Dissent and Political Culture*. 1st ed. New York: Routledge, 1995.

Durkheim, Emile. *The Elementary Forms of the Religious Life*. Translated by Joseph Ward Swain. London: Free Press, 1965.

"Dyke March Los Angeles." *Divas Magazine* 2, no. 4 (2002): n.p.

Easton, Dossie, and Janet Hardy. *The Ethical Slut: A Practical Guide to Polyamory, Open Relationships & Other Adventures*. 2nd ed. Berkeley, Calif.: Celestial Arts, 2009.

Ehrenreich, Barbara. "The End of Naive Feminism." *Catholic New Times*, October 10, 2004. Academic OneFile.

Eley, Geoff. "Nations, Publics, and Political Cultures: Placing Habermas in the Nineteenth Century." In *Habermas and the Public Sphere*, edited by Craig Calhoun, 289–339. Boston: MIT Press, 1992.

Eller, Cynthia. *Living in the Lap of the Goddess*. New York: Crossroads Press, 1993.

Elliott, Charlene. "Pink! Community, Contestation, and the Colour of Breast Cancer." *Canadian Journal of Communication* 32, no. 3/4 (2007): 521–36.

Elshtain, Jean Bethke. *Public Man, Private Woman*. 2nd ed. Princeton, N.J.: Princeton University Press, 1993.

Emmett, Ayala. *Our Sisters' Promised Land: Women, Politics, and Israeli-Palestinian Coexistence*. Ann Arbor: University of Michigan Press, 2003.

Enke, A. Finn. "The Education of Little Cis: Cisgender and the Discipline of Opposing Bodies." In *Transfeminist Perspectives in and beyond Transgender and Gender Studies*, edited by Anne Enke, 60–77. Philadelphia: Temple University Press, 2012.

Enke, Anne. *Finding the Movement: Sexuality, Contested Space, and Feminist Activism*. Durham, N.C.: Duke University Press, 2007.

Essoglou, Tracey Ann. "Louder Than Words: A WAC Chronicle." In *But Is It Art? The Spirit of Art as Activism*, edited by Nina Felshin, 333–72. Seattle: Bay Press, 1995.

Faludi, Susan. *Backlash: The Undeclared War against American Women*. 15th anniversary ed. New York: Broadway Books, 2006.

Farrar, Margaret E., and Jamie L. Warner. "Rah-Rah-Radical: The Radical Cheerleaders' Challenge to the Public Sphere." *Politics & Gender* 2, no. 3 (2006): 281–302. doi:10.1017/S1743923X06060090.

Fernandes, Leela. *Transforming Feminist Practice: Non-violence, Social Justice and the Possibilities of a Spiritualized Feminism*. San Francisco: Aunt Lute Books, 2003.

Ferree, Myra Marx, and Beth B. Hess. *Controversy and Coalition: The New Feminist Movement across Four Decades of Change*. 3rd ed. New York: Routledge, 2000.

Finnegan, Margaret. *Selling Suffrage*. New York: Columbia University Press, 1999.

Flesher Fominaya, Cristina. "Collective Identity in Social Movements: Central Concepts and Debates." *Sociology Compass* 4, no. 6 (2010): 393–404. doi:10.1111/j.1751-9020.2010.00287.x.

Foucault, Michel. *Power/Knowledge: Selected Interviews and Other Writings, 1972–1977*. Edited by Colin Gordon. 1st American ed. New York: Vintage, 1980.

Frankenberg, Ruth. *White Women, Race Matters: The Social Construction of Whiteness*. Minneapolis: University of Minnesota Press, 1993.

Fraser, Nancy. "Rethinking the Public Sphere: A Contribution to the Critique of Actually Existing Democracy." *Social Text*, no. 25/26 (1990): 56–80.

Fried, Amy. "'It's Hard to Change What We Want to Change': Rape Crisis Centers as Organizations." *Gender and Society* 8, no. 4 (1994): 562–83.

Fukumura, Yoko, and Martha Matsuoka. "Redefining Security: Okinawan Women's Resistance to U.S. Militarism." In *Women's Activism and Globalization: Linking Local Struggles and Transnational Politics*, edited by Nancy Naples and Manisha Desai, 239–66. New York: Routledge, 2002.

Gabbidon, Shaun L., and Helen T. Greene. *Race and Crime*. 1st ed. Thousand Oaks, Calif.: Sage Publications, 2005.

Gender and Multi-Cultural Leadership Project. "Elected Officials of Color by Gender." *Gender and Multi-Cultural Leadership Project*, 2007. http://www.gmcl.org/maps/national/gender.htm.

———. "United States: Federal Elected Officials of Color." *Gender and Multi-Cultural Leadership Project*, 2007. http://www.gmcl.org/maps/national/federal.htm.

Ghaziani, Amin. *The Dividends of Dissent: How Conflict and Culture Work in Lesbian and Gay Marches on Washington*. Chicago: University of Chicago Press, 2008.

Ghaziani, Amin, and Gary Alan Fine. "Infighting and Ideology: How Conflict Informs the Local Culture of the Chicago Dyke March." *International Journal of Political and Cultural Sociology* 20, no. 1–4 (2008): 51–67.

Gilman-Opalsky, Richard. *Unbounded Publics: Transgressive Public Spheres, Zapatismo, and Political Theory*. Lanham, Md.: Lexington Books, 2008.

Gilmore, Gerry. "Washington Mall Hosts Annual Salute to Public Servants." *Defense LINK News*, May 6, 2004. http://www.defenselink.mil/news/May2004/n05062004_200405067.html.

Gilmore, Ruth Wilson. "You Have Dislodged a Boulder: Mothers and Prisoners in the Post-Keynesian California Landscape." *Transforming Anthropology* 8, no. 1–2 (1999): 12–38.

Glenn, Evelyn Nakano. "From Servitude to Service Work: Historical Continuities in the Racial Division of Women's Work." *Signs: Journal of Women in Culture and Society* 18, no. 1 (1992): 1–43.

Gonyea, Don. "Jesting, McCain Sings: 'Bomb, Bomb, Bomb' Iran." *National Public Radio*, April 20, 2007. http://www.npr.org/templates/story/story.php?storyId=9688222.

Goodman, Amy. "CODEPINK Activist Barred from Capitol after Calling Rice 'War Criminal.'" *Democracy Now!* Free Speech TV, November 2, 2007. http://www.democracynow.org/2007/11/2/codepink_activist_barred_from_capitol_after.

Gopinath, Gayatri. *Impossible Desires: Queer Diasporas and South Asian Public Cultures*. Durham, N.C.: Duke University Press, 2005.

Gordon, Avery F. *Ghostly Matters: Haunting and the Sociological Imagination*. 2nd ed. Minneapolis: University of Minnesota Press, 2008.

Gordon, Linda. *Woman's Body, Woman's Right: Birth Control in America*. New York: Penguin Books, 1990.

Gore, Dayo, Jeanne Theoharis, and Komozi Woodard. *Want to Start a Revolution? Radical Women in the Black Freedom Struggle*. New York: New York University Press, 2009.

Gould, Deborah B. *Moving Politics: Emotion and ACT UP's Fight against AIDS*. Chicago: University of Chicago Press, 2009.

Greenberg, Kae. "Still Hidden in the Closet: Trans Women and Domestic Violence." *Berkeley Journal of Gender, Law & Justice* 27, no. 2 (Summer 2012). http://genderlawjustice.berkeley.edu/issues/volume-27/still-hidden-in-the-closet-trans-women-and-domestic-violence-by-kae-greenberg/.

Greer, Germaine. "These 'Slut Walk' Women Are Simply Fighting for Their Right to Be Dirty." *Telegraph*, May 12, 2011. http://www.telegraph.co.uk/health/women_shealth/8510743/These-slut-walk-women-are-simply-fighting-for-their-right-to-be-dirty.html.

Haaken, Janice. "Cultural Amnesia: Memory, Trauma, and War." *Signs: Journal of Women in Culture and Society* 28, no. 1 (2002): 455–57.

Habermas, Jürgen. "The Public Sphere: An Encyclopedia Article (1964)." Translated by Sara Lennox and Frank Lennox. *New German Critique* 3 (1974): 49–55.

———. *The Structural Transformation of the Public Sphere: An Inquiry into a Category of Bourgeois Society*. Boston: MIT Press, 1991.

Halberstam, Judith. *Female Masculinity*. Durham, N.C.: Duke University Press, 1998.

———. *In a Queer Time and Place*. New York: New York University Press, 2005.

Hall, Cheryl. "Recognizing the Passion in Deliberation: Toward a More Democratic Theory of Deliberative Democracy." *Hypatia* 22, no. 4 (2007): 81–95.

Hanhardt, Christina B. "Butterflies, Whistles, and Fists: Gay Safe Street Patrols and the New Gay Ghetto, 1976–1981." *Radical History Review* 100 (2008): 60–85.

———. *Safe Space: Gay Neighborhood History and the Politics of Violence*. Durham, N.C.: Duke University Press, 2013.

Haraway, Donna Jeanne. *When Species Meet*. Minneapolis: University of Minnesota Press, 2008.

Harvey, Sheridan. "Marching for the Vote: Remembering the Woman Suffrage Parade of 1913." In *American Women: A Library of Congress Guide for the Study of Women's His-*

tory and Culture in the United States, edited by Sheridan Harvey, Janice Ruth, Barbara Orbach Natanson, Sara Day, and Evelyn Sinclair, 32. Washington, D.C.: Library of Congress, 2001.

Hauser, Christine. "Demonstrators Toe the Line on Jobs." *International Herald Tribune*, September 2, 2004. http://www.highbeam.com/doc/1P1-98630436.html.

Helman, Sara, and Tamar Rapoport. "Women in Black: Challenging Israel's Gender and Socio-political Orders." *British Journal of Sociology* 48, no. 4 (1997): 681–700.

Hemmings, Clare. *Why Stories Matter: The Political Grammar of Feminist Theory*. Durham, N.C.: Duke University Press, 2011.

Herd, Pamela, and Madonna Harrington Meyer. "Care Work: Invisible Civic Engagement." *Gender & Society* 16, no. 5 (2002): 665–88.

Hobson, Janell. "Should Black Women Oppose the SlutWalk?" *Ms. Magazine Blog*, September 27, 2011. http://msmagazine.com/blog/blog/2011/09/27/should-black-women-oppose-the-slutwalk/.

"Home." *Reverend Billy & the Church of Stop Shopping*. Accessed December 2, 2012. http://www.revbilly.com/.

"Home Page of Disability Pride Parade." 2014. http://www.disabilityprideparade.org/.

Homsher, Deborah. *Women & Guns: Politics and the Culture of Firearms in America, Expanded Edition with Primary Source Material*. Armonk, N.Y.: M. E. Sharpe, 2001.

Hubbard, Phil. "Sex Zones: Intimacy, Citizenship and Public Space." *Sexualities* 4, no. 1 (2001): 51–71.

Hull, Akasha Gloria. *Soul Talk: The New Spirituality of African American Women*. Rochester, Vt.: Inner Traditions, 2001.

Hunter, Mary Ann. "Cultivating the Art of Safe Space." *Research in Drama Education* 13, no. 1 (2008): 5–21. doi:10.1080/13569780701825195.

"Ida Cox, Blues Woman of the Times." *African American Registry*, 1993. http://www.aaregistry.org/historic_events/view/ida-cox-blues-woman-times.

INCITE! Women of Color Against Violence, ed. *The Color of Violence: The Incite! Anthology*. Cambridge, Mass.: South End Press, 2006.

———. *The Revolution Will Not Be Funded: Beyond the Non-profit Industrial Complex*. Cambridge, Mass.: South End Press, 2007.

Independent Living Resource Center of San Francisco. "5th Annual Disability Pride Parade & Festival 2014." 2014. http://www.ilrcsf.org/events/.

Intertribal Friendship House. *Urban Voices: The Bay Area American Indian Community*. Tucson: University of Arizona Press, 2002.

Iveson, Kurt. *Publics and the City*. Malden, Mass.: Wiley-Blackwell, 2007.

Jacobs, Andrew. "Banner-Bearing Protester at Convention Is Acquitted." *New York Times*, June 24, 2005. http://www.nytimes.com/2005/06/24/nyregion/24protest.html.

Jacobs, Sue-Ellen, Wesley Thomas, and Sabine Lang, eds. *Two-Spirit People: Native American Gender Identity, Sexuality, and Spirituality*. Chicago: University of Illinois Press, 1997.

Jameson, Fredric. "The Cultural Logic of Late Capitalism." In *Postmodernism, or, The Cultural Logic of Late Capitalism*. Durham, N.C.: Duke University Press, 1999.

Jeffreys-Jones, Rhodri. *Peace Now! American Society and the Ending of the Vietnam War*. New Haven, Conn.: Yale University Press, 1999.

John McCain's "Bomb Bomb Iran" Parodied by CODEPINK!, 2007. http://www.youtube.com/watch?v=WND78uw8ku4&feature=youtube_gdata_player.

Johnson, Gaye Theresa. *Spaces of Conflict, Sounds of Solidarity: Music, Race, and Spatial Entitlement in Los Angeles*. Berkeley: University of California Press, 2013.

Kafer, Alison. *Feminist, Queer, Crip*. Bloomington: Indiana University Press, 2013.

———. "Gender and Disability in the Amputee-Devotee Community." In *Gendering Disability*, edited by Bonnie G. Smith and Beth Hutchinson, 107–18. New Brunswick, N.J.: Rutgers University Press, 2004.

Kapur, Ratna. "Pink Chaddis and SlutWalk Couture: The Postcolonial Politics of Feminism Lite." *Feminist Legal Studies* 20, no. 1 (2012): 1–20. doi:10.1007/s10691-012-9193-x.

Katzenstein, Mary Fainsod. "Feminism within American Institutions: Unobtrusive Mobilization in the 1980s." *Signs* 16, no. 1 (1990): 27–54. doi:10.2307/3174606.

Kelly, Caitlin. *Blown Away: American Women and Guns*. New York: Pocket, 2004.

Khanna, Akshay, Priyashri Mani, Zachary Patterson, Maro Pantazidou, and Maysa Shqerat. "The Changing Faces of Citizen Action: A Mapping Study through an 'Unruly' Lens." Working paper. Institute of Development Studies, Brighton, U.K., June 2013. https://www.ids.ac.uk/files/dmfile/Wp423.pdf.

Klapper, Melissa R. "'Those by Whose Side We Have Labored': American Jewish Women and the Peace Movement between the Wars." *Journal of American History* 97, no. 3 (2010): 636–58.

Knezevic, Dubravka. "Marked with Red Ink." In *Radical Street Performance: An International Anthology*, edited by Jan Cohen-Cruz, 52–64. New York: Routledge, 1998.

Kostash, Myrna. "Visible Silence: Women in Black in Edmonton." *Signs: Journal of Women in Culture and Society* 29, no. 2 (2004): 591–93. doi:10.1086/378547.

Krause, Sharon. "Lady Liberty's Allure Political Agency, Citizenship and the Second Sex." *Philosophy & Social Criticism* 26, no. 1 (January 1, 2000): 1–24. doi:10.1177/019145370002600102.

Kristinn. "Second Amendment Sisters SAFER Rally, After Action Report." *Free Republic*, May 9, 2004. http://www.freerepublic.com/focus/f-news/1132479/posts.

Kuppers, Petra. Introduction to *Somatic Engagement*, edited by Petra Kuppers, 9–18. Oakland: Chainlinks, 2011.

———. "'your Darkness Also / rich and beyond Fear': Community Performance, Somatic Poetics and the Vessels of Self and Other." *M/C Journal* 12, no. 5 (2009). http://journal.media-culture.org.au/index.php/mcjournal/article/view/203.

Ladd, Kevin I., and Bernard Spilka. "Inward, Outward, Upward Prayer: Scale Reliability and Validation." *Journal for the Scientific Study of Religion* 45, no. 2 (2006): 233–51.

Landes, Joan B. *Feminism, the Public, and the Private*. New York: Oxford University Press, 1998.

Lederer, Laura. *Take Back the Night*. 1st ed. New York: Harper Perennial, 1980.

Lee, Henry K. "New Accusations against Santa Rosa Deputy Who Shot Boy." *SFGate*, January 7, 2014. http://www.sfgate.com/crime/article/New-accusations-against-Santa-Rosa-deputy-who-5122862.php#src=fb.

Lee, N'Tanya, Don Murphy, and Juliet Ucelli. "Whose Kids? Our Kids! Race, Sexuality, and the Right in New York City's Curriculum Battles." *Radical America* 25, no. 1 (1993): 9–21.

Lefebvre, Henri. *The Production of Space*. Malden, Mass.: Wiley-Blackwell, 1991.

Leitner, Helga. "Spaces of Encounters: Immigration, Race, Class, and the Politics of Belonging in Small-Town America." *Annals of the Association of American Geographers* 102, no. 4 (2012): 828–46.

Lesbian Avengers. "Communiqué No. 3: From the Frontline." 1993. Folder "Lesbian Avengers, NY (1)." Lesbian Herstory Archives, Brooklyn, N.Y.

———. "Lesbian Avengers March on Washington Schedule." 1993. Folder "Lesbian Avengers, NY (1)." Lesbian Herstory Archives, Brooklyn, N.Y.

Lomax, Tamura. "SlutWalk: A Black Feminist Comment on Media, Messages and Meaning." *WIMN's Voices: A Group Blog on Women, Media, AND . . .*, May 27, 2011. http://www.wimnonline.org/WIMNsVoicesBlog/?p=1447.

Lorde, Audre. *A Burst of Light: Essays*. Ithaca, N.Y.: Firebrand Books, 1988.

———. "Uses of the Erotic: The Erotic as Power." In *Sister Outsider: Essays and Speeches*. Freedom, Calif.: Crossing Press, 1984.

Loyd, Jenna M. "'Peace Is Our Only Shelter': Questioning Domesticities of Militarization and White Privilege." *Antipode* 43, no. 3 (2011): 845–73.

———. "'War Is Not Healthy for Children and Other Living Things.'" *Environment and Planning D: Society and Space* 27, no. 3 (2009): 403–24. doi:10.1068/d12107.

Ludlow, Jeannie. "From Safe Space to Contested Space in the Feminist Classroom." *Transformations* 15, no. 1 (Spring 2004): 40.

Lugones, Maria, and Elizabeth Spelman. "Have We Got a Theory for You! Feminist Theory, Cultural Imperialism, and the Demand for the 'Women's Voice.'" *Women's Studies International Forum* 6, no. 6 (1983): 573–81.

MacDonald, Christine. "Rose-Colored Clashes." *Washington City Paper*. January 11, 2008.

MacKinnon, Catharine A., and Andrea Dworkin, eds. *In Harm's Way: The Pornography Civil Rights Hearings*. Cambridge, Mass.: Harvard University Press, 1998.

Maier, Shana L. "Are Rape Crisis Centers Feminist Organizations?" *Feminist Criminology* 3, no. 2 (2008): 82–100. doi:10.1177/1557085107310623.

Manalansan, Martin F. "Race, Violence, and Neoliberal Spatial Politics in the Global City." *Social Text* 23, no. 3–4 (2005): 141–56.

Mansbridge, Jane. *Why We Lost the ERA*. Chicago: University Of Chicago Press, 1986.

"Marching Moms." *PBS Online NewsHour*, May 12, 2000. http://www.pbs.org/newshour/bb/politics/jan-june00/moms_5-12.html.

Marinucci, Carla. "S.F. Woman Hauled Away for Interrupting President." *San Francisco Chronicle*, September 3, 2004. http://www.sfgate.com/politics/article/S-F-woman-hauled-away-for-interrupting-president-2728080.php.

Martinez, Elizabeth. "Caramba, Our Anglo Sisters Just Didn't Get It." *Network News (National Women's Health Network)*, December 1992.

———. "Unite and Rebel! Challenges and Strategies in Building Alliances." In *The Color of Violence: The Incite! Anthology*, edited by INCITE! Women of Color Against Violence, 191–95. Cambridge, Mass.: South End Press, 2006.

Matthews, Nancy A. *Confronting Rape: The Feminist Anti-rape Movement and the State*. New York: Routledge, 1994.

McClish, Carmen. "Activism Based in Embarrassment: The Anti-consumption Spirituality of the Reverend Billy." *Liminalities: A Journal of Performance Studies* 5, no. 2 (2009): 1–20.

McGee, Dylan. *Loretta Ross*. Makers Profile, accessed September 2, 2013. http://www.makers.com/loretta-ross.

Miller-Young, Mireille. "Hip-Hop Honeys and Da Hustlaz: Black Sexualities in the New Hip-Hop Pornography." *Meridians* 8, no. 1 (2008): 261–92.

Million Mom March. "About the Million Mom March." *Million Mom March*. Accessed June 18, 2005. http://www.millionmommarch.org/about/#whywemarch.

———. "How We Started." *Million Mom March*. Accessed February 18, 2007. http://www.millionmommarch.org/aboutus/2000march/.

"Million Mom March / Brady Campaign to Prevent Gun Violence." Accessed February 1, 2014. http://www.bradycampaign.org/?q=programs/million-mom-march.

Miriam, Kathy. "Branding Feminism." *Dialectical Spin: Radical Feminism in Other-Land*, October 23, 2011. http://kmiriam.wordpress.com/tag/katha-pollitt/.

———. "Feminism, Neoliberalism, and SlutWalk." *Feminist Studies* 38, no. 1 (2012): 262–66.

Mitchell, Don. *The Right to the City: Social Justice and the Fight for Public Space*. New York: Guilford Press, 2003.

Mitchell, Don, and Lynn Staeheli. "Permitting Protest: Parsing the Fine Geography of Dissent in America." *International Journal of Urban and Regional Research* 29, no. 4 (2005): 796–813.

Mitchem, Stephanie. "Sankofa: Black Theologies." *Cross Currents* 50, no. 1–2 (Spring 2000): 177–84.

Mookherjee, Monica. "Affective Citizenship: Feminism, Postcolonialism and the Politics of Recognition." *Critical Review of International Social and Political Philosophy* 8, no. 1 (2005): 31–50.

Moraga, Cherríe, and Gloria Anzaldúa, eds. *This Bridge Called My Back: Writings by Radical Women of Color*. 2nd ed. New York: Kitchen Table Press, 1984.

Mothers in Charge. "Home." *Mothers in Charge: Stop the Violence*, 2009. http://www.mothersincharge.org/.

"Mothers in White—Madres en Blanco / Demand Answers & Action Now!" IndyBay, January 7, 2014. https://www.indybay.org/newsitems/2014/01/01/18748639.php.

Moynihan, Colin. "Ejected at '04 Convention, a Protester Gets $55,000." *New York Times*, November 15, 2008. http://www.nytimes.com/2008/11/16/nyregion/16settle.html?_r=2&oref=slogin&.

Muñoz, José Esteban. *Cruising Utopia: The Then and There of Queer Futurity*. New York: New York University Press, 2009.

———. *Disidentifications: Queers of Color and the Performance of Politics*. Minneapolis: University of Minnesota Press, 1999.

———. "Feeling Brown: Ethnicity and Affect in Ricardo Bracho's *The Sweetest Hangover (and Other STDs)*." *Theater Journal* 20, no. 1 (2000): 67–79.

Munt, Sally. "The Lesbian Flâneur." In *Mapping Desire: Geographies of Sexualities*, edited by David Bell and Gill Valentine, 114–25. New York: Routledge, 1993.

Murphy, Gael, Medea Benjamin, and Victoria Cunningham. "Women Use Weather Balloon to Lift 40-Foot Pink Banner in Front of White House with the Message: 'Women Say: Fire Bush,'" March 7, 2004. http://www.commondreams.org/news2004/0308-04.htm.

Murphy, Meghan. "We're Sluts, Not Feminists: Wherein My Relationship with Slutwalk Gets Rocky." *Feminist Current*, May 7, 2011. http://feministcurrent.com/2585/were-sluts-not-feminists-wherein-my-relationship-with-slutwalk-gets-rocky/.

Nanes, Susan Rachel. "'The Constitutional Infringement Zone': Protest Pens and Demonstration Zones at the 2004 National Political Conventions." *Louisiana Law Review* 66, no. 1 (2005): 189–232.

Neely, Brooke, and Michelle Samura. "Social Geographies of Race: Connecting Race and Space." *Ethnic and Racial Studies* 34, no. 11 (2011): 1933–52. doi:10.1080/01419870.2011.559262.

Nelson, Jennifer. *Women of Color and the Reproductive Rights Movement.* New York: New York University Press, 2003.

Ochoa, Maria, and Barbara K. Ige, eds. *Shout Out: Women of Color Respond to Violence.* 1st ed. Emeryville, Calif.: Seal Press, 2008.

Ong, Aihwa. *Buddha Is Hiding: Refugees, Citizenship, the New America.* Berkeley: University of California Press, 2003.

Ordona, Trinity. *Coming Out Together: An Ethnohistory of the Asian and Pacific Islander Queer Women's and Transgendered People's Movement of San Francisco.* New York: Routledge, 2007.

Palmer, Anna, and Elizabeth Brotherton. "CODEPINK: Upping the Protest Ante." *Roll Call.* December 4, 2007.

Pardo, Mary. *Mexican American Women Activists.* Philadelphia: Temple University Press, 1998.

Payne, Paul. "Police Say Andy Lopez Shooting Investigation 'Nearing the End.'" *PressDemocrat.com*, January 9, 2014. http://www.pressdemocrat.com/article/20140109/articles/140109603.

Perucci, Tony. "Guilty as Sin: The Trial of Reverend Billy and the Exorcism of the Sacred Cash Register." *Text and Performance Quarterly* 28, no. 3 (2008): 315–29.

Peterson, LaToya. "Slutwalk, Slurs, and Why Feminism Still Has Race Issues." *Racialicious*, October 6, 2011. http://www.racialicious.com/2011/10/06/slutwalk-slurs-and-why-feminism-still-has-race-issues/.

Phelan, Shane. *Sexual Strangers: Gays, Lesbians, and Dilemmas of Citizenship.* Philadelphia: Temple University Press, 2001.

Plaid, Andrea. "Does SlutWalk Speak to Women of Color?" *AlterNet*, June 22, 2011. http://www.alternet.org/story/151390/does_slutwalk_speak_to_women_of_color.

Podmore, Julie A. "Lesbians in the Crowd: Gender, Sexuality and Visibility along Montréal's Boul. St-Laurent." *Gender, Place & Culture: A Journal of Feminist Geography* 8, no. 4 (2001): 333–55.

Pollitt, Katha. "Instead of a Riot, a Riot of Pink." *Nation*, August 30, 2004. http://www.thenation.com/blogs/protest?pis=1726.

———. "Talk the Talk, Walk the SlutWalk." *Nation*, June 28, 2011. http://www.thenation.com/article/161728/talk-talk-walk-slutwalk.

"Postponing Bartholdi's Statue Until There Is Liberty for Colored as Well." *Cleveland Gazette*, November 27, 1886.

Povinelli, Elizabeth A. *The Empire of Love: Toward a Theory of Intimacy, Genealogy, and Carnality*. Durham, N.C.: Duke University Press, 2006.

Price, Margaret. "The Bodymind Problem and the Possibilities of Pain." *Hypatia* 30, no. 1 (2015): 268–84. doi:10.1111/hypa.12127.

"Protect Minnesota / Minnesota Gun Safety and Gun Violence Prevention." Accessed February 1, 2014. http://www.protectmn.org/.

Puwar, Nirmal. *Space Invaders: Race, Gender and Bodies Out of Place*. New York: Berg Publishers, 2004.

Radical Women's Group. "Burial of Weeping Womanhood." In *Dear Sisters: Dispatches from the Women's Liberation Movement*, edited by Rosalyn Baxandall and Linda Gordon, 25. New York: Basic Books, 2000.

Ramos, Miguel. "Mojuba: Sacred Lukumí Invocation." n.d. http://ilarioba.tripod.com/articlesmine/Mojuba.htm.

Ratner, Lizzy. "Axis of Eve Is Just Beating around the Bush." *San Francisco Chronicle*, May 23, 2004. http://www.sfgate.com/opinion/article/Axis-of-Eve-is-just-beating-around-the-Bush-2756764.php.

Reagon, Bernice Johnson. "Coalition Politics: Turning the Century." In *Home Girls: A Black Feminist Anthology*, edited by Barbara Smith, 343–56. New Brunswick, N.J.: Rutgers University Press, 1983.

Reed, Miriam. *Margaret Sanger: Her Life in Her Words*. Fort Lee, N.J.: Barricade Books, 2003.

Reverend Billy and CODEPINK in Hillary Clinton's Office, 2007. http://www.youtube.com/watch?v=v2szVFFJnYo&feature=youtube_gdata_player.

Reverend Billy and CODEPINK Thank Russ Feingold, 2007. http://www.youtube.com/watch?v=AJMYJK6jc1M&feature=youtube_gdata_player.

Reverend Billy and CODEPINK Visit Obama's Office, 2007. http://www.youtube.com/watch?v=WVoFzFu45as&feature=youtube_gdata_player.

Rhomberg, Chris. *No There There: Race, Class, and Political Community in Oakland*. Berkeley: University of California Press, 2004.

Ringrose, Jessica, and Emma Renold. "Slut-Shaming, Girl Power and 'Sexualisation': Thinking through the Politics of the International SlutWalks with Teen Girls." *Gender and Education* 24, no. 3 (2012): 333–43.

Roberts, Dorothy. *Killing the Black Body: Race, Reproduction, and the Meaning of Liberty*. New York: Vintage, 1997.

Ross, Loretta. "The Color of Choice: White Supremacy and Reproductive Justice." In *Color of Violence: The INCITE! Anthology*, ed. INCITE! Women of Color Against Violence, 53–65. Cambridge, Mass.: South End Press, 2006.

Roth, Lisa. Interview with the author, June 2002.

Rothenberg, Tamar. "'And She Told Two Friends': Lesbians Creating Urban Social Spaces." In *Mapping Desire: Geographies of Sexualities*, edited by David Bell and Gill Valentine, 165–81. New York: Routledge, 1995.

Rothstein, Betsy. "Meet Midge, the Protester in Pink—the Hill." *Hill*, March 27, 2007. http://thehill.com/capital-living/23913-meet-midge-the-protester-in-pink.

Roy, Carole. *The Raging Grannies: Wild Hats, Cheeky Songs, and Witty Actions for a Better World*. Montreal: Black Rose Books, 2004.

Ruddick, Sara. *Maternal Thinking: Toward a Politics of Peace*. Boston: Beacon Press, 1995.

Ruhl, P. Lealle. "Disarticulating Liberal Subjectivities: Abortion and Fetal Protection." *Feminist Studies* 28, no. 1 (2002): 37–60.

Rupp, Leila J. *Worlds of Women: The Making of an International Women's Movement*. Princeton, N.J.: Princeton University Press, 1997.

Russell, Emily. *Reading Embodied Citizenship: Disability, Narrative, and the Body Politic*. New Brunswick, N.J.: Rutgers University Press, 2011.

Russo, Ann. "The Feminist Majority Foundation's Campaign to Stop Gender Apartheid." *International Feminist Journal of Politics* 8, no. 4 (2006): 557–80. doi:10.1080/14616740600945149.

Ryan, Mary P. *Women in Public: Between Banners and Ballots, 1825–1880*. Baltimore, Md.: Johns Hopkins University Press, 1992.

Sandoval, Chela. *Methodology of the Oppressed*. 1st ed. Minneapolis: University of Minnesota Press, 2000.

"San Francisco Trans March." 2014. http://www.transmarch.org/.

Sangtin Writers and Richa Nagar. *Playing with Fire: Feminist Thought and Activism through Seven Lives in India*. 1st ed. Minneapolis: University of Minnesota Press, 2006.

Santora, Marc. "With Spare Passes in Hand, Hecklers Found It Surprisingly Easy to Crash the Party." *New York Times*, September 3, 2004. http://www.nytimes.com/2004/09/03/politics/campaign/03floor.html?pagewanted=print&position=.

Schalk, Sami. "Metaphorically Speaking: Ableist Metaphors in Feminist Writing." *Disability Studies Quarterly* 33, no. 4 (2013). https://www.academia.edu/4662975/Metaphorically_Speaking_Ableist_Metaphors_in_Feminist_Writing.

Scheper-Hughes, Nancy. "Maternal Thinking and the Politics of War." *Peace Review: A Journal of Social Justice* 8, no. 3 (1996): 353. doi:10.1080/10402659608425979.

Schott, Linda. "The Woman's Peace Party and the Moral Basis for Women's Pacifism." *Frontiers: A Journal of Women Studies* 8, no. 2 (1985): 18–24. doi:10.2307/3346048.

"Second Amendment Sisters—Self-Defense Is a Basic Human Right." Accessed February 1, 2014. http://www.2asisters.org/.

Sedgwick, Eve Kosofsky. *Touching Feeling: Affect, Pedagogy, Performativity*. Durham, N.C.: Duke University Press, 2003.

Serano, Julia. "Reclaiming Femininity." In *Transfeminist Perspectives in and beyond Transgender and Gender Studies*, edited by A. Finn Enke, 170–83. Philadelphia: Temple University Press, 2012.

"Sexual Assault Awareness Month." *National Sexual Violence Resource Center (NSVRC)*. Accessed July 29, 2011. http://www.nsvrc.org/saam.

Shadmi, Erella. "Between Resistance and Compliance, Feminism and Nationalism: Women in Black in Israel." *Women's Studies International Forum* 23, no. 1 (2000): 23–34. doi:10.1016/S0277-5395(99)00087-4.

Shimizu, Celine Parreñas. *The Hypersexuality of Race: Performing Asian/American Women on Screen and Scene*. Durham, N.C.: Duke University Press, 2007.

Silliman, Jael, Marlene Gerber Fried, Loretta Ross, and Elena Gutierrez. *Undivided Rights: Women of Color Organizing for Reproductive Justice*. Cambridge, Mass.: South End Press, 2004.

Simon, Roger, and Claudia Eppert. "Remembering Obligation: Witnessing Histories of Historical Trauma." In *The Touch of the Past: Remembrance, Learning, and Ethics*, by Roger Simon, 50–64. New York: Palgrave Macmillan, 2005.

Skeggs, Beverley. "The Toilet Paper: Femininity, Class and Mis-recognition." *Women's Studies International Forum* 24, no. 3–4 (2001): 295–307. doi:10.1016/S0277–5395(01)00186–8.

SlutWalk Toronto. "From the Ground Up: A Response to an Open Letter and the Beginning of an Action Plan for Better Work with Our Communities." *SlutWalk Toronto*, October 17, 2011. http://www.slutwalktoronto.com/from-the-ground-up.

———. "Initial Response to an Open Letter from Black Women's Blueprint." *SlutWalk Toronto*, September 25, 2011. http://www.slutwalktoronto.com/initial-response-to-an-open-letter-from-black-womens-blueprint.

———. "Racism and Anti-racism: Why They Matter to SlutWalks." *SlutWalk Toronto*, October 31, 2011. http://www.slutwalktoronto.com/racism-and-anti-racism.

———. "WHO." *SlutWalk Toronto*. Accessed December 6, 2012. http://www.slutwalktoronto.com/about/who.

Smith, Andrea. *Conquest: Sexual Violence and American Indian Genocide*. Cambridge, Mass.: South End Press, 2005.

———. "Introduction: The Revolution Will Not Be Funded." In *The Revolution Will Not Be Funded: Beyond the Non-profit Industrial Complex*, 1–18, edited by INCITE! Women of Color Against Violence. Cambridge, Mass.: South End Press, 2007.

———. "Native American Feminism, Sovereignty, and Social Change." *Feminist Studies* 31, no. 1 (2005): 116–32. doi:10.2307/20459010.

Sparks, Holloway. "Dissident Citizenship: Democratic Theory, Political Courage, and Activist Women." *Hypatia* 12, no. 4 (1997): 74–110.

Spirit Drumz. "Welcome to Spirit Drumz." *Spirit Drumz*, 2009. http://www.spiritdrumz.org/.

"Spittoons and Quills but No Laptops, Please." *Bloomberg Businessweek*, March 12, 2006. http://www.businessweek.com/stories/2006–03–12/spittoons-and-quills-but-no-laptops-please.

Springer, Kimberly. *Living for the Revolution: Black Feminist Organizations, 1968–1980*. Durham, N.C.: Duke University Press, 2005.

Squires, Catherine R. "Rethinking the Black Public Sphere: An Alternative Vocabulary for Multiple Public Spheres." *Communication Theory* 12, no. 4 (2002): 446–68.

Staeheli, Lynn A. "Publicity, Privacy, and Women's Political Action." *Environment and Planning D: Society and Space* 14, no. 5 (1996): 601–19.

Starr, Amory, Luis A. Fernandez, and Christian Scholl. *Shutting Down the Streets: Political Violence and Social Control in the Global Era*. New York: New York University Press, 2011.

Stengel, Barbara S. "The Complex Case of Fear and Safe Space." *Studies in Philosophy and Education* 29, no. 6 (2010): 523–40. doi:10.1007/s11217–010–9198–3.

Stimpson, Catherine R. Foreword to *Women Strike for Peace: Traditional Motherhood and Radical Politics in the 1960s*, by Amy Swerdlow, ix–xii. Chicago: University of Chicago Press, 1993.

Sturken, Marita. "Masculinity, Courage, and Sacrifice." *Signs: Journal of Women in Culture and Society* 28, no. 1 (2002): 444–45.

Swan, Rachel. "Sistahs Steppin' Out." *East Bay Express*, August 24, 2011. http://www.eastbayexpress.com/oakland/sistahs-steppin-out/Content?oid=2967081.

Swerdlow, Amy. "Ladies' Day at the Capitol: Women Strike for Peace versus HUAC." *Feminist Studies* 8, no. 3 (1982): 493–520.

———. *Women Strike for Peace: Traditional Motherhood and Radical Politics in the 1960s.* Chicago: University of Chicago Press, 1993.

Tahir, Hufsa. "Toronto March to Redefine 'Slut.'" *Excalibur: York University's Community Newspaper*, March 30, 2011. http://www.excal.on.ca/news/toronto-march-to-redefine-%E2%80%98slut%E2%80%99/.

Taylor, Diana. *The Archive and the Repertoire: Performing Cultural Memory in the Americas.* Durham, N.C.: Duke University Press, 2003.

———. *Disappearing Acts: Spectacles of Gender and Nationalism in Argentina's "Dirty War."* Durham, N.C.: Duke University Press, 1997.

Teish, Luisah. *Jambalaya: The Natural Woman's Book of Personal Charms and Practical Rituals.* New York: Harper & Row, 1988.

Terada, Rei. *Feeling in Theory: Emotion after the "Death of the Subject."* Cambridge, Mass.: Harvard University Press, 2001.

Thompson, Becky. "Multiracial Feminism: Recasting the Chronology of Second Wave Feminism." *Feminist Studies* 28, no. 2 (2002): 336–60.

Traister, Rebecca. "Ladies, We Have a Problem." *New York Times*, July 20, 2011, sec. Magazine. http://www.nytimes.com/2011/07/24/magazine/clumsy-young-feminists.html?_r=3&pagewanted=1.

Trigilio, Jo. "Complicated and Messy Politics of Inclusion: Michfest and the Boston Dyke March." *Journal of Lesbian Studies* 20, no. 2 (2016): 234–50. doi:10.1080/10894160.2016.1083835.

Tuck, Eve, and K. Wayne Yang. "Decolonization Is Not a Metaphor." *Decolonization: Indigeneity, Education & Society* 1, no. 1 (2012). http://decolonization.org/index.php/des/article/view/18630.

Turbin, Carole. "Refashioning the Concept of Public/Private: Lessons from Dress Studies." *Journal of Women's History* 15, no. 1 (2003): 43–51. doi:10.1353/jowh.2003.0038.

"US Judge Restarts Wrongful Death Lawsuit Filed by Andy Lopez's Parents." *KTVU.com*, July 11, 2014. http://www.ktvu.com/news/news/crime-law/us-judge-restarts-wrongful-death-lawsuit-filed-and/ngdmJ/.

Utne, Nina. "Think Pink." *Utne Reader*, April 2003. http://www.utne.com/2003-03-01/ThinkPink.aspx.

Vaid, Urvashi. *Virtual Equality: The Mainstreaming of Gay and Lesbian Liberation.* New York: Anchor, 1996.

Valentine, David. *Imagining Transgender.* Durham, N.C.: Duke University Press, 2007.

Valentine, Gill. "Living with Difference: Reflections on Geographies of Encounter." *Progress in Human Geography* 32, no. 3 (2008): 323–37. doi:10.1177/0309133308089372.

Vance, Carole, ed. *Pleasure and Danger: Toward a Politics of Sexuality*. Boston: Routledge and Kegan Paul, 1984.

Walia, Harsha. "Slutwalk—to March or Not to March." *Racialicious*, May 19, 2011. http://www.racialicious.com/2011/05/19/slutwalk-%E2%80%93-to-march-or-not-to-march/.

Walt, Vivienne. "L.A. Killers' 'Wake Up Call to America to Kill Jews.'" *Salon News*, August 11, 1999. http://archive.salon.com/news/feature/1999/08/11/jcc_shooting/.

Warner, Michael. *Publics and Counterpublics*. New York: Zone Books, 2005.

Warrington, Molly. "'I Must Get Out': The Geographies of Domestic Violence." *Transactions of the Institute of British Geographers* 26, no. 3 (September 1, 2001): 365–82. doi:10.1111/1475-5661.00028.

Weiss, Margot. "Gay Shame and BDSM Pride: Neoliberalism, Privacy, and Sexual Politics." *Radical History Review* 100 (2008): 87–101.

Wheeler, Tim. "Women Send Pink Slips to White House in Anti-war Action." *People's World*, March 8, 2003.

White, E. Frances. *Dark Continent Of Our Bodies: Black Feminism & Politics of Respectability*. Philadelphia: Temple University Press, 2001.

White House Vigil for ERA v. Clark, 1983, http://www.prop1.org/legal/845271.htm.

Women Against Violence in Pornography and the Media. "Press Release: Take Back the Night." October 29, 1978. WAVPM Collection, GLBT Historical Society, San Francisco.

"WOMEN! Take Liberty in '86." Flyer, 1986. Marches folder. ONE Archives Foundation, Los Angeles, Calif.

Wood, Nichola, Michelle Duffy, and Susan J. Smith. "The Art of Doing (Geographies of) Music." *Environment and Planning D: Society and Space* 25, no. 5 (2007): 867–89. doi:10.1068/d416t.

Wright, Melissa. "Femicide, Mother-Activism, and the Geography of Protest in Northern Mexico." *Urban Geography* 28, no. 5 (2007): 401–25.

Young, Iris Marion. "Asymmetrical Reciprocity: On Moral Respect, Wonder, and Enlarged Thought." In *Intersecting Voices: Dilemmas of Gender, Political Philosophy, and Policy*, 38–59. Princeton, N.J.: Princeton University Press, 1997.

———. "Communication and the Other: Beyond Deliberative Democracy." In *Intersecting Voices: Dilemmas of Gender, Political Philosophy, and Policy*, 60–74. Princeton, N.J.: Princeton University Press, 1997.

Zamora, Jim Herron. "Oakland, Gays in the Mainstream, East Bay City Ranks Third in Nation for Gay and Lesbian Households." *San Francisco Chronicle*, June 25, 2004. http://www.sfgate.com/cgi-bin/ article.cgi?f=/c/a/2004/06/25/BAGC47AU0M33.DTL&hw=oakland&sn=048&sc=332.

Zeiger, Susan. "Finding a Cure for War: Women's Politics and the Peace Movement in the 1920s." *Journal of Social History* 24, no. 1 (1990): 69–86.

Zucker, Alyssa N., and Laina Y. Bay-Cheng. "Minding the Gap between Feminist Identity and Attitudes: The Behavioral and Ideological Divide between Feminists and Non-labelers." *Journal of Personality* 78, no. 6 (December 2010): 1895–1924. doi:10.1111/j.1467-6494.2010.00673.x.

Index

ELIZABETH CURRANS is an associate professor of Women's and Gender Studies at Eastern Michigan University.

The University of Illinois Press
is a founding member of the
Association of American University Presses.

Composed in 10.5/13 Minion Pro
with Frutiger LT Std display
by Lisa Connery
at the University of Illinois Press

University of Illinois Press
1325 South Oak Street
Champaign, IL 61820-6903
www.press.uillinois.edu